LINCOLN'S BOYHOOD

A Chronicle of His Indiana Years

By FRANCIS MARION VAN NATTER

Foreword by Karl Detzer

Public Affairs Press, Washington, D. C.

Copyright, 1963, by Public Affairs Press
419 New Jersey Avenue, S.E., Washington 3, D. C.

Printed in the United States of America
Library of Congress Catalog Card No. 63-10816

FOREWORD

Francis M. Van Natter and I were sergeants together nearly half a century ago at an arid Mexican Border camp called Llano Grande. We shared puptent, mosquito net, water bag, conversations and confidences those long nights while coyotes yelped and the horses whinnied in a mesquite corral just beyond the saddle tent.

Those nights under low desert stars Van Natter liked to talk of pioneers in the American midlands, and to compare our thirsty inconveniences with the hazards and occasional agonies of tall Kentucky and Virginia men who grubbed hungry farmsteads out of the Indiana wilderness. Particularly he talked of how young Abe Lincoln's 'teen-age years on the stern frontier had shaped both his fortitude and the splendor of his character.

For this book Van Natter searched diligently among small events and the half-remembered characters Lincoln encountered in the raw, new land between 1816 and 1830. Carefully researched, fully annotated, this colorful narrative of a little known period of Lincoln's life not only is a rousing story, full of surprises for the average reader, but also is a thoughtful evaluation of how his hard boyhood helped build Lincoln, the man, and assure his splendid place in world history.

This is a book not only for Lincoln enthusiasts, but for anyone who appreciates a good story for its own sake.

KARL DETZER
Roving Editor
The Reader's Digest

PREFACE

The twofold purpose of this book is to present the story of Abraham Lincoln's early everyday life and to trace the influence of that early period upon his White House behavior. He was seven when he entered Indiana in 1816 and twenty-one when he left there in 1830. Those were his fourteen formative years.

Lincoln lived those impressionable years in the Indiana pocket country, a triangular area between the Ohio and Wabash rivers, which contains all of Pigeon Creek. In a letter to Secretary of War Stanton, the President called the area "my old boyhood home." His secretaries, John G. Nicolay and John Hay, wrote of the settlers there: "Among these people, and in all essential respects one of them, Abraham Lincoln passed his childhood and youth." There his mother and only sister died and were buried. There he greeted his stepmother. There he received his basic education, felt the pinch of hard times, took note of political upheavals and attempted social reforms. There he saw slavery; this region was border country, part slave and part free. Before he was out of his teens the slavery issue threatened to dissolve the Union and caused great concern among his Pigeon Creek neighbors. Long afterward Lincoln returned and wrote a poem about the place:

> *"Now twenty years have passed away*
> *"Since here I bid farewell*
> *"To woods and fields and scenes of play*
> *"And schoolmates loved so well."*

Although considerable material relating to Lincoln's formative years has been destroyed by fire and flood, what remains clearly indicates that much of his greatness is tracable to his Indiana years. "You all know how these early impressions last longer than any others," he said.

In preparing this book the author was assisted by numerous individuals and institutions. Several people who started with him fell along the trail during the twenty-two years he spent accumulating data pertaining to this little-known period of Lincoln's life. He is grateful to everyone.

Foremost among the author's helpers was Eli L. Grigsby of Gentryville, who furnished affidavits and spent long hours pointing out places where Lincoln lived his Pigeon Creek years. Mrs. Mina G.

Cook of Rockport, set before the author the rich collection of Lincoln biographical notes which her father, Joseph D. Armstrong, began gathering in Southern Indiana three years prior to the outbreak of the Civil War. William Fortune of Indianapolis gave access to the Lincoln material he collected following that war.

Other Indiana citizens who generously cooperated were John Gentry of Gentryville, Dr. J. Edward Murr of Washington, Davis Enlow of Lincoln City, Professor Andrew M. Sweeney of Indianapolis, Charles T. Baker and Charles Todd Enghof of Grandview, William L. Barker of Boonville, A. H. Bergenroth of Troy, Miss Anna C. O'Flynn, Judge Curtis G. Shake and Lafayette Johnson of Vincennes, John W. McCoy of Evansville, Mrs. Bess V. Ehrmann, Hilbert Bennett, Benjamin Huffman and E. Grant Gentry of Rockport, Senator Jesse E. Wade and Major George W. Kimball of Mount Vernon, Ora Brown and S. Grant Johnson of Dale.

Outside the state liberal help came from George Burton Cunningham of Chenault, Mrs. R. G. Higdon of Frankfort and William H. Townsend of Lexington, Kentucky; Oliver R. Barrett and Eleanor Gridley of Chicago and M. L. Houser of Peoria, Illinois; Captain John T. Clemens, custodian of the Lincoln Museum, Ford Theater, and Captain O. H. Oldroyd of Washington, D. C.; Fletcher Chenault of Cape Girardeau, Missouri.

Dr. Louis A. Warren allowed the author to browse for weeks in the great Lincolniana collection of the Lincoln National Life Foundation at Fort Wayne. Dr. Paul M. Angle, Secretary of the Illinois State Historical Society, was equally cooperative. The Henry E. Huntington Library and Art Gallery, San Marino, California, kindly gave permission to quote from their valuable Herndon-Lamon Lincoln Collection. The staffs of the Newberry Library of Chicago, the Chicago Historical Society, the Louisiana State Museum, the Indiana State Historical Library, the New Harmony Working Mens Institute, and the librarians and county officials at Boonville, Cannelton, Evansville, Mount Vernon, Rockport, Vincennes, Indiana and at Marion, Arkansas, also lent willing hands. The directors of the Southwestern Indiana Historical Society made it as easy as possible for the author to examine the Society's files.

At the Library of Congress Dr. C. Percy Powell of the Manuscript Division, Colonel Willard Webb, Chief, Stack and Reader Division, and Frank Louraine, Senior Reference Assistant, always stood ready to lighten the author's task of research. Dr. Anson Phelps Stokes, Canon of Washington Cathedral, and Dr. J. C. Hindle, of Bodleian

Library, Oxford University, discovered that the "Lincoln Book of Sermons" fragment was Dr. Matthew Hole's *Practical Discourses.* Harold E. Christie assisted in organizing the material.

The one to whom the author owes his greatest debt of gratitude is his wife. She copied voluminous notes, drove thousands of miles to collect material, and time after time has spoken encouraging words when the task of completing a life of Lincoln in Indiana looked hopeless.

FRANCIS MARION VAN NATTER

Vincennes, Indiana

CONTENTS

CHAPTER ONE

INTO THE BIG TIMBER

Abraham Lincoln was still losing his first set of teeth when his parents began loading the wagon to move from Kentucky to Indiana. He was puzzled as he looked at his father, Thomas, and at his Knob Creek neighbors standing in a circle in front of the Lincoln log cabin a few rods west of the Louisville-Nashville turnpike. Thomas Lincoln was telling them that he was fixing to move over into the big timber, where he aimed to clear the land and do all kinds of crop raising.

A gust of raw November wind whipped through the crowd. Neighbors glanced uneasily at one another. When George Redmond asked why Tom Lincoln didn't stay on the Knob Creek farm, Tom answered that he wanted to get out of the slave country and that he was sore tired of finding his land titles plumb worthless.

"You got friends here," remarked Redmond, who had resigned the job of road surveyor so Tom could have it.[1] The point was a good one but Tom had his heart set on going across the Ohio River. Over there was plenty of free land and all he had to do was settle on it. "I'll get along a heap better," he explained.

Doubt showed in the rugged faces of his neighbors. Abraham looked at them and then at the broad turnpike. Down it was a promise of adventure, of things new and exciting to a boy past seven. Along that road he often had seen men on horseback swinging big ox-whips, driving Negro slaves to Southern markets. He wondered what it would be like in Indiana. From the circle of friendly faces, Abe glanced to the southward at Muldraugh's Hill—a steep, craggy-sided benchland rising four hundred feet into the air. On its top, in the Redmond graveyard, his infant brother, Tom, was buried. Moving to new country meant leaving all these ties behind. He listened to his father talking about a cooper's job in the big timber, making brandy casks for a man by the name of Reuben Grigsby.

"Thought you aimed to farm?" said Redmond.

Tom replied he would do that, too; Grigsby had leased him eight acres of gladly land for three years and everybody knew such land was far better than middling fair for crop raising.[2] Redmond shook his head. "Sure hate to see you folks leave."

1

It was morning in late November, 1816, and the Lincolns were ready to start when Abraham with his mother and his nine year old sister, Sarah, climbed Muldraugh's Hill and stood at the head of Baby Tom's grave, where lay a flat piece of limestone with the initials T. L. chiseled into it.[3] Abraham watched his mother kneel and pat the little mound. When she arose he saw tears in her tired, gray eyes; as she slowly led him away he felt her cold fingers around his hand. They followed a narrow path down the steep, rocky hillside, crossed the turnpike and went to the loaded wagon in front of their cabin.

While Mrs. Lincoln and Sarah climbed to the seat, Abraham walked to the hogpen. When Tom finished laying down the rail fence, Abe and his big dog chased the hogs out of the pen and onto the road ahead of the wagon. His father waved an arm. "Start on," he said.

Nancy Hanks Lincoln brushed her brown hair from her high, slanting forehead and slapped the reins together. "Get up," she clucked to the team. As the horses leaned against their collars the heavy wagon groaned and the tar-bucket swung back and forth from the tailgate, like a black pendulum. Traveling northward along Rolling Fork of Knob Creek the movers soon were out of sight of the cabin and Muldraugh's dreary hilltop. The farther they went the more each hour appeared like the preceding one to Abe as he helped his father drive the hogs.

It seems incredible that any man would take hogs into a strange country reported to be full of wild ones, but it must be remembered that Tom Lincoln was a self-reliant man. Since wild hogs were the run-down offspring of others turned loose by earlier settlers, Tom was taking no chances; he was taking along his own winter supply of hogmeat.[4]

Early in December Abraham entered an entirely new world. Before him now lay the Ohio River, half a mile wide and slow moving. On its muddy surface he saw steamboats funnelling up smoke from their twin smokestacks. Whistles blew and steam hissed. Flatboats loaded with cattle, barrels and hay drifted by and on down river.

Where the road ended at the river's bank the Lincolns drove onto Ephriam Thompson's ferry. As Thompson poled off from the Kentucky mudbank Abe watched richly dressed men and women step into skiffs, sit down and direct their Negro slaves to oar them across to the other shore.

"Well, she's in," said Thompson. "And she come in free."

"I heard she did," said Tom Lincoln.

"Who come in free?" asked Abe. Thompson, working the wide-bladed steering oar, answered, "Indiana." Back in April, he explained, President Madison had approved the enabling act to admit the state into the Union. In June delegates had met at Corydon and framed a constitution. The Ordinance of 1787 forbade slavery in the Northwest Territory; that same prohibition was written into the state's new constitution. Free education, open to all, also was written in. A regular state-wide election had been held in August; a governor, a lieutenant-governor and county sheriffs were chosen by free men. The first General Assembly had convened at Corydon in November and voted for James Monroe for President of the United States. The Assembly was still in session.

The crossing completed, Thompson snubbed his ferry into the Indiana mudbank at Bates Landing near the mouth of Anderson River.[5] Up the Ohio a little way Abraham could see slaves helping their masters and mistresses out of the skiffs at the town of Troy.

When his family drove off the boat and onto the land Abe noticed his father's swarthy face glow with happiness. Abe shoved his hands into the pockets of his buckskin pants and stared into the dark forest. He wondered why his father was so cheerful when in those woods just ahead lurked bears, wildcats, panthers, wolves, and maybe Indians. "Pap, what's free over here?" he asked. "Everything!" replied Tom Lincoln. "Men free. Land free for the homesteading. Everything's free."

Abe turned to his mother and saw that her angular face wore an unusual look of melancholy.[6] He could not understand why she should be sad today. Maybe it was because this was the Lincolns' fourth move: Elizabethtown, Hodgensville, Knob Creek, and now Indiana. Maybe, too, she was thinking of Baby Tom on Muldraugh's hilltop. He sidled up to her: "Pap says everything's free over here." His mother smiled. Sarah's childish face brightened. His father's one good eye sparkled with joy. "Everything!" Tom Lincoln repeated gaily, raised an arm and sang out, "Start on!"

With the help of the dog Abe put the hogs in line.

The home-seekers moved northward into the wilderness, leaving behind them the broad Ohio—that river which separated slave from free soil, mint julep from applejack. They struck the Troy-Vincennes trail and angled northwestward, heading for their pole-house and gladly land in the Pigeon Creek country sixteen miles away. Shortly, fallen trees and dense thickets of briars and underbrush choked the narrow bumpy trail. Whiteoaks, hickory, red gum, sassafras darkened every foot of the way. Yellow clay hills now rolling, now steep, made it hard for the horses to pull the heavy wagon.

The farther the movers penetrated the big timber the faster their
troubles increased. They had all they could do to keep their drove
of hogs together, for panthers were stalking them. Above the con-
fusion Abraham heard his father say it was somewhere along here
that he met Reuben Grigsby last summer.[7] As night approached
great flocks of passenger-pigeons settled down to roost, their weight
breaking off the treetops. Disturbed by snapping limbs the pigeons
flapped about, creating booming noises. When the frosty night closed
in and blacked out everything but the green eyes of wild animals,
the Lincolns made camp on the trail, threw up a hogpen of brush and
stretched out for a night's rest.

But there was no rest, no peace. Panthers screamed. Late-hiber-
nating bears grunted. Wolves howled. The hogs squealed and ran
back and forth. In spite of all Tom, Abe and the dog could do the
hogs finally broke out of the pen and disappeared. Resigned to his fate,
yet holding to the faith of Job, Thomas Lincoln reverently bowed his
head and lamented, " 'Tis the heavy hand of Providence laid upon me.
Whom the Lord loveth He chasteneth." [8]

Next day the movers made better time. Their wagon jolted along
the blazed trail so rapidly that toward nightfall they reached the
Pigeon Creek country and entered a cleared area right east of the forks
of Buck Horn Creek. They pulled up to the pole-house, half-faced
camp or hunter's camp as it was variously called. With tinder,
flint-and-steel, Tom Lincoln fired the big logheap in front of the new
home. Almost at once roaring flames lighted the place and drove
chill from the night air.

Standing on the southeast side of a gentle slope in the small clearing
the pole-house, which the Grigsbys had helped Tom build, was nothing
more than a three-sided shed of whiteoak and black cherry logs.
Twenty feet long and sixteen feet wide, the house set at a slight
angle. Its southeast open side faced the blazing logheap. A stick-
and-mud chimney occupied most of the rear or northwest side.[9]

Tom took a pair of heavy andirons out of the wagon and arranged
them on the tamped-clay hearth. With logs burning in the fireplace
and in the heap out front, the pole-house quickly heated.

Nancy brought in iron kettles and other utensils and cooked supper
over the open fire.

Before the family began to eat their cornbread and slim ration of
smoked hogmeat, Tom returned thanks, a ceremony he kept up most

of his life: "Fit and prepare us for humble service, we beg for Christ's sake. Amen." [10]

After supper Abe helped his father carry in dry twigs and pile them on the clay floor. Nancy and Sarah spread bear and deer skins over the brush. "Beds are ready," announced Nancy.

A stinging cold December wind cut through the clearing. But the wall of fire out front heated the wind and puffed warmth into the pole-house. Tired and sleepy from the day's long, rough journey Abraham rubbed his gray eyes with his fists, trying hard to keep awake. By the dancing firelight he saw his mother look at him, his father and Sarah. He saw her bow her head. "Remember our God is a prayer-hearing God," he heard her say. [11]

"Amen," said Tom and led the family in kneeling on the earthen floor beside the beds.

Next morning the Lincolns had a good look at their new home. Except for the small clearing about the pole-house, all they saw was virgin timber and unbroken wilderness. [12] Frost-bitten sawbriars and wild grapevines entangled the underbrush. Acorns littered the ground.

Mrs. Lincoln picked up a wooden bucket: "Where's that spring?"

Tom motioned to the left. Indian-file Nancy Hanks Lincoln, Sarah and Abe followed Tom southward along a trail through the silent woods until they came to a ridge of hills forming a shallow natural bowl. They noticed that the hillsides had been cleared and set out in apple and peach trees. Tom waved an arm: "It's all Grigsby's."

The trail made a quick descent to a pool of clear, bubbling water. Overflow water angled westward in a shallow stream and ran under a hewn-log structure daubed with clay and roofed with clapboards. When Abe wanted to know who lived there Tom explained it was the Grigsby still-house in which whiskey mash had to be kept warm or it wouldn't work properly. Grigsby's whiskey had the reputation of being so dry it would burn like a candle. It sold for $1.25 a gallon when the market price in Vincennes, Indiana, was only seventy-five cents.

Tom pushed open the thick, heavy still-house door and went inside, Abe at his heels. Warm fumes—moist and rancid—clawed their throats. The room was a compact structure, twelve feet square and ten feet to the eaves. Along one of its plastered walls was the still: an iron vat with a copper coil leading into an iron pipe. The pipe, at the bottom of a wooden trough, extended nearly a foot outside the house. As fresh air chilled the tube, clouds of steam arose and raw liquor dripped into an iron kettle embedded in the stream of cold water flowing from the bubbling pool.

Abe and his father stepped out into the wintry air. A few yards away Abe saw two circular stones. One, resting flat on the ground, was perhaps eight feet in diameter and had running around its perimeter a trough about eighteen inches wide and three inches deep. The other one, thirty inches high, stood upright in the trough. "What are they for?" asked Abe. Carefully Tom explained that the contraption was a stone mill; to work it Reuben Grigsby hitched a horse to the beam and rolled the smaller stone around inside the trough of the other. Apples tossed into the trough were crushed to a pulp. This was Grigsby's first step in the art of making applejack.[13]

Impressed by the Grigsby liquor-producing plant, Abe slowly looked in all directions. Through an opening in the orchard, on a knoll a hundred and fifty yards to the southward, he saw an enormous two-story hewn-log house with a spacious lean-to. He turned inquiringly to his father. "Grigsby's place," said Tom. "They got seven boys."

Nancy Hanks Lincoln and Sarah, using gourds, had dipped water from the pool and filled the big bucket. "We're ready to go," said Nancy. Tom took the pail. "I'll tote it," he added and led the return to the pole-house.

While Nancy and Sarah went about making the half-faced camp liveable, Thomas and Abraham set to work pushing the wilderness back from their leased eight-acre tract of land. Tom cut down the small trees and trimmed off the limbs. And as Abe piled the brush over the stumps and fired the heaps the ringing of Tom's axe filled the clearing.

It was in the dark of the moon which, according to Tom Lincoln's superstitious belief, was the right time to deaden trees by girdling them. Tom chopped a deep notch around each trunk, through bark and sapwood. After a while he handed the axe to Abe, "I got to get to work on the casks." They were needed for the Grigsby apple brandy run on Christmas Eve;[14] Tom walked away, leaving to Abe the job of clearing the land.

Although the sharp cold wind nipped Abraham's face and the hickory axe handle stung his palms, he worked as faithfully as if his father were watching him. At noon he returned to the pole-house and ate cornbread and hogmeat. By supper-time he was, as pioneers said, "dog-tired and hog-hungry." That night he slept soundly on his bed of bearskins and dry brush.

Day after day Abe worked in the clearing. Stumps which he had set on fire with brush piled around them burned day and night until a heavy rain seemed to have put out the fire. To his surprise three or four days later the stumps burst into flame as if lighted by spirits.

The Lincolns had been in Indiana only a few weeks before Abe saw Reuben Grigsby, Sr. Before sunup one morning a middle-aged man, wearing a chicken feather in his hat, limped along through the woods. He moved silently. Abe watched him climb onto the top rail of a fence and face eastward. Just as the sun rose over the horizon the man flapped his arms and crowed like a rooster. Reuben Grigsby, Sr. was going through religious rites learned while a captive boy among Indians. When Abraham mentioned it to his father, Thomas repeated what he had heard others say, "Reuben Grigsby, he's just like an Indian." [15]

Each Sabbath Day all work stopped in the Lincoln household; the Lincolns were devout Primitive Baptists. Mrs. Lincoln took down her Bible with its chapter footnotes by the Reverend Frederick Ostervald [16] and read to Abe and Sarah. To own a farm was the highest aim of many pioneers, but Nancy put ability to read the Bible above land ownership: "I would rather Abe would be able to read the Bible than to own a farm if he can't have but one." [17] If her son could read the Bible, she added, he also would be able to read other books.

On Monday mornings Mrs. Lincoln and Sarah, carrying the family's soiled clothing, soap and a tightly covered iron kettle filled with glowing coals, trudged to the wash-place below the Grigsby spring. There they started a fire. One morning they found a fourteen year old boy waiting for them: "I'm Aaron Grigsby." "Proud to meet you," said Mrs. Lincoln. "Proud to meet you," echoed Sarah. [18] "I'll help you," said Aaron as he at once set about dipping wash water.

As Christmas neared Thomas Lincoln worked very hard at cask making. Astride his shaving-horse, grasping his drawing-knife with both hands, he carefully tapered flawless, seasoned whiteoak staves and matched their ends precisely. At regular intervals the tattoo of his cooper's hammer broke the forest stillness. By Christmas Eve he had finished the casks for the apple-brandy run.

Christmas Day, 1816, in Indiana was a hopeful one for the Lincolns. While the flaming log-heap puffed warmth into the pole-house, Mrs. Lincoln sang her favorite hymn:

> *"Come thou fount of every blessing*
> *"Tune my heart to sing Thy praise."*

Though not a slave in Kentucky was more humbly sheltered than they, unlike the slave, the Lincolns were free. Here on Pigeon Creek the backwoodsman's idea of freedom was: "A man has the right to do anything but injure his neighbor." [19] In the Lincoln three-sided shed that day, hatred of human slavery burned as brightly as did the logs in the great roaring fire out front, for Thomas and Nancy were conscious of the wrongs of slavery and the rights of man as expounded by Thomas Jefferson and Thomas Paine.[20] The Lincolns believed in the Declaration of Independence dictum that all men are created equal and the teachings in Genesis that God created man in His own image.

By early February the family had moved out of their temporary shelter and into a one-room log cabin about half a mile to the northward. This house, facing south, had a stick-and-mud chimney in the west end and a log cut out in the southeast corner for a window. It had two doors.[21]

A day or so before his eighth birthday Abraham saw a flock of wild turkeys slowly approaching the new cabin. He poked his father's rifle-gun in a crack between the wall logs, aimed at the big leader of the flock, fired, then said: "I killed one." [22] Wild turkey for supper that evening was a welcome change from the usual wild hog meat. Carpenter and cooper by winter, Thomas Lincoln was a busy farmer in the summer. Wild hogs had been bothering him so much lately that he decided to fence the leased eight acres before planting time. Taking Abe with him, Tom went into the woods and selected a stand of straight whiteoak timber. He chopped down a tree, trimmed it and cut it into fence-rail lengths. Abe watched his father make a cleft with the axe and drive in a forged iron wedge.[23] Then, rhythmically swinging a maul, Tom Lincoln drove a dogwood glut deep into the widened cleft, moving wedge and glut methodically along. At last the log popped open from end to end, glistening in the sunlight. Tom split the halves into quarters and the quarters into eighths. He leaned on the maul handle and rested for a while; picked up the axe and passed it over to Abe: "Here, try your hand."

Abe tackled an oak log. His muscles already hardened and his palms calloused by work in the clearing he, too, swung axe and maul smoothly, rhythmically. With each stroke the maul gradually grew heavier. Soon Abe was grunting and sweating. "The quarters won't be nigh so hard," Tom commented with a grin. Another swing with the maul and the log popped open. Abe split the two halves into eight fence rails. Although hardly more than a child, he now was doing a man's work. Together, he and his father fenced in the clearing.[24]

An increase of sun spots alarmed the Lincolns and their fellow Pigeon Creekers. They feared total darkness and prolonged frost. Only last summer green corn had frozen in the fields and ice had damaged fruit and vegetables. Already 1816 was being called Eighteen Hundred and Froze to Death. Would the coming summer be worse?

But spring came and blotted out the sun spots. While creamy dogwood blossoms lighted the somber Indiana woodlands, redbuds dotted the yellow hillsides.[25] Encouraged by these favorable signs, Tom Lincoln hitched a yoke of oxen to a wooden moldboard plow and with Abe driving, broke the land. When he believed the chill had left the ground he and Abe planted the field in corn and flax.[26]

Instead of another freezing summer the 1817 season was a growing one, warm and normal. The corn crop was good and the flax yield big. Now the Lincolns were taking food and clothing from the rich topsoil. With cash money received for making the Grigsby casks and abundant crops harvested, the Lincolns were far from being hard up.

And then Mrs. Lincoln's kinfolk, Uncle Tom and Aunt Betsy Sparrow, with their eighteen year old foster son, Dennis F. Hanks, moved in from Kentucky. Tom Lincoln quartered them in the old pole-house. The Sparrows were almost the only parents Nancy Hanks Lincoln had ever known. They had reared her to womanhood. Dennis Hanks, whom Abe called Denny, was a genial youth, full of songs and stories. He faced life as he found it: "I came into the world through nature's back-door." [27] Abe liked Denny's homely philosophy.

Feeling a new security, the Lincolns decided to take up some of the free land. Tom, Abe and Denny went a mile north of the Grigsby still-house where, pioneer fashion, they read the record in the bark by piling brush heaps on four corners of a patchwork quarter section of land. Locally it was described as rolling upland middling fair, sad, brushy and sorry. A swamp bordered it on the north; black-slashes and salt or deer licks nearly closed it in on its northeast corner.

Early in October, 1817, Thomas Lincoln told his family goodbye and set out for the U.S. Land Office at Vincennes, sixty miles north-westward on the Wabash River. While Thomas was away Nancy enlivened the cabin by telling Abe, Sarah and Denny legends and Bible stories. She went over Dilworth's *Speller* as she had done in Kentucky. Some words she seemed to underscore: "The heart of the prudent seeketh knowledge . . . we must do to all men as we like to be done to."

When Thomas Lincoln returned from Vincennes he happily showed the family Receipt No. 8499, dated October 15, 1817, given to him by Receiver Nathaniel Ewing. It read: "To Thomas Linkern of Perry County, Indiana." It acknowledged his payment of $16 as "a deposit on account of Land for which he intends to apply." The receipt officially described the land as "the S.W. qu. Section No 32 in Township No 4 S of Range No 5 W containing 160 acres at two Dollars and— cents per acre." [28] Assured of owning a farm, the Lincolns began building a hewn-log house on a windy knoll about a half mile north of their second house. Below it fifty yards westward was a spring of cold, pure water.

Swinging a foot adz in helping to build his third Indiana home, Abraham learned that the mud-sill was a very important log for it was placed at the bottom of every well-built cabin. After a few years, he was told, the mud-sill became a fixed part of both cabin and earth. About eighteen by twenty feet, this new home had a split-board roof, its first layer pegged down and the rest weighted with poles thrown across it. [29] Cracks between wall logs were chinked with clay. Directly opposite one another, in the north and south walls, were doors of split shakes fastened with wooden hasps. Whang leather latch-strings hospitably invited all passers-by. Two windows in the south wall let in some daylight. Pieces of sandstone carefully fitted together formed a hearth in the east end. Wooden pegs above the fireplace crotched Tom Lincoln's gun. Another set of pegs formed a ladder to the dark loft. [30]

The family moved in and settled down for the winter. Tom cut a big log from a tree trunk, hitched a horse to it and dragged it into the house. After he and the boys had rolled it into the cavernous fireplace for a backlog, they led the horse across the puncheon floor and out at the opposite door. His family comfortably lodged in the new house, Thomas Lincoln again set out for the Federal land office at Vincennes.

During the day Abraham worked in the clearing, but in the evening he took out his *Aesop's Fables*, [31] an old edition full of rough wood-cut illustrations, and, sitting on a three-legged stool in front of the blazing logs in the fireplace, tried to read the book. His mother helped him over the hard places and explained to him the tacked-on morals. Aesop, a spindle-shanked slave, quickened young Abe's imagination. Using his mother's comments and earthy philosophy, he constructed fables of his own.

Other evenings Abe watched his mother sit down to her little spinning wheel in front of the fireplace and carefully load the dogwood distaff with flax grown on the leased eight acres. She fastened the distaff into the arm of the wheel and worked the treadle with one foot. A gentle whirr filled the cabin as she drew out the thread and he watched her expertly size it. Abe knew she was proud of her spinning ability; as a girl she had won many prizes at spinning parties because her thread was the longest and finest.[32] "All the women that were wise hearted did spin with their hands," she often quoted from Exodus XXXV.

For an hour or more Abe sat near his mother. Then she took her foot off the treadle and the music of her spinning faded, giving way to the moan of the night wind across the top of the stick-and-mud chimney. Abe climbed the peg ladder to the loft and lay down on his sack of corn shucks.[33] Another winter day had ended.

During the holidays Thomas Lincoln returned from Vincennes and handed Nancy a second receipt given him by the Land Office Receiver, dated December 26, 1817. Again made out to "Thomas Linkern," it read: "The sum of sixty four dollars which with the sum of Sixteen Dollars heretofore paid by him, per receipt No. 8499 dated the 15th of October 1817 is in full the first installment of the purchase of the S.W. qt. Section No. 32 in township No. 4 S of Range 5 w." [34]

Nancy's face lit up. That piece of paper meant that she and Tom had paid for one-fourth of a 160 acre farm. Their title would be good. They wouldn't have to move any more.

The spring of 1818 was pleasant but the summer set in oppressively hot and sticky. While vegetation steamed in the bottom lands along Buck Horn and Pigeon Creeks, frog ponds gave off heavy, pungent fumes. Slimy water filled sloughs and black slashes. Men grubbing in the nearby fields were almost suffocated. Lassitude, drowsiness and general weakness slowed the people. Many did not feel well. Dull pains shot up and down their legs. Pulses slowed. Vomiting followed loss of appetite. A dark brown film coated their tongues. Violent trembling seized their bodies. The loathsome disease called "milksick" by Lincoln's neighbors had come upon them.

With lancet in hand "yarb doctors" bled the stricken settlers. Mistaking the disease for what was locally called "buck ager," those doctors prescribed tea made of corn husks and boiled roots. But neither the bleeding nor the tea did any good. Shortly, to the dismal croak of bullfrogs and the drone of clouds of mosquitoes, death cut

down scores of victims. "It's the trembles!" moaned Lincoln's neighbors.[35]

A little white flower called snake-root was accused of spreading the
plague.   The plant which was the cause of the sickness, was the
poisonous *espatorium urticae folyum.*[36]   Some folk claimed they had
seen snakes nibbling at it or curled around it.   Cows eating it soon
reeled, staggered, fell to the ground exhausted and paralyzed, but not
before their owners had drunk the infected milk.

Up to this time Nancy Hanks Lincoln had been regarded by her
neighbors as unsociable, more interested in spinning or reading than in
returning calls and exchanging gossip.   All that was now forgotten, for
she was going from cabin to cabin nursing the sick and comforting the
sorrowing.   By early September deep lines furrowed her sharp, angular
face.   Her shoulders drooped.   She was very, very tired.   She, too, was
infected with the noxious milksick; but even though she may have
known she was infected, her pitying nature drove her on her mercy
errands.[37]

For support and comfort Nancy had the doctrine of fatalism as
expressed in the creed of her Primitive Baptist Church and restated
over and over in her Ostervald Bible. In footnotes to the first chapter
of I Kings, Ostervald warned, "Nothing can hinder the execution of
the designs of Providence, that whatever men do to prevent them,
only serves to hasten them."   From Dilworth's *Speller* she often
had read to Abraham "Divine Providence disposes of all things most
wisely."   Her Primitive Baptist creed put it simply: "What is to be
will be and we can do nothing about it." [38]

Mrs. Lincoln's uncle, Thomas Sparrow, apparently aware of his
infected condition prepared his last will and testament.   On September 21, 1818, he signed it by making his mark, an X.   Nancy Hanks
Lincoln, a witness to the will, also signed by mark.[39] From the
Sparrow will it is quite evident that Mrs. Lincoln could not write even
her name; yet she was not illiterate.   It was not uncommon during
pioneer days in Indiana to find people who could easily read the printed page but could barely make out a word of script. Many could
print letters but could not write them.   The fact that Mrs. Lincoln
read the Bible and other books to her children shows she was not entirely unlettered.

Thomas Sparrow bequeathed by will all his goods and chattels to his
wife "Elizabeth Sparrow so She can do as She pleases with it until
her death."   After that the "whole property is to fall to Dennis Hanks
when he comes of age."

Scarcely had the ink dried on his mark before Thomas Sparrow was dead. Along a dark, rough trail his body was hauled to a hilltop a quarter of a mile south of the Lincoln cabin. There was no funeral service; only a few words were said over his open grave. Then clods of yellow clay were shoveled over his coffin. "A time will come when all men must be put in the dust," Abe's *Speller* foretold.

Soon after the last shovelful of clay fell on Uncle Tom's grave, Aunt Betsy died.[40] The shock of these two deaths cut into Nancy's fast ebbing strength. She struggled on; she was only thirty-five. One could not hinder the designs of Providence.

While Nancy continued her mercy errands, Thomas Lincoln, cooper and cabinet maker, worked day and night at making coffins, refusing to accept payment for his services. Abe helped by whittling out neat wooden pegs with which Tom pinned together the coffin boards.

Almost a mile southeast of the Lincoln cabin Mrs. Peter Brooner lay ill with milksickness. Mrs. Lincoln visited her and tried to ease her suffering. "I believe I will have to die," moaned Mrs. Brooner. "Don't talk that way," admonished Mrs. Lincoln. "You may outlive me yet." During the night of September 28th Mrs. Brooner died; Thomas Lincoln whipsawed another coffin. Neighbors buried her on the hilltop close to the graves of Uncle Tom and Aunt Betsy Sparrow.[41]

Heedless of her ebbing strength, Nancy visited more stricken neighbors. Then pangs of milksickness seized her. She went bravely to bed on her cornshuck tick in a corner of the cabin. Her dark skin turned sallow and her gray eyes sank deep into their sockets. Now neighbor women came to nurse her. William Wood came also. "I sat up with her all one night," he recalled.[42]

As vomiting set in, Nancy obviously realized her last hour was near. She beckoned to Abraham: "I am going away from you and I shall not return." The words came slowly. Abe wiped his eyes with a fist and his chin trembled. He heard her voice, now very low and labored: "I know you will be a good boy. Be kind to Sarah and to your father. I want you to live as I have taught you and to love your heavenly Father." He tried to answer her but sobs broke his words. "Remember our God is a prayer-hearing God," he heard her whisper.[43] He saw cold sweat break out on her high, slanting forehead. Gradually her tired body relaxed. And so on Monday, October 5, 1818, Abraham Lincoln saw his mother die.

While compassionate neighbor women washed and laid out Nancy Hanks Lincoln, Abe sat in the cabin doorway weeping. He was whittling out more wooden pegs, the last thing he could do for his mother.—

Nearby, Thomas Lincoln worked on Nancy's coffin. With his whip-saw he ripped boards out of a black cherry log taken from the pole-house.⁴⁴ He smoothed the surfaces with his jack-plane. Carefully he felt the wood with his sensitive fingers; blind in one eye, Tom was this day having difficulty seeing through a mist clouding the other.

Neighbors placed Nancy Hanks in the coffin and Thomas pegged down the lid. Reuben Grigsby brought up his ox-drawn mudsled and gentle hands put the long box upon it. The oxen pulled out onto the wilderness trail which Mrs. Lincoln recently had walked to tend sick neighbors. Slowly the procession moved southward that October day. Behind the sled walked Abraham, his sister, father and Dennis Hanks. They followed it over clay ridges and across weedy draws. Unmindful of the golden leaves of the hickory and maple, the dull red sweet gum and scarlet sumac, Abe Lincoln saw only the jolting mud-sled and heard only the earth grating under its wooden runners.

When they reached the mound-wrinkled hilltop, the sled halted at an open grave alongside Mrs. Brooner's resting place. There stood Peter Brooner and his two motherless sons, Henry and Allen. There also was William Roberts, a neighbor who had helped dig Mrs. Lincoln's grave. Over by a big whiteoak tree stood Joseph Gentry and Nathaniel Grigsby, Abe's friends.⁴⁵

— Abraham, with Sarah, Thomas and Dennis, watched the black cherry coffin eased down into the narrow pit and heard clods thud on the lid. The grave filled and the thudding died away.—

Peter Brooner reached across the new mound and clasped Thomas Lincoln's hand. "We are brothers now," he said sadly.⁴⁶ Thomas Lincoln nodded.

— With slow, dragging feet the Lincolns and Dennis Hanks walked back down the trail, leaving the lonely mound on the hilltop for the lonely cabin on the knoll. Gazing southward, Abe watched the hilltop grow purple in the twilight. Crowding through his mind were the words from his mother's favorite hymn:

> "Praise the mount—O, fix me on it!
> "Mount of God's unchanging love."

Inside the cabin Abe felt a heavy stillness. The old cornshuck tick was empty; the spinning wheel was silent. Only across the stick-and-mud chimney faintly moaned the rising night wind. —

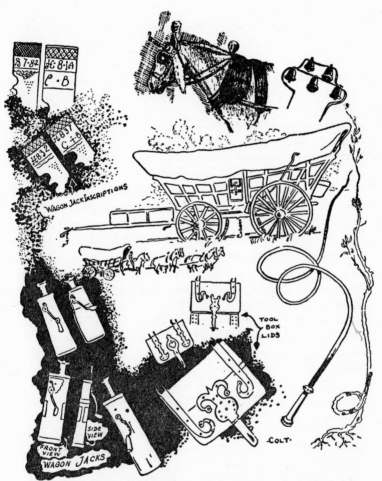

Conestoga wagon equipment. (Indiana Historical Bureau).

Chapter Two

THE DREAM

As eleven year old Sarah (everyone called her Sally) went about learning her duties of housekeeper for her father, brother and Dennis Hanks, winter came on and nipped the white snake root, halting the milksick terror. But that terror had deepened a belief in the supernatural among Lincoln's neighbors. Some were sure a ghost was riding every gust of wind. Others were just as sure Old Splithoof had been unchained and would take up lodging in wild hogs. Word reached the community that a regular old haunt had appeared down along Honey Creek a little way to the southward. A pot of gold was said to have been buried there by a river pirate. Maybe the haunt guarding it was the ghost of one of Mike Fink's victims. No one cared to pry into the matter.

Not only did ghosts occupy a high place in the supernatural world of Lincoln's fellow Pigeon Creekers, but all the well known signs were carefully observed. Abe heard his neighbors say that if a male pig were neutered in the Zodiac sign of the heart the pig would surely die . . . Never lay a fence-worm in the dark of the moon else the rails would sink into the ground . . . Never lay clapboard shingles in the light of the moon or they would curl up . . . If a hoe or other sharp tool were carried through a house an early death in the family living there could be expected . . . Only a silver bullet would injure a witch whose image had been drawn on a clapboard . . . A hen owl hooting in the north meant the coming of bad weather . . . Watch out for a bird flying in through a window: it foretokened sorrow . . . Dreams, the people believed, foretold events.

One morning Tom Lincoln said to Abe, Dennis and Sally, "I had a wonderful dream last night. I dreamed I rode through a path to a strange house. A woman was sitting at the fireside. I distinctly saw her features." He paused. "She was peeling an apple," he solemnly added.[1] He gazed into the fireplace, then looked up at Sally.

More than a year had passed since the death of Nancy Hanks Lincoln. And during that time little Sally had tried hard to brighten the cabin and make it homelike. But the girl's efforts had not been too successful. In spite of the fact that the Lincoln farm now was

16

abundantly stocked with hogs, cattle and horses, that fine crops of wheat and corn had been gathered, the wilderness still squeezed in and beat a dreary tattoo on the cabin.[2] Even the antics of Abe's pet cat did not dispel the gloom. What the place needed was a woman.

That dream of a woman paring an apple so fired Tom Lincoln's imagination that he got out his best clothes, told Abe, Sally and Dennis he wouldn't be gone long, and set out late in November, 1819, for Elizabethtown, Kentucky. There, in 1797, he had helped Samuel Haycraft build a mill on Severns Valley Creek. There he had worked as a cabinet maker. There on June 12, 1806, he had married Nancy Hanks. And there, Sarah had been born.[3] It was toward Elizabethtown, then, that Tom turned when his dream bade him look for a new woman to care for the Lincoln household.

While Sally went on running the house she, Abe and Denny speculated on what might be happening over in Kentucky. Then one December day they saw a four-horse wagon drive up and Thomas Lincoln help down a woman who was about five feet, eleven inches tall. "I got you a new mother," he said. They saw that her dark hair was neatly curled and that her gray eyes looked at them in a friendly way. She was about thirty-one years old. Abe and Sally went up to her: "Proud to meet you."

The new mother was Sarah Bush Johnston, widow of the Elizabethtown jailer, Daniel Johnston. She and Thomas Lincoln had been married by the Reverend George L. Rogers, a Methodist minister, December 2, 1819, at ten o' clock in the morning at Benjamin Chapeze's big log house in Elizabethtown.[4]

On the day before their marriage, Tom Lincoln paid off the widow's debts, amounting to about twelve dollars. For that sum Tom got not only a wife for himself and a stepmother for Abe and Sally, but also a bed and bedding, a forty-dollar bureau, a set of knives and forks, a table, a clothes-closet, and three stepchildren—Elizabeth, aged twelve; Matilda, eight; and John D. Johnston, three. Moreover, his new brother-in-law, Ralph Crumes (or Croome) provided the four horses and wagon.[5]

Straightway the children made friends. "My earliest recollections of Abe," said Matilda Johnston, "is playing—carrying water about one mile—had a pet cat that would follow him to the spring."[6]

With eight people and a cat crowded into an eighteen by twenty foot log cabin it was clear the place would have to be run systematically or a lot of feelings were going to be hurt. The second Mrs. Lincoln bent to her task of making the place more comfortable. She persuaded

Tom to replace the rickety doors of split-shakes with battened ones. She carpeted the puncheon floor with freshly tanned deer skins.[7] And she gave Abe and Sarah a mother's care.

Sarah Bush Lincoln had neither the brilliant mind nor the sensitive nature of Nancy Hanks Lincoln. But she was thoughtful, methodical, even tempered. Nancy Hanks had been a dreamer; Sarah Bush was a practical woman. Nancy Hanks had been inclined to coldness; Sarah Bush was very sociable. But, like Nancy Hanks, Sarah Bush was industrious and essentially religious. Her quiet ways soon won her stepchildren's affection. Abe liked her: "She proved to be a good and kind mother."[8]

While Sarah Bush went about mothering Abe and Sally, the Pigeon Creek-Buck Horn Valley busybodies ranted, " 'Pon my word, Tom Lincoln's woman's body ain't cold yet and here he's up and married again!"[9] It was hinted that Tom Lincoln had first proposed to Sarah Bush, had been turned down and then married Nancy Hanks. Paying no attention to the gossip, Mrs. Lincoln went on with her home-making chores.

All the family had gone to bed one night except Abe, who wanted to read by the firelight. When Tom growled about this Mrs. Lincoln spoke up plainly: "You leave Abe be. Let him read there if he wants to." Tom protested, "He's keeping us awake." Mrs. Lincoln was firm: "The boy is trying to study things out." Tom said no more.

Abe grinned at his stepmother. After throwing hickory bark and dry sassafras twigs onto the fire, he stretched out full length on the sandstone hearth, on his back, his head toward the blaze. He raised his book above his breast and went on with his reading.

Thomas Lincoln, Mrs. Lincoln recalled, "could read a little and could scarcely write his name: hence he wanted Abraham to learn and he encouraged him to do it in all ways he could." But Tom didn't like to see Abe read all night. Abe, according to his stepmother, "would not quit reading till his father made him climb the ladder and go to bed." If, however, Abe had waited for her "to tell him to go to bed he would (have waited) till doomsday," she declared.[10]

CHAPTER THREE

NEIGHBORS

Abe's neighbors fell into one of the three classes of immigrants who preceded the Lincolns into Indiana: hunters, squatters and old-timers. As soon as game grew a bit scarce the hunters moved on. Squatters, who usually had been in trouble back home, did not want neighbors and when new-comers increased the squatters abandoned their small gardens and got out. Old-timers moved in and stayed. To them the frontier code of freedom was more binding than any statute.[1]

Like many old-timers, Thomas Lincoln came ahead of his family and spied out land. About three miles southwest of the site Lincoln selected for his pole-house, lived a family of squatters, all brothers. Before the Lincolns moved in the brothers had cleared an acre of ground and built a log cabin on it. Because of their strange goings-on the neighbors called their cabin The Mysterious House.

The moment the Lincolns moved into the Pigeon Creek-Buck Horn Valley country the gamblers moved out.[2] Did they know Tom Lincoln? Over in Kentucky they had been gamblers. And according to the records of Cumberland County, Burksville, Kentucky, Thomas Lincoln had been constable, 1802-1804.[3] Did these men fear ex-Constable Lincoln? Their sudden abandonment of the place left an unsolved mystery in Buck Horn Valley and Tom Lincoln said nothing to help solve it.

A mile or so east of the gamblers' cabin Reuben Grigsby had built his great two-story hewn-log house, and was already well settled when, in the frosty summer of 1816, he met Thomas Lincoln on the bleak Indiana wilderness trail.

Lincoln said, "My name's Tom Lincoln. I'm looking for a location." Grigsby eyed him shrewdly: "I'm Reuben Grigsby."

"I'm a carpenter by trade," Lincoln added. Grigsby studied Tom's swarthy face then replied, "That suits me. I'm looking for a cooper." That's how Tom Lincoln got the job of making casks for the Grigsby still-house.[4]

During that first winter in Indiana when Abe saw Reuben Grigsby he asked his father why Grigsby limped. "Indians," said Tom.

Abraham knew by heart his father's experience with Indians; and

Reuben Grigsby's childhood experience matched Tom Lincoln's. Abe could vividly retell how in May, 1786, his grandfather Abraham, for whom he had been named, had been tomahawked to death by Wabash Indians at Long Run near Hughes Station, Kentucky. And how an Indian grabbed up seven year old Thomas, carrying him under one arm down the lane. "Don't kill me," Thomas had cried. The Indian stopped and looked back at the cabin. A half-moon trinket glittered on his breast. Tom's brother, Mordecai, in the cabin, fired and killed the Indian. Little Tom fled back home.[5]

When Reuben was four years old a band of sun-worshipping Indians entered his home near Bardstown, Kentucky. His father was away. Reuben scampered up the stick-and-mud chimney and tried to hide. But an Indian yanked him down and made him watch while other Indians killed his three older brothers and a sister. Then the Indians started north, carrying Reuben and driving his mother as she carried her baby.

When Mrs. Grigsby tired so she could not walk fast enough to please her captors, they killed her. The baby cried. They held it by the heels and dashed its head against a tree. And when the Indians grew weary of carrying Reuben they threw him into a river. An old squaw swam out and rescued him. Again they threw him in. And again the squaw rescued him. The tribe let her keep Reuben. Soon afterward he developed what was called white swelling. With herb poltices the old squaw doctored and saved his leg. But that leg never grew as much as the other, making him always limp when he walked.

For seven years Reuben Grigsby lived with the Indians. During those years, from four to eleven, he acquired many of their customs. He talked very little and was overly cautious. He went through their religious rites. "He's just like an Indian," said his neighbors.[6]

Common childhood suffering appeared to draw Thomas Lincoln and Reuben Grigsby together. The Ten O'clock Line—that imaginary zigzaging line drawn across Indiana in 1809—only a few miles north of Pigeon Creek—to separate roaming Indians from white land-seekers, held a deeper significance for Grigsby and Lincoln than it did for the average settler.

In the Grigsby household were seven sons: Aaron, Ruben, Jr., Charles, Redmond, William, Nathaniel and James. Quickly Nathaniel, known as Nattie, and Abe became close friends. Meanwhile, Aaron and Abe's sister, Sally, met regularly at the spring on washdays.

By early 1818, movers from Virginia, North Carolina, Tennessee,

Kentucky and some eastern states, were coming into the Pigeon
Creek community. Like Thomas Lincoln they sought free homestead
land, commonly called Congress land. Among them was James Gentry,
a wealthy slave-holder from near Maceo, Kentucky, just across the
Ohio River from Hanging Rock (Rockport), Indiana. Gentry sold his
slaves, and with his wife and ten children, moved in and took up a
thousand acres of land adjoining the Lincoln farm.[7]

Abraham and Nathaniel Grigsby made friends with one of the sons,
twelve year old Joseph, forming a three-way boyhood companionship
which, for frank exchange of ideas, can hardly be matched in youth
history. According to Pigeon Creek standards the Grigsby and Gentrys
were very wealthy and the Lincolns were decently poor. The Grigsbys
and Lincolns were anti-slavery; the Gentrys were pro-slavery. The
Grigsbys and Gentrys were close-fisted thrifty; the Lincolns often did
favors for people without pay. Usually the Lincolns gave the other
fellow just a little bit the best of the bargain. These things the three
boys observed, discussed among themselves and reached conclusions
satisfactory to their youthful viewpoints.

Joe and Nattie also discussed Abe. Lincoln "was truthful and
industrious, always working with his own hands when he was not at
school or studying at home," said Nattie.[8]

Into the community moved another wealthy man, seventy year
old Thomas Turnham, a Revolutionary War soldier opposed to
slavery. Turnham entered Congress land across Pigeon Creek bottoms
and the deer licks, right north of Thomas Lincoln's farm. It wasn't
long until his son, David, and Abe were friends.

In spite of pestilence and other hardships, travelers, movers and
traders, in increasing numbers, made their way through the Indiana
wilderness. They followed the road—scarcely more than a trail—
which passed the Lincoln home. Some told tales about yellow fever;
some boasted of fights with bears and panthers; some described Harmonie on the Wabash River where the Angel Gabriel conversed with
Father George Rapp. Rapp preached the doctrine of the dual sexual
nature of Adam and then demanded strict celibacy of all Rappites.

Many incidents in the early life of Abraham Lincoln were intimately
tied to the passing of these travelers. One day Abe's father, anxious
to share the hospitality of the Lincoln cabin, hailed a weary horse-
man. "Light, stranger, and rest your saddle," Tom invited. The
stranger sat his horse and asked, "How is the road ahead?" Tom
walked to the rail-fence to answer the man's question. Out ran Abe
and hooked a skinny leg over the top rail. "Stranger, what's the news?"

he called anxiously. "Hush up," said Tom and went on telling about the condition of the road.

Only for a moment did Abe hush up. "Stranger, what is the news where you come from?" he cried. Tom Lincoln straightened out an arm and brushed Abe off the fence. Humiliated but not conquered, Abe Lincoln and Dennis Hanks, with whom he had been playing, crawled alongside the fence worm to a spot beyond the reach of Tom's powerful arm. There Abe waited and thought over what next to do. When he saw the man rein his horse to leave, Abe pleaded: "Say, stranger, what is the news?"[9] After the stranger had told him and ridden away, Abe said to Dennis, "Pap don't think it's polite to ask folks questions. But Denny, I reckon I wasn't born polite. There are so many things I want to know and how else am I a-going to get to know them?"[10]

One place Abe could get to know things was at Noah Gordon's horse-mill; men and boys from miles around congregated there, told jokes and swapped stories. On a late afternoon Abe Lincoln and David Turnham rode to the mill a mile and a quarter south of the Lincoln cabin. Finding a line-up they waited, as was customary, to take their turn.

Abe pulled his sack of shelled corn off his old gray mare's back and watched the mill, which seemed to him to be grinding unnecessarily slowly. "My hound pup can eat all the meal that thing'll grind in a day and then howl for his supper," he commented to Turnham. About sundown Abe's turn came. After hitching his mare to the long driving sweep he crawled onto the end seat. "Get!" he ordered. Around and around walked the horse, the wooden cog-wheels revolving and growling as they turned the shafts which drove the millstones.

Miller Gordon stood on the grinding floor methodically dipping his toll box into the hopper, taking out the mill's pay.

"Get up!" Abe shouted as he urged his old nag to step faster, but she acted as if she didn't like the idea at all. Louder roared the grinding stones and the song of the mill filled the brushy hollow while fragrance of broken corn grains floated out onto the evening air. Still faster Abe wanted the horse to step. He hit her a whale of a whack with his gad and yelled, "Get up!" That instant the old mare let drive a shoeless hoof squarely onto Abe Lincoln's forehead. He fell back, limp and senseless. Noah Gordon stopped the mill, jumped from the floor and examined Abe. The boy was bleeding, possibly to death.

David Turham ran for Tom Lincoln who arrived with a wagon and

hauled Abe home.[11] Neighbors flocked in and helped to lay out
Abe's body. All night they kept the wake. The next morning
a mourner exclaimed, "Look! He's coming back to life!" Another
cried, "He's coming straight back from the dead!" Abe jerked all over.
Slowly he rolled his tongue, then blurted his unfinished indictment
of the horse: "You old hussy!" [12]

The experience of being unconscious for several hours and then
completing a sentence caused Lincoln to speculate a great deal on the
workings of the mind. Finally he explained the phenomenon to his
satisfaction: "Just before I struck the old mare my will through the
mind had set the muscles of my tongue to utter the expression, and
when her heels came in contact with my head the whole thing stopped
half-cocked, as it were, and was only fired off when mental energy or
force returned." [13] Being "apparently killed for a time," as he put it,
may have influenced Lincoln to compose some verse about time as
an "empty vapor." [14]

During the forenoon of November 28, 1820, while looking out of his
cabin door, Abe saw Mrs. Margaret McFarland, widow of the local
shoemaker, walking up the trail. She had her four children with her.
Her husband and two other children had died of milksickness and were
buried near Nancy Hanks Lincoln. Abe knew that times were very
hard for the widow—so hard that Dr. Stephen P. Cissna, the local
physician, was sending her baskets of food. Back in Kentucky the
Lincolns and McFarlands had been friends.

"Pap, what you reckon is the matter now?" Abe asked. "She'll tell
us," said Tom. Mrs. McFarland came to the door: "Folks, would
you mind keeping my children until tomorrow?" Mrs. McFarland
blushed. "I'm going down to Rockport," she murmured.

Abe heard a horse's hoofbeats. He turned and saw Dr. Cissna. Mrs.
McFarland added: "Dr. Cissna and I are going down there to be
married." She climbed up on the horse behind the doctor. As they
rode away Abe heard the doctor sing out, "I've told the boys to have
the preacher on hand." The next morning they returned on the same
horse. Tom Lincoln called to them, "Light, folks and rest your saddle."
They got down and came into the cabin. When they reached Rockport, they explained there was no preacher on hand and the boys had to
go to the country and bring in the Reverend James L. Thompson, a
Methodist minister. The wedding feast got underway at two o'clock
in the morning in the Brown Tavern and lasted until sunup.

Mrs. Cissna looked at her four children and said to Mrs. Lincoln,
"I want to pay you for their trouble."

"We don't want any pay," replied Mrs. Lincoln. "They ain't been a bit of trouble," Tom assured her. "We're proud to help you." Abe, feeling differently about it, asked, "Pap, why don't you ask her for her shoemaker's tools and call it even?"

Mrs. Cissna smiled. Her social position had just risen from shoemaker's widow to doctor's wife. "Of course, Abe, you can have those tools. I won't need them any longer," she said.[15]

When not reading by the fireplace Abe Lincoln tried his hand at the cobbler's art. He also found time to go hunting in order to supply the family table with fresh meat. One cold afternoon he and Joe Gentry went deep into the forest to hunt wild turkeys. Night shut down so dark the boys could not see a turkey roosting on a limb shoulder high. They tossed a blanket and some skins on the ground, rolled up in them and dropped off to sleep. Snow fell and covered them completely. Just before morning a herd of wild hogs came along looking for a warm place. Lincoln nudged Gentry,"Wake up, Joe. We're going to have company." The hogs rooted through the snow and crawled in bed with the hunters.[16]

Feeding on pecans, acorns, pig-nuts, beechnuts—all called mast by backwoodsmen—wild hogs put on meat which, though not of the firm quality of corn-fed hogs, was much relished by Lincoln's root-grubbing, hungry neighbors.

As winter grew colder Lincoln and his friend, John Tuley, who lived about two miles to the southwest, decided to trap game with a pen of poles. They built one eight feet square, notching its corners as if they were building a hewn-log house. They covered it with slabs except at the exact center which they left open to let in daylight. From the center to outside they dug a channel, deep and rather narrow. To bait the trap they dropped shelled corn into the channel. Quails, turkeys, wild hogs followed the corn trail to the center of the pen. Unable to figure a way out the victims became panicked, kept looking up at the center opening and stayed there until Abe and John removed them.[17]

To add venison to the family diet and buckskin to the family wardrobe, Abe would take his father's rifle gun and walk northeastward a short way to the deer licks along Prairie Fork of Pigeon Creek. There David Turnham, living north of the licks, joined him. During the night deer came to lick the gray, saline earth as buffalo had done for centuries. Such crusty areas being without vegetation made it easy for hunters to get in good shots. "Abe was not so fond of a gun as I was," Turnham recalled.[18]

Throughout the growing season Abe helped his father with the farm work. Eventually bears got into Tom Lincoln's cornfield and damaged the greening ears. More bears broke into the pens and killed his fattening hogs. " 'Tis the heavy hand of Providence laid upon me. Whom the Lord loveth He chasteneth," Abraham heard his father again lament.[19]

Abe described the troublesome situation in verse:

> "When first my father settled here,
> " 'Twas the frontier line;
> "The panther's scream filled night with fear,
> "And bears preyed on the swine.

Since Lincoln's neighbors also were having bear trouble a bear hunt was organized. With a pack of dogs, men and boys set out to destroy the marauders. Abe described the onset of the hunt:

> "Now to elude the eager pack
> "Bear shuns the open ground
> "Through vines, he shapes his track,
> "And runs it round and round.
> "Across the glade he sweeps for flight
> "And fully is in view
> "The dogs, now fired by the sight,
> "Their cry and speed renew." [20]

The hunters chased the bears to Cow Pond. There Matthew Rogers cornered one but had run out of ammunition. Grabbing Mason J. Howell's butcherknife, Rogers waded in and fought the bear face to face. At the second or third blow the knife blade broke off in the bear's jaw. Maddened by pain the bear mauled and bit Rogers fiercely. Howell went to Rogers' rescue. Swinging a heavy club, he struck the bear hard between the eyes. Nine bears were killed in that hunt.[21]

On the edge of Pigeon Bottoms, northwest of the Lincoln cabin, was a stand of firewood timber. With his keenly sharpened axe over his shoulder, a book in one pocket and a hunk of cornbread in another, Abe Lincoln went whistling along the deer path to his day's work. His stepsister, Matilda Johnston, followed, moving over the dead leaves as softly as his pet cat. Because there was danger in crashing trees and glancing axe, Matilda's mother had forbidden her to go with him into the woods. When close enough the girl sprang onto Abe's back, throwing him off balance. In the fall she cut her foot on the axe blade.

Blood spurted. Matilda screamed. Abe got up, took out his handkerchief and bound the wound. "What will we tell mother as to how this happened?" he asked. "I'll tell her," said Matilda, "I cut my foot on the axe. That will be no lie." Lincoln shook his head: "That won't be all the truth, the whole truth. Tildy, you tell the whole truth and trust your mother." [22]

As if in celebration of Abraham Lincoln's thirteenth birthday, a big road was laid out between Evansville, forty miles to the southwest on the Ohio, and Corydon, the Indiana State capital, sixty miles to the east. This new road following the old blazed trail, passed alongside the Lincoln cabin. A little way to the eastward it crossed the three hundred mile long Louisville-Vincennes-St. Louis highway over which stage coaches lumbered, carrying passengers and mail. Soon homeseekers, missionaries, fur-traders, cut-throats, runaway slaves, politicians, slave-hunters, New Harmony communists, soldiers patrolling for "bad" Indians, were passing Abe Lincoln's door. It was the full pageant of the roaring Hoosier frontier. And at every opportunity young Abe ran to the fence, swung a leg over the top rail and called out: "Stranger! What's the news where you come from?"

From travelers Abe learned that aging American men wanted ginseng. In China ginseng was selling for its weight in silver. The demand was much greater than the supply. "Chew a root of ginseng," wrote an elderly man in the Vincennes *Western Sun*. "It gives an uncommon warmth and vigor to the blood and frisks the spirits beyond any cordial. It will even make old age amicable by rendering it lively." [23]

Abe knew there was a rich patch of the valuable root just below the place where Matilda had cut her ankle on his axe; he and Joe Gentry sharpened their grubbing hoes and went to work. They dug ginseng in the spring rains; they dug it in the summer heat. Some days they made as much as seventy cents. They were happy that digging up the fountain of youth for romantically inclined old men was such a rewarding activity.

Early one morning, instead of going to the ginseng patch, Abe Lincoln streaked it four miles over the hilly Troy-Vincennes trail to the home of Shadrach Hall, the tanner. Wesley Hall, about Abe's age, opened the cabin door. Abe went in and sat down. "How are all the folks?" Mrs. Hall asked. "Oh, they're all well," said Abe. After a pause he added: "Mother sent me here to borrow your fine-toothed comb." Mrs. Hall eyed him apprehensively "What's the matter?"

Abe studied the puncheon floor: "Mother thinks we got creepers."

Mrs. Hall threw up her hands: "You reckon it's a fact?" Abe reckoned it was: "We don't have any comb with teeth fine enough to catch them. Mother thought you might let us borrow yours."

Mrs. Hall pointed to a newspaper on the floor and ordered Wesley, "Put your head over that!" She bent down and combed his hair. Frightened lice rattled onto the paper. She groaned "Why, Wesley Hall! Your head is just alive with creepers!" She examined her other son Squire. "All you young-uns got creepers!" she cried. "Abe, put your head down there!" Again she combed. Abe's head was alive with the things, too. "You all were playing together last week!" she stormed. Where did Abe get them? He couldn't explain; maybe travelers brought them along with the news.[25]

One traveler by the name of William Jones brought a general store and meat market, in 1823, and opened where the Boonville-Corydon road crossed the Rockport-Bloomington highway, two miles southwest of the Lincoln cabin. That was the beginning of a town. Abe asked Jones for the jobs of cutting pork and rendering lard and got both.[26] The pay was not much but the jobs gave Lincoln an opportunity to talk with people who traded at the store. Also here he began reading Jones' copy of the Vincennes *Western Sun & General Advertizer,* a weekly newspaper which came to the store. It was the first newspaper Lincoln ever read regularly.[27]

From the outset William Jones' background interested Abraham Lincoln. Born in Vincennes on January 5, 1800, William was three years old when his father, Peter Jones, was appointed Esquire Justice of General Quarter Sessions of the Peace for Indiana Territory at the capital, Vincennes. He was seven when his father was elected to the Board of Trustees of Vincennes University. Its president was William Henry Harrison, Territorial Governor. At ten, William saw his father organize the Light Horse Company to defend the old city against Tecumseh, the powerful Indian chief. Tecumseh and his three hundred warriors had come bent on breaking the Ten O'Clock Line Treaty and eventually driving white settlers from the whole western country. It was this Ten O'Clock Treaty line which Lincoln and his fellow Hoosiers called "the frontier line."

After Indiana entered the Union, Captain Peter Jones, in violation of the State Constitution and the Ordinance of 1787, openly sold Negro slaves at the door of his tavern.[28] In an inventory of his estate dated September 1, 1819, listed between a meat axe and a keg of brandy, were the names of seven Negro slaves ranging in value from $25 for

Phillip to $400 for Jonathan.[29]   That same year widow Sarah Jones,
serving as administratrix for the captain's estate, paid $40 to Vincen-
nes University for a year's tuition for her son, William, to study Latin,
Greek, English Grammar, Mathematics and Geography.   Thus the
appraised value of the slave, Jonathan, equalled the cost of ten years
of university training for his young master, who was now Abe Lincoln's
employer.[30]

The estate settled, William Jones, in company with Gideon Romine,
left Vincennes and came to Pigeon Creek community.   Since 1815,
Gideon Romine, son of the nearby prosperous Lincoln neighbor, Christopher Romine, had been tending bar in the Jones tavern at Vincennes.
Bartender Romine's services were estimated to be worth $200 a year.[31]
At the crossroads, in upper Spencer county, Jones established his
general store and hired Abe Lincoln.   The store became the shopping
place for political fixers, slave-hunters (called "nigger-ketchers" and
"patter-rollers"), story tellers, drunks, horse buyers, gamblers, social
reformers.   Lincoln met them all, and took advantage of the opportunity to ask the news.

Even when Lincoln was not working, William Jones encouraged him
to hang around the place.   It was good business for Jones; Abe told
jokes, made up parodies, recounted news he had just read in the Vincennes *Sun*. Sometimes Abe put on the dog by carrying a cane. "It was
a freak of mine," he said. "My favorite one was a knotted beech stick.
I carved the head myself." [32]   He began work on another cane but
left it unfinished.   Jones laid it away.   "Abe was warmly attached
to Bill Jones," Dennis Hanks recalled.[33]

William Jones' success with the general store caught the sharp
business eye of Lincoln's wealthiest neighbor, James Gentry.   Gentry
opened a store in competition, about one hundred yards to the westward and across the Corydon road from the enormous Gentry two-
story hewn-log house.   When his store was going well, James Gentry
laid out a town and persuaded people to buy his lots and build on
them.   The new town grew rapidly.   Because of increasing traffic over
the New Harmony-Boonville-Corydon road, the United States Government established a post office there and named it Gentry's Store.

Meanwhile Lincoln worked irregularly for Jones.   Sometimes he
would take a smoothly shaved clapboard over to an old stump near
the Gentry establishment, sit down and figure on it.   Once John W.
Lamar and his father came by.   When Mr. Lamar pointed to him and
said "Abe, you'll amount to somebody someday," Abe paid no apparent attention.   Several times after that John and his father went by

the stump. And Abe Lincoln was always there either writing on the clapboard or reading a book or newspaper, while other men and boys were loafing.[34]

Ambitious to control the whole town, James Gentry bought Jones' store and renamed the area about it Gentryville. Jones moved perhaps half a mile west of Gentryville, on the New Harmony-Boonville road, and set up a new store. He took Abe Lincoln along with him. Customers followed.[35] At the new store Abe increased his free entertainment by telling bigger tales and more news from the Vincennes *Sun*. Also, he began taking a great interest in local, state and national politics. "Abe is a well-posted politician," Jones said proudly.[36]

The growing success of Jones' new establishment cut into the profit of Gentry's store and even hurt the sale of town lots. So Gentry persuaded Jones to move back to Gentryville. This time Jones opened up at the southwest corner of the crossroads. Again Abe Lincoln and his stories moved with him and again the town started booming along with Jones' business.

With hope of offsetting Jones' competition, James Gentry built still another store—across from Jones on the southeast corner of the crossroads. He took Benjamin and Gideon Romine into partnership with him and called the firm the Gentry-Romine Store.[37] Though as shrewd in his dealings as Gideon Romine, James Gentry was not as proficient in business arithmetic. Someone asked him what per cent he was making on the sale of goods. "God bless your soul, I don't know anything about your per cent. But I know when I buy an article in Louisville for a dollar and sell it here in Gentryville for two dollars I double my money every time," replied Gentry.[38]

To Abraham Lincoln's delight John Baldwin opened a blacksmith shop in the northwest angle of the crossroads, about a hundred feet north of Jones' store. Here Abe watched Baldwin, grimy and soot-covered, rest his great muscular arms on the long bellows shaft and pump it up and down. When a horseshoe in the roaring forge glowed to a white heat, Baldwin seized it with tongs and pounded out a melody on the anvil. And while Baldwin pounded, Abe listened to stories the blacksmith told, some decently funny, some off color, but all with nubs as sharp as plow points. "John Baldwin is Abe's particular friend," said Dennis Hanks.[39]

About the time Baldwin was starting the blacksmith shop, Peter B. Whittinghill was putting up a corn-cracker down the road west of Gentryville. Now Abraham Lincoln had his first glimpse of industry and the employment of factory labor. That glimpse was enlarged when the Gentry family began operating a cotton gin a short way southeast of the old Gentry store. In a little while cotton chopping was as familiar to Lincoln as corn hoeing.

The growing community soon attracted two slick-tongued high-hatted Kentucky horse-buyers who rode into town. Seeing them enter Gentry's store, Abe moseyed over and listened to their big talk. "We're going up north of Elizabeth to buy horses," he heard them say. That gave Abe an idea for a bit of fun. Visiting Gentryville housewives, he explained his scheme and borrowed tin pans and brass kettles. He hurried north on the Rockport-Bloomington road, over the bridge beyond Saltzman's Spring, the neighborhood fist-fighting ground, and hid. While he waited he tied the kettles and pans to his clothing. About sundown he saw the horse-buyers riding up Saltzman's Hill. Abe let them get within a stone's throw before he staggered out, rattling his kitchenware armor, yelling and waving his arms. The frightened horses reared and refused to go any farther. The men spurred them. Abe fell down, pretended to be trying to get up, yelled and fell back again. The horses bucked and snorted. Abe staggered to his feet and headed for the buyers, still yelling and pounding his pans and kettles.

Clutching their high hats, the men wheeled their horses and fled back toward Gentryville. Abe rattled into town and was greeted with loud whoops. "Where are the buyers?" he asked.⁴⁰ "Look!" said a loafer, pointing eastward. All Lincoln saw was a cloud of dust settling down in the twilight.

Once again it was spring and Tom had set Abe to plowing for corn. With John D. Johnston, still a mere child, holding the plow handles, Abe drove the horse straight across the field, plowing a shallow furrow. "Get up!" Abe shouted, but the old horse continued to saunter along. Suddenly, however, it threw up its head and almost trotted across the field. At the end of the furrow Abe examined the horse's head. "Why, it's a big chin fly," he said and knocked the fly off. "But, Abe," lamented John, "that's all that made him go!" ⁴¹

The corn was about ready to be laid by and Tom wanted the field finished; so he put bells on the yoke of oxen Abe was working. As long as Tom could hear the bells he felt sure Abe was busy. But one drowsy summer day—good corn-growing weather—the bells tinkled merrily on while Abraham Lincoln slept under a walnut tree, holding a book in his hand. His oxen, feeding on the corn, kept the bells going.

Joe Gentry, crossing the field, went over to Lincoln and shook him: "Wake up, Abe! Wake up! Your oxen are eating the tops off your corn." Lincoln rubbed his eyes and drowsily answered, "Oh, that's all right, Joe. It'll grow out again." [42]

When the corn grew too high to plow Abe cut the weeds with the hoe and hilled each stalk at its roots. It tasseled and went into ears. Following a rain, the sun burst out steaming hot, forcing the ears to grow so rapidly Abe was sure he could hear them crackling: "The rain makes the corn laugh." [43]

Needing another ox, Tom Lincoln went up to the home of William Wood, an enterprising farmer who lived midway between Gentryville and Elizabeth, about a mile and a half north of the Lincoln farm. A night or two later the ox, named Buck, bought by Tom, broke out and wandered off home and Tom sent Abe to bring the animal back. Abe found Buck contentedly grazing in a field. After helping to drive the ox into a barnlot, Mr. Wood offered a rope: "You can lead Buck with this." "No," said Abe, "I won't lead him. I'll ride that ox home and make him pay for his smartness."

While Abe cut a gad, the entire Wood family came out to see the show. He leaped onto the ox's back and waved at Wood's attractive daughter, Elizabeth. Buck stood immovable. "Get out of here!" yelled Abe. Buck didn't move. Abe jammed his heels hard into Buck's flanks. Resenting that, Buck jumped high into the air and came down with a jolt on all fours. Around and around the barnlot the ox leaped and bawled, swayed, kicked, bucked, did everything an ox could do to throw off a rider. But Abe Lincoln stuck on tighter than a hungry tick, for Elizabeth Wood was watching him. Her father shouted, "Better get off and lead him! He'll break your neck against that fence!"

On and on went the struggle between Abe Lincoln and Buck. "Have the bars down 'gin we get around again!" finally yelled Abe.

Wood ran to the bars, but before he could lay them down Buck made another circuit and headed straight for him. Frantically, Wood jumped aside. The ox leaped the bars and headed down the road, Lincoln sticking on. They covered the first mile in no time. Buck slowed to a walk. Then Abe laid it on heavy with the gad. Panting, his tail drooping, the ox went into a jog trot. As they entered the Lincoln barnyard, Abe grinned at Tom and patted Buck: "I gentled him, Pap." [44]

Fall and winter passed and on the stormy night of May 8, 1825, Abe Lincoln went to sleep in his cabin loft unaware that the Marquis de Lafayette of France, aboard the steamboat *Mechanic,* was passing an Ohio River point only sixteen miles away. Since August 16, 1824, the day Lafayette landed at Castle Garden, New York, the whole United States had been sizzling with patriotic fervor.[45] Lincoln had read in the Vincennes *Western Sun* and heard travelers, pausing in Gentryville, tell of the amazing receptions being given to the American Revolutionary War General, who was now the nation's guest. Bands played "See the Conquering Hero Comes." Cannon boomed salutes. People sang the "Marseillaise." Transparencies, showing Lafayette in heroic pose, illuminated coffeehouses and roadside taverns. Beneath arches of fire and flowers banners read:

> *"Lafayette, Friend of Liberty*
> *"Welcome to the Land of Liberty."*

Lafayette was scheduled to come up the Ohio River. But when? None of Lincoln's neighbors was more interested in the General's visit than was Thomas Turnham, who had served under Lafayette at Brandywine and had been wounded and had fought at Yorktown when Washington and Lafayette forced Cornwallis to surrender.

Through the winter of 1824-1825, when not working in the Jones store, Abe cut cordwood for the Turnhams. Eagerly he listened to the old Revolutionary War veteran describe battles for American independence, tell how Lafayette and Washington acted under gunfire. Already the sixty-eight year old Marquis de Lafayette had travelled, by stage-coach and boat, more than four thousand miles in America. From New York to New Orleans, to St. Louis, not a single accident had marred his journey. But he had yet to sail up the Ohio River along the Indiana shore.

Lincoln slept but, before daylight on May 9th, startling news jarred him and his neighbors wide awake: "Lafayette's boat's been wrecked!" Through pouring rain Hoosiers scurried over logs, down trails, across black slashes to the overhanging rock southeast of Troy. Nearby they saw the steamboat *Mechanic* impaled on snags which were poking up through crevices of jagged flint. "Where's Lafayette?" neighbors asked. Those who had come earlier pointed to a house across the river. "He's been oared over there," they said.[46]

Fragmentary accounts picked up and pieced together showed that the *Mechanic's* paddlewheels had been turning very rapidly, a dangerous thing in broad daylight and certainly hazardous at night. Lafayette was asleep in the ladies' cabin when, about midnight, the vessel hooked onto the flint rocks. The captain of the vessel had shouted, "A snag!" General Lafayette jumped out of his berth; his son, George Washington Lafayette, ran on deck. "Quick," ordered

the captain, "put Lafayette in the boat!" Water was pouring in the
Mechanic. She was settling fast, her boilers hissing. "They're going
to blow up!" someone cried. Lafayette boarded a small lifeboat, and
through the cold pelting rain the captain steered the small boat to the
Indiana bank and landed under the overhanging rock. Wet and shiver-
ing the great Frenchman clambered ashore and sat down on a water-
soaked mattress while an attendant, with a candle, built a fire near
a gurgling spring of cold water. As they had pulled away the *Mechanic*
went down, taking with her the General's hat, all his papers and his
carriage.[47]

From midnight until nine o'clock Lafayette occupied the chilly edge
of the Indiana wilderness, only a few miles southeast of the spot where
the Lincolns had landed in December, 1816. It was such tales of the
famed Frenchman that helped Abe form an opinion of him. Similarly,
he formed opinions of Washington, of George Rogers Clark, of Thomas
Turnham, of other Revolutionary War soldiers. "Pillars of the Temple
of Liberty" he called them.[48]

Excitement over Lafayette died down and Abe resumed work on the
Lincoln farm. He and Sally had hauled a load of manure out of the
pole barn and returned for more. But Abe had neglected to lay up
the bars when Sally first drove the wagon into the barnlot and their
spotted colt, tied to its mother, broke loose, ran through the fence
opening and right into the clothesline full of washing which Sally and
Mrs. Lincoln had put out that morning. It knocked down the props, got
tangled in the wet clothes and trampled them into the dirt. Mrs.
Lincoln and Sally helped Abe chase the colt, around trees and between
outhouses. Sally became so angry she panted, "You're a bulger!"
Later when a Kentucky horse-buyer named Glenn came by and offered
a good price for the colt, Abe urged, "Sell Bulger, Pap. With that
much money I reckon we could buy another forty acres."[49] Tom
Lincoln gave in and jokingly repeated his favorite tale about a horse
trader he had known in Kentucky who always required a guarantee
with each bill of sale: "I warrant him sound in skin and skeleton and
without faults or faculties."[50]

By late spring of 1825, easy going, ever helpful Thomas Lincoln was
again in trouble. He had endorsed a neighbor's note which was coming due and the neighbor refused to meet it. Tom explained to Abe:
"I've got it to pay. And it's going to sweep away just about everything we got—unless I can hire you out."[51]

"All right, hire me out," agreed Abe. Regretfully, Tom added,
"Reckon I'll have to hire out Sally, too."

Hoping to find employment, Abe walked to the Josiah Crawford home, two miles south. There, the year before, he had daubed their unbarked round-log cabin. Also he had borrowed their copy of David Ramsay's *Life of Washington*, taken it home, allowed it to get wet and topped corn to pay for the damage.[52] Moving in from Kentucky, the Crawfords had shortly become outstanding citizens of Buck Horn Valley. Their religious zeal appealed to their neighbors, they being so devout they had named their children Abel, Samuel, Joseph, Ruth and Mary. Josiah Crawford, generally called Cy, was known as a yarb-and-root doctor and tooth puller. But his wife, Elizabeth, was looked upon as a "real" doctor. She had several medical books in her possession; had read them and tried diligently to practice what they recommended. By profession she was both midwife and general practitioner. With pill bags strapped to her saddle, Elizabeth Crawford rode horseback in all kinds of weather; rode to all parts of the wilderness for more than fifteen miles around.[53] Raising his coonskin cap, Abe greeted the Crawfords: "I want a job of work to help Pap out a little." They hired him at twenty-five cents a day and Cy Crawford put him to work building a strong, cage-like hogpen. Wolves and panthers had been getting into the ordinary pen and killing his fattening hogs. After splitting heavy whiteoak rails Abe notched them at the ends and fitted them together as securely as he would the timbers of a hewn-log house. He notched more rails and covered the pen. It was hard work. "My greatest pleasure when taking a rest after splitting rails," he said, "was to play a solo on my Jews' harp." [54] He finished the pen; Crawford's hogs were not again molested by prowling wolves and panthers.

Crawford pointed to a place just east of his house. "I need a water well there," he told Abe. With pick and shovel Lincoln went to digging. He got hungry and ate heavily. After a meal as he left the table Cy would trip him. "There was a tight scuffle," wrote Mrs. Crawford. Sometimes Abe threw Cy and sometimes Cy threw Abe. "They was always playing pranks on each other." [55]

But work and pranks stopped on the Crawford farm June 23, 1825; for that day Agnes Gentry was marrying Benjamin Romine. Weddings always attracted Pigeon Creekers, although none before had attracted such wide social interest. Agnes' father, James Gentry, was "the rich man of a poor neighborhood," wrote Lincoln.[56]

The Gentrys and Romines enjoyed a standard of living higher than nearby settlers. While both families had carpets on their floors, the Romines had the added luxury of glass pulls on their bureau drawers.

Reproductions of this drawing were distributed throughout Indiana during the 1860 Presidential campaign.

Clothing for both families came either down the Ohio River from Cincinnati or up the Mississippi from New Orleans. The Romines operated one of the biggest distilleries in the valley. The Gentry cotton gin drew patronage from thirty miles around. Both families flatboated their farm produce down river to cotton and sugar plantations. And Lincoln worked for both families. "He was always reading and thinking," declared John Romine.[57]

After the Reverend Young Lamar had performed the wedding ceremony, Abe went back to the Crawford farm, picked up his tools and resumed his job of well-digging. When the well was finished it was deep, cylindrical and neatly walled with limestone.

Sarah, meanwhile, had showed up and the Crawfords had hired her, also. Mrs. Crawford left Sally Lincoln to work in the house and went with Abraham to the corn field to pull fodder off the stalks. Since Abe was over six feet tall, Elizabeth Crawford said he could beat her in reaching the higher blades. Day after day as they worked down the corn rows they discussed the past, present, and future. One time Abe confided he intended to be somebody someday: "Mrs. Crawford, I don't always intend to delve, grub, shuck corn, split rails and the like." [58]

Evenings in the Crawford home Lincoln kindled a fire, took a book from the shelf and sat up late reading and ciphering by the blaze. Unmindful of the Crawfords watching him, he worked sums on their wooden shovel. Sometimes he wrote on planed boards. Using either a charred stick or red keel which he had picked up from the creek bed, he filled shovel and board with words and figures. He wiped them off and put on more. Always he was up early in the morning for the day's work.[59] "Abe worked hard and faithful," said Mrs. Crawford. "When he missed time he would not charge for it." [60]

For nine years—ever since December, 1816, when they first met at the wash place—Sarah Lincoln and Aaron Grigsby had been growing fonder of one another. Now a rather shy, strong, healthy girl of eighteen, Sally was not excitable. "She'll do to tie to," observed Mrs. Crawford.[61] Once when Sarah and Aaron were enjoying an evening together, the Crawford's four year old son, Samuel, spied on them and reported to his mother, "I saw Aaron sparking Sally. I saw him kiss her". Mrs. Crawford scolded "Stop watching Sally and Aaron, or you won't get to go to the wedding." [62]

The Crawfords needed a larger house for their five growing children. At the same time, Tom Lincoln desperately needed more money with which to pay installments due on his wayward neighbor's note. So Tom got the job of carpenter work. "You help Cy whipsaw the boards," he said to Abe.   ..

Still working for twenty-five cents a day, Abe's lot was to be under sawyer in the pit. When he looked up he could see Crawford, as top sawyer, standing on the scaffold, watching the gauge to get the right thickness of the planks. But, down in the pit, when Abraham Lincoln yanked at the end of the heavy saw, sawdust rained on him. He shook his head to dislodge it from his eyes, ears and nose. Crawford pulled up the saw; Abe looked up at Crawford's long nose, blue with its network of veins. Blue-nose Crawford some people called him. Abe pulled the saw down; and each down pull brought a new storm of sawdust. Being under sawyer in that pit probably was the hardest work Abe Lincoln ever did. When each day ended he went to the Crawford home tired out. But at sixteen Abe Lincoln was remarkably healthy. After he had eaten supper he forgot his weariness. Then he teased his sister and the Crawford girls, Ruth and Mary, pulled their hair and played tricks on them until they ran squealing from the room.

One time Abe's tomfoolery annoyed Sally so much Mrs. Crawford said, "Abe, you ought to be ashamed of yourself! What do you expect will become of you?" Abe replied, "Be President of the United States." [63] Mrs. Crawford scoffed: "You'd make a pretty President with all your tricks, now wouldn't you?" Abe didn't mind such words; he set forth his reasons for pushing aside everything else to read a book or work a problem: "I'll study and get ready and some day my chance will come". "From early youth," according to Ward Hill Lamon, "he seemed conscious of a high mission . . . a vision of grandeur and of gloom." [64]

Not long after his chat with Mrs. Crawford, Abe was astonished to hear how constant, hard study could affect some ambitious youths. One of his most brilliant schoolmates became very sick mentally. "In my poetizing mood I could not forget the impression his case made upon me," he wrote. Here are two stanzas of Lincoln's poem about the boy:

> *"And when at length, tho drear and long,*
> *"Time soothed your fiercer woes,*
> *"How plaintively your mournful song*
> *"Upon the still night rose!—*
> *"To drink its strains I've stole away,*
> *"All silently and still,*
> *"Ere yet the rising god of day*
> *"Had streaked the Eastern hill."* [65]

Indian Summer rolled around and Abe Lincoln found new interests. About two miles southwest of his home and a little north, half way between the swimming hole and the Grigsby still-house, was a medium high plateau called Flat-top Hill. There camped a band of sun-worshipping Indians. Coming from the northwest they had set up their wigwams on their old camping grounds. Each fall they came to hunt, fish and visit with their white friend, Reuben Grigsby, Sr., the man who had been their captive for seven years, from four to eleven years of age. With a feather in his hat, old Reuben limped about the camp or sat smoking with the painted warriors. Abraham Lincoln had only to walk to Flat-top Hill to see Grigsby go by with the Indians to a clearing and face eastward. And as the sun rose over the dark forest Lincoln saw the white man do in company with the warriors, what so often he had seen him do alone: mount a log or a stump and reverently flap his arms while he crowed like a rooster.

The fishing and hunting season ended, the Indians left for their homes somewhere in the northwest, Reuben Grigsby going with them. Sometimes he was gone for weeks; but he never told where he had been. This mystery of his goings made his neighbors say, "Reuben, he's just like an Indian." [66]

A friendly Kickapoo Indian, Johnny Kongapod, seems to have been a very welcome visitor to Pigeon Creek and young Lincoln was quite taken up with him. It was claimed Johnny could forecast weather, especially thunder and lightning; and he often repeated Indian camp-fire tales. Johnny's talents so fascinated Lincoln that he wanted to do something for the Indian. Probably having heard the nearby settlers, recently come from Scotland, quote the following epitaph from a gravestone back in Edinburghshire:

> "Here lie I, Martin Eldinbrode,
> "Ha' mercy on my soul, Lord Gode,
> "As I would do were I Lord Gode,
> "And thou wert Martin Eldinbrode," [67]

Using that epitaph as a model, Abe wrote the following appeal for presentation to the Great Spirit on behalf of the talented Kickapoo:

> "Here lies poor Johnny Kongapod;
> "Have mercy on him gracious God,
> "As he would do if he was God,
> "And you were Johnny Kongapod." [68]

Pigeon Baptist Meetinghouse Thomas and Abraham Lincoln helped build in 1820. (Sketch by John H. Rowbottom).

CHAPTER FOUR

MORE NEIGHBORS

Indian summer faded into cold winter. One blustering night Abe, nursing a sore toe, sat with the family in front of the fireplace. Through the driving blizzard which lashed the cabin, drifting snow high against its walls, they heard a faint "Hel-lo!" Tom Lincoln opened the door and called, "Who's here?" "Me," answered a shaking voice. "That you, Wesley?" Tom shouted. "Well, you get right down out of that saddle and come on in here out of the weather." He hurried to the big road, helped Wesley Hall slide a sack of corn-meal off the horse. "Abe! Oh Abe!" Tom yelled. "Come on out here and get Wesley's grist while I put up his horse! The boy's mighty nigh froze, I reckon."

With one shoe on Abe Lincoln hobbled into the snow storm, limping on the ball of his bandaged foot. As light from the open door fell on Abe, Wesley noticed Abe's condition. "Split my big toe open with the axe in the clearing today," explained Abe. Wesley laughed: "I've measured that toe many a time with shavings under your pap's work-bench."

Abe picked up the sack of cornmeal with one hand and, tossing it across his arm, headed toward the cabin with Wesley, leaving Tom to put the horse in the pole stable.

Hall sat down in front of the fireplace and began to thaw out. In came Tom Lincoln; slapping his hands together, he sat down and asked, "You got mighty cold, I reckon?" Wesley nodded. Mrs. Lincoln: "Bet you're mighty hungry, too." Wesley: "Mrs. Lincoln, I ain't had nothing to eat 'cept parched corn since morning." Pointing to a big bank of embers in one end of the fireplace, Mrs. Lincoln added: "We ain't got any cornmeal to make bread with. We're just out. But we got some potatoes in there a-baking and we'll give you a bite to eat pretty soon." Wesley: "Just help yourself out of my meal sack."

Sarah Bush Lincoln opened Wesley's bag and scooped up a measure of meal. Then she hollowed out a turnip, filled it with lard, and lit one end of a tow wick which she had dropped inside and pulled through a notch cut in the turnip rim. She handed the grease lamp to Wesley and a butcher knife to Abe. "You boys go out and get me some bacon," she said.

Abe led the way to the little pole smokehouse. While Wesley held up the light, Abe found a side of bacon and cut a half-moon out of it. After a hearty supper, Wesley relaxed in front of the fireplace. Tom said, "Now, Abe, you get down your book and read to us." Abe gathered an armload of dry sassafras brush from a corner of the cabin and stirred up a big fire. When the flames were going evenly, he took from the shelf where he kept his books Benjamin Franklin's autobiography.[1] He read aloud until bedtime.

While Tom banked the fire, Abe and Wesley climbed the peg ladder to the loft. An upright post held crossed bed rails, the ends of which were fastened into holes bored into the west and north wall logs. Planks lay across the rails with a sack of dry leaves on top. The boys crawled into bed, covered themselves with bearskins, and drifted off to sleep.

By the time Lincoln was seventeen, February 12, 1826, he had reached his full height of six feet and four inches. His hands were too big for his thin body and his legs too long for his buckskin pants. Several inches of shinbone showed. His muscles were as hard as dornicks.[2] Whenever he appeared at log rollings a joyous whoop went up, for his great strength was an asset to any team. Ten to twenty men gathered at a settler's cabin. With axes and handspikes they went to the deadening ground or clearing. Organizing two teams, they tried to defeat each other in piling the most logs into a mountainous heap. And the team which enrolled Abe Lincoln usually defeated the other.[3]

One day, due to his height, Abe bumped his head against the top of the Lincoln door frame and his stepmother said, "Abe, I don't care so much about the mud you track in on my floor for I can scrub that up; but you must be more careful about my whitewashed ceiling."

Patiently waiting until she was away from the cabin, Abe persuaded neighborhood children to wade in a mud puddle. Afterward he led them into the cabin and, one by one, he picked them up and marched them upside down across the spotless whitewashed ceiling. Scarcely had the children fled out of sight before Mrs. Lincoln returned. Wondering what she would do, Abe watched her examine the muddy footprints, drop into a split-bottomed chair and break into a hearty laugh. He started for the door.

Mrs. Lincoln: "Where are you going?" "Wait and see." He went

to the lime barrel, mixed a batch of whitewash and re-whitewashed the
ceiling, beams and all.[4]

Appreciating his stepmother's kindness, Abe always seemed eager
to help her. He walked with her to the dozen or more deer licks a few
hundred yards northeast of the cabin. There he scooped up the crusty,
saline earth and mixed it with hickory ashes in a hopper. With Mrs.
Lincoln directing, he poured water over the mixture, and, as the
brackish water dripped from the hopper, caught it in kettles. Over a
slow fire they boiled the water until only salt remained.

In 1826 Abe left home and went down the Ohio five miles, to the
mouth of Anderson River, half a mile below Troy. There James
Taylor operated a ferry near the spot where the Lincolns had landed
in 1816. Abe asked Taylor for the job of ferryman and got it. From
the ferry's deck he could look across the half-mile wide Ohio River
and see low, flat plantations in Kentucky. On calm days he could
hear the mournful songs of Negro slaves as they chopped cotton or
stemmed tobacco.

Taylor's ferry, which James McDaniel, a native of Scotland, had
established, was a sort of flatboat built to carry only a wagon and
team, or some livestock. Aprons and railings held on the cargo. A
cable, running through pulleys at each end of the boat, was made fast
to trees on the banks of the Anderson River. By letting out one
line and hauling in on the other, Lincoln snubbed the boat upstream.
Sometimes he went to the stern and swung back and forth on a long
sweep, propelling the ferry across the narrow, deep river. Taylor paid
him six dollars a month for the job.

But for that six dollars Abe also worked as Taylor's hired hand.
He was up first in the morning, started a fire in the kitchen stove, took
care of Taylor's horses and kept an eye on the ferry as he plowed
Taylor's fields. In butchering time Taylor sub-hired him. Abe
hated that bloody job, considered rough but expert labor, for which
Taylor's neighbors paid Taylor thirty-one cents a day. But although
he was tired and depressed by the work, Abraham Lincoln continued
to study and get ready. He slept upstairs with Green B. Taylor, the
ferryman's seven year old son. "Abe usually read 'til near midnight,"
according to Taylor.[5]

From the ferry's deck, youthful Abe Lincoln also saw the commerce
of the great Mississippi valley passing; saw craft of all kinds go by
bound for Cincinnati and Pittsburgh, St. Louis and New Orleans.
Steamboats snorted up to the Indiana side of the Ohio. Negro
slaves coonjined firewood back to their vessels. Huge flatboats drifted

lazily downstream while dancers on deck jigged to tunes scraped off by heavy footed fiddlers. Keelboats crept up stream, their white crews heaving at poles and ropes, pulling their lives out for a few dollars and a skinful of whiskey. Broadhorns slid by, carrying hoop-poles and pumpkins to Louisiana plantations and the Red River country.

Sometimes Abe sauntered up to Troy where the log-house lined streets were crowded with boatmen, river pirates, Negro slaves, prostitutes, gamblers, planters. Around Gamage Williams' tavern swirled the town's life. Troy's most successful merchant was Reuben Bates, who in 1812 established a store below town and now operated one of the best boat landings along the Ohio. There Abe Lincoln watched the Bates flatboats push off, loaded with pork, corn, hay, beeswax; saw Bates keelboats tie up with merchandise poled all the way from New Orleans, a thousand miles down river.[6]

Negro clog dancers fascinated Abe. He had seen them oar their masters across from Kentucky to trade in Troy. And while their owners traded, he saw the slaves dance in the streets. He tried to do some of the steps. That attracted passersby who laughed and waved their whiskey bottles, urging Lincoln to go to it. Black slaves grinned and hoed it down. Abe's long legs swung and missed the rhythm. But he kept on trying. Taking a liking to him, the Negroes showed him the steps in slow motion. While the crowd shouted and emptied their bottles, Abe concentrated on clog dancing. He caught on. According to Moss Emacoal, a neighbor of the Lincolns, "Abe got to be one of the best clog dancers in Southern Indiana."[7]

When the Trojans, as the young men of Troy were called, tired of the town's uproar some one would suggest, "Let's go down to the ferry and listen to Long Abe tell his stories." Aboard Taylor's ferry Long Abe retold stories from *Aesop's Fables* and other books, sometimes embellishing them outlandishly. He mimicked well-known political spell-binders and circuit riding preachers. Evoking laughter came easy to him. Yet he found time to put out and tend a tobacco patch, to play his Jew's harp, and to wander back into the hills.

About half a mile north of the ferry was—and still is—a high bluff of shale. In prehistoric ages the Anderson River had been a large stream, and had sculptured ornate pillars and balconies into its stony banks. Crevices separate the balconies. Forty feet up one of these crevices and eight feet below the floor of a balcony, now almost erased by more than a century of frosts and rains, are initials chiseled half a foot high in the stone: A L.

Lincoln left the Taylor ferry on time to arrive home by August 2,

1826, for on that day his sister, Sarah, was marrying Aaron Grigsby. The romance, begun at the Grigsby spring on washday nearly ten years before, had grown with each passing year.

Adhering to the Pigeon Creek-Buck Horn Valley custom, the groom with his attendants left his parents' two-story log-house in time to reach his bride's one-room cabin precisely at noon. The Reverend Charles Harper saw to it that all went according to custom. In his marriage records he wrote: "I Married these on the Same within." [8] The ceremony over, the infare got underway. Contents of the Grigsby still-house were liberally offered, much honor being due Aaron as the first born of Reuben's seven sons. [9]

Abe furnished a part of the entertainment by writing a piece called "Adam and Eve's Wedding Song." No one sang more gaily than Mrs. Josiah Crawford in whose home Aaron had long courted Sally. [10] Where did Lincoln get the idea for his song? Less than thirty miles west of the Lincoln cabin were thriving settlements of Scotch and English immigrants. Several had come to Indiana early in 1817 and by 1826 had built good homes and were well established citizens. They brought with them songs of their native land. [11] Among those songs must have been "When Adam Was First Created," a ballad very popular with aged people then living back on the ancient Scottish-English border. The ballad appeared about 1740 in *The Ladies Evening Book of Pleasures* and had five stanzas of eight lines each. Lincoln's adaptation for Sally's wedding has eight stanzas of four lines each.

> "*As Adam was resting in slumber*
> "*He lost a short rib from his side.*
> "*And when he awoke 'twas in wonder*
> "*To see a most beautiful bride.*"

Lincoln's version went like this:

> "*The Lord then was not willing*
> "*The man should be alone*
> "*But caused a sleep upon him*
> "*And took from him a bone.*"

Neither the peasant balladist nor Geoffrey Chaucer in his *Canterbury Tales,* quoted directly from the Bible in describing the short-rib operation. But Lincoln wrote into his song part of Genesis II, 18 and 21: "It is not good that the man should be alone . . . and closed up the flesh thereof."

The old balladist said that woman "was not taken out of his head, sir, to rule and to triumph in man." Lincoln made that line read: "To show she must not rule him."

The balladist wrote: "Nor was she taken out of his foot, sir, By him to be trampled upon." Abe's version:

> "*This woman was not taken*
> "*From Adam's feet we see*
> "*So he must not abuse her*
> "*The meaning seems to be.*"

Lincoln and the balladist agreed that the short-rib operation took place in a garden. Lincoln said it happened while Adam "dwelt in Eden's shade"; the balladist placed things in a garden "planted by nature." However, they disagreed over the reason woman was made from the man's rib. The balladist contended "she was taken out of his side, sir, His equal co-partner to be." Seventeen year old Abe Lincoln held differently:

> "*This woman she was taken*
> "*From under Adam's arm*
> "*So she must be protected*
> "*From injuries and harm.*" [12]

In the last two lines Abe gave Aaron Grigsby a broad hint to be very considerate of Sarah. The Lincoln family led in singing Abe's song, naturally using the early ballad air: [13]

Subsequently Aaron and Sarah set up housekeeping in a one-room log house about three quarters of a mile northeast of Aaron's parents' big home and not far from the abandoned Lincoln pole-house. [14]

When in the fall Abe returned to his job on the ferry the slow-moving, muddy Ohio beckoned him to go with it down to the Mississippi, down to the sea. Abe decided to go, but first he must convince his father and stepmother the trip would be good for him. All summer he had carefully hoed and wormed his tobacco patch at every moment he could spare from the ferry. Now he cut, cured, and stemmed the enormous leaves. He had two hogsheads of prime tobacco. His father had a surplus of corn and potatoes. Farm products flatboated down the Mississippi—below Natchez or Memphis—always sold, at big profits, to slave-owners.

All Abe needed was a small one-man flatboat. He went home and asked permission to build a boat and make the trip. Still hard up for money, Tom Lincoln enthusiastically approved Abe's plan, but Sarah Bush Lincoln said, "No, it's too venturesome." She warned of highwaymen lurking in the canebrakes, of river pirates who slit their victims' throats and tossed their bodies into the river. Abe stood up and almost cracked his head against the whitewashed ceiling: "Mother, I can take care of myself." Mrs. Lincoln muttered to herself. And when Abe urged "Pap needs the money," she snapped: "Not that bad!" Abe hung around home several days, coaxing his stepmother to let him go. She gave in very reluctantly.

Abe hurried back to the Taylor ferry and in his spare time built a small flatboat. The job took a lot longer than he had expected and once his cargo of tobacco, corn and potatoes was stacked on the river bank it appeared too much for his small craft. Winter was coming on and soon the Ohio River would be closed in with ice. That worried him. Seeing his opportunity fading, Abe sat on Taylor's ferry and disconsolately thought over his problem. He remembered that Jefferson Ray was building a good sized boat up the Anderson River. Maybe he could arrange to ship on with him. He hurried to Ray. "Jeff, could you use an extra hand?" he asked. Jeff, a few years older than Abe, answered, "I reckon I could." Abe added, "I want to make a trade with you. I'll go along with you at the oar if you will take my tobacco and other stuff and pay me the difference."

Ray agreed,[15] and the flatboat, made bottomside up, was rolled on logs down to the river, turned over and launched. Lincoln helped stow on board pork, corn, apples, and cabbage. Then he rolled on his two hogsheads of tobacco and his father's corn and potatoes. The boys loosened the check rope and shoved their flatboat away from shore. With Jeff at the steering oar and Abe at the bow oar, the voyage down river was underway. At seventeen, Abe Lincoln was making his first trip to Southern markets.

Oars bending in the stubborn current, the two Hoosiers drove their craft-with-a-house on it, as flatboats were called, into the Ohio River's channel and swung down stream. Following old rivermen's tradition, Abe joined Ray in an Indian war whoop and then they sang the flatboatmen's chanty:

> *"Hard upon the beech oar!*
> *"She moves too slow—*
> *"All the way to Shawneetown,*
> *"Long while ago!"* [16]

Deftly bucking his bow oar, Abe kept the boat out of eddies, propelled it around snags, yanked it around sawyers, held it firmly in the channel. If he lived to get back home he would be entitled to wear the flatboatman's nickname: *"Half-horse, Half-alligator."*

Down past Rockport, past Evansville, past the broad mouth of the Wabash River with its cypress swamps and crane towns, the boat moved. When darkness shut in and woodcutters' fires lit up the banks, Ray steered the boat to land. Abe hopped ashore and made check line and breast line fast to trees to prevent the boat from moving on down stream during the night. Early in the morning they were again on their way. Seemingly endless yanking filled day after day. The Hoosiers passed Shawneetown, flatboatmen's idea of paradise. They drifted safely past Cave-in-the-Rock, hideout of the old river pirate, Mike Fink, and still a brigands' nest although Mike was long dead. Just one blast from bandit chieftain Sturdevant's horn could bring a hundred cutthroats.

Abe and Jeff felt their flatboat heave under them as they sloshed into the cross current pouring out from the Cumberland River. "Hold her steady," Jeff cautioned. "Steady she is," said Abe. They held the boat to its course. On and on they drifted. Now the Ohio was widening and river craft increasing. The boys bore left. Before them spread out a lake about a dozen miles across. They held to a steady course. In a moment the current of the Ohio shoved them into the broad Mississippi, tossing them around like twigs. Lincoln saw a barrel of Ray's apples roll off the boat and into the river; as he watched them float out of the barrel and bob away in all directions he also saw that Ray was feeling the loss keenly. "Jeff," said Abe, "what is lost is lost. Let's look to the future." Slowly Jeff nodded, but at the same time he seemed to be counting his apples one by one as they disappeared forever.[17]

Soon the young flatboatmen entered the country where cotton was

king. They crept along the Arkansas and Tennessee shores, peddling
Ray's cargo and Tom Lincoln's corn and potatoes to the planters.
Memphis hove in sight. Here, it is believed, Lincoln got rid of his
tobacco. Memphis was a roaring river town in 1826. In its infamous
Pinch-Gut district gamblers slashed one another with long knives;
flatboatmen bit off one another's noses or gouged out eyes for favors
from prostitutes. Outlaws sneaked in from the Natchez trace, spotted
homeward going boatmen and waylaid them. Abe settled with Ray,
crossed the river just above Memphis, entered Crittenden County,
Arkansas Territory, went to Sheriff William D. Ferguson and applied
for a job on his plantation. Because Ferguson's place bordered
Wappanocca Lake, the Sheriff was called "Wappanocca." He hired
Lincoln and put him to work chopping firewood for steamboats.
There he worked alongside Negro slaves,[18] cutting tupelo gum, which,
he soon found out, was a much harder job than chopping Indiana
whiteoak and hickory.

Abe was back home in time for his eighteenth birthday. He celebrated it by grasping the extreme end of an axe handle and holding
the axe at arm's length from his body.[19] Probably not another man in
Buck Horn Valley could do that. Abe's great strength amazed many.
William Wood declared, "Abe could sink an axe deeper in wood than
any man I ever saw." Standing six feet four inches tall, Abe towered
above all his Hoosier neighbors. His long shin bones usually showed
far below his buckskin pants, so men and boys called him Long Shanks.
Said Tom Lincoln: "Abe looks like he has been chopped out with
an axe and needs a jack plane to smooth him down." [20]

Although good natured and generous, Abe was disliked by some
Pigeon Creekers. Still, along with scores of his neighbors, he was invited to the dedication of Jesse Isaac's new puncheon floor, one of the first
dressed floors in Spencer County. Knowing the affair would be a
regular old hoe-down, Abe pulled on his coonskin cap and, swinging
his knotted beech cane, lit out early in the evening for the Isaac double
hewn-log house three miles north of Gentryville. As he stepped into
the long room with its whitewashed walls and ceiling dazzling in the
candle light, he saw that the floor already was cleared. While the
fiddlers tuned, people in little groups talked excitedly. When the
fiddlers started playing the caller clapped his hands and cried, "Swing
your partners!" Did Abe Lincoln swing a girl? "Gosh, no!" said
Moss Emacoal. "Abe got off in a corner and clog-danced better'n ary
nigger. He told his funny stories. Why that feller in no time was
surrounded by men and boys." [21] Lincoln's antics infuriated the women,

for he was robbing them of partners. But he paid no attention to their protests. He went right on dancing and telling outlandish tales while the men laughed and asked for more. Jesse Isaac's wife thought he almost ruined the floor-warming.

Although Abe could clog-dance, he could not sing very well. According to Dennis Hanks, "Abe sometimes attempted to sing but always failed. Sometimes we spent a little time at grog in Gentryville." On some of these occasions Denny raised his voice in Abe's grocery-store favorite:

> *"The turbaned Turk that scorns the world,*
> *"And struts about with his whiskers curled*
> *"For no other man but himself to see!"*

A few more drinks and, with Denny still leading, the Gentryville boys pounded the table until the bottles jingled in tune to:

> *"Hail Columbia, happy land!*
> *"If you ain't drunk, then I'll be damned!"* **22**

Late one freezing night Lincoln, David Turnham and some other Pigeon Creekers were on their way home from Gentryville when they saw a horse, saddled and bridled, standing in the road. Nearby they found the neighborhood drunk stretched out on the ground, half frozen. "Leave him lay," the boys said, "Come on." Lincoln disagreed: "No, that's not right." He picked up the sot, slung him over a shoulder and walked about eighty rods to Denny Hanks' cabin. There Abe kindled a fire and sat up until daylight, rubbing the man's numbed hands. "It was mighty clever in Abe to tote me to a warm fire that cold night," the man told John Hanks, who had moved from Kentucky in 1822.**23**

David Turnham said almost everybody around Pigeon Creek drank their dram, "preachers and Christians included." But some drank too many drams and brought tragedy to their families. One such case undoubtedly inspired Lincoln to write his *John Anderson's Lamentations*:

> *"O sinners! poor sinners take warning by me*
> *"The fruits of transgression behold now and see*
> *"Much intoxication my ruin has bin*
> *"And my dear companion have barbarously slain*
> *"In yonder cold graveyard her body doth lie*
> *"Whilst I am condemned, and shortly must die."* **24**

Lincoln also tried his hand at writing an article on temperance. He showed it to William Wood, who liked it so well he showed it to the Reverend Aaron Farmer, a Baptist preacher who was quite pleased with it and sent it to an Ohio newspaper. When it was published Abe was overjoyed at seeing his words in print. His "piece excelled for sound sense anything that my paper contained," Wood boasted.[25] Whether writing, clog-dancing, fighting, rail-splitting, log-rolling or book-learning, Lincoln surpassed other boys of the neighborhood.

Being eighteen, Abe now was subject to militia duty. Under the laws of Indiana he was required to furnish his own rifle, powderhorn and ammunition, and to be at the drill field on regimental muster day. From here on he must be ready at all times to march across the Ten O'Clock Line and into upper Indiana to quell any Indian uprisings. Abe had no gun, his father apparently having disposed of their long rifle. Since he had little money with which to buy another, he made a deal with his youthful neighbor, Henry Brooner, to buy a gun in partnership with him. Leaving on foot for the sixty mile trip to Vincennes, where they planned to purchase the gun, they hit an ancient buffalo trace. Only recently the great herds had ended their semi-annual trek along the high ridge to the salt licks. This trace, between Louisville and Vincennes was clearly marked with holes the bull buffaloes had made.

Century-old Vincennes was not unknown to Lincoln. He had heard his father and William Jones describe the place. From reading the *Western Sun*, he knew something about the town's commerce and leading citizens. He was not surprised to see Negro slaves working there in violation of the slavery prohibitions in the Indiana State Constitution and the Ordinance of 1787 or to hear the townspeople speaking French as they strolled up and down the cherry-tree lined streets.[26] He saw the little French houses of *poteaux en terre* with gardens in the back. At the foot of Market Street and a few rods down the Wabash River, he saw marks of the buffalo crossing and nearby the ruins of Fort Sackville which Colonel George Rogers Clark and his "American Long Knives" had captured in February, 1779, taking as prisoners General "Hair-Buyer" Hamilton and his British garrison. On the site of Saint Xavier's log church, where Clark had forced Hamilton to sign the articles of surrender, Father John L. Champomier was building the Cathedral of Vincennes. After shopping around town for a while, Lincoln and Brooner bought a rifle for fifteen dollars and left for home.[27]

In May, 1827, Abraham Lincoln had his first military experience. Muster grounds for Training Day were on the flat-topped section of Blue Bill Harris' Hill about a mile southeast of the Lincoln home. There "Lincoln and other young men of the neighborhood went to drill up," said Nathaniel Grigsby.[28] Tall, gangling Abe was by no means the most soldierly looking militiaman on that hill, but certainly he was one of the most eager to learn. He took his training seriously. After all, Indians had massacred his grandfather, the first Abraham Lincoln, in the spring of 1786; and his widowed grandmother had donated the family musket to General George Rogers Clark's Long Knives to use against the marauders. Fear of an uprising kept Lincoln and his Pigeon Creek neighbors in a constant state of uneasiness.[29]

A short while after Training Day, Buck Horn Valley was hit by a furious storm which uprooted big trees, blew down hewn-log houses, snatched up people and cut a wide swath through the forest. Abe visited Sarah, who was expecting a child, to see how she fared. The storm, worst in Spencer County history, had barely missed her tiny cabin.

A woman living along Pigeon Creek, a mile southwest of the Lincoln cabin, had foretold the storm. Lincoln's neighbors neither feared her as a witch nor consulted her as Saul had consulted the witch of Endor. They went to her in times of trouble; they listened to her foretell happenings. To them she was what they called her: The Miracle Woman. Early on the day of the storm some people were passing her cabin when she hailed them. "We are going to have an awful hurricane before nightfall," she warned. "How can you tell?" they asked. "I see two small haystacks made of fog down there in the middle of the meadow." Naturally, the passersby were a bit skeptical of her prophecy, for the morning was bright and clear and they saw no fog in the meadow. But the storm did strike. And in its wake was left greater belief in the Miracle Woman.[30]

With stories of miracle women, spirit-rappers, mad-stones, witches, signs, omens, plus his father's belief in dreams, crowding his youthful mind, Abe Lincoln could scarcely be criticized for being superstitious. "I can't help being this way," he confessed. "My father was like this before me."[31]

Nevertheless Abe was capable of wholesome skepticism—sometimes about his neighbors. Again hard up, his father hired Abe out to cut corn for Neighbor Carter at ten cents a day. Carter, a sharp bargainer, offered to buy at a high price a few acres of Tom Lincoln's farm. Ever trusting Tom, taken in by the glittering offer, allowed Carter to write the deed; but before he signed it, he handed it to Abe. "Read it over," he said.

Carefully, Abe read the paper, his black eyebrows puckering, his big mouth setting harder and harder; then he handed it back to his father. "Better watch out, Pap," he cautioned. Carter protested. Tom's good eye stared at Abe. "What's the matter?" Abe stared right back: "If you sign that deed, Pap, you've sold our whole farm." Whirling on Neighbor Carter, Tom Lincoln thundered, "Somebody's lied and 'tain't Abe!" [32]

About to become a mother, Sarah Lincoln Grigsby lay on her pole-bed while a raw January wind drove snow and rain through the cracks between the logs of the tiny cabin. Apparently neither a doctor nor the experienced local midwife, Mrs. Josiah Crawford, was present. Nature was just taking its course.

Worried that all was not going well with Sarah, Aaron ran for help to his parents' home, three quarters of a mile southwestward. There he and his father, Reuben Grigsby, Sr., yoked a team of oxen to the big sled and drove back to the cabin. With great tenderness they lifted Sarah from her bed, wrapped her in bear and deer skins and laid her on a pallet of straw in the bottom of the sledbox. Reuben cracked his long ox gad and away the sled moved across fields and through woods, snow and mud slithering under the runners. It wound down hillsides and through valleys, jolting over snags and rough ground, with every jolt sharpening Sarah's labor pains. When the sled stopped in front of the two-storied Grigsby house, the men carried Sarah into a big room where Aaron's mother tried to make her comfortable. [33]

The Lincoln family physician, Dr. Edmund Moore, a native of Ireland, had recently moved from Rockport, Indiana, to Morgan County, Illinois. [34] Of course, that was too far away to call him; as soon as it became apparent that a doctor was needed quickly, another was called. When he arrived, he was so drunk the Grigsbys had to put him to bed even though Sarah's condition was becoming more alarming. Then Mrs. Josiah Crawford turned up. But with all her midwifery skill she could now do little for Sarah. William Barker, brother of Mrs. Reuben Grigsby, Sr., came with his wife and little daughter, Millie. Barker went to bed but was awakened about midnight by his wife. "Sally's getting worse! Get Dr. Davis quick!" she exclaimed.

Dr. Davis lived to the westward in Warrick County. Although Pigeon Creek, due to rain and melting snow, was out of its banks, Barker made it to the Davis home, but flood waters forced him and the doctor to take a circuitous route back to the Grigsbys, consuming valuable time. When Dr. Davis arrived he could do nothing for Sarah. It was too late. Her child, a boy, was still-born.[35] On Sunday, January 20, 1828, just three weeks before she would have been twenty-one, Sarah Lincoln Grigsby died.

Aaron and his ten year old brother Redmond ran all the way to the Lincoln home where they found Abe standing in the smokehouse doorway. Abe sensed something was wrong: "What's happened?" Aaron looked at the ground and answered brokenly, "Sally just died."

A haze floated before Abe's eyes, blotting out the world about him. Hiding his lean face in his big hands, he slowly sat down on the doorsill and sobbed. Since their mother's death, he and Sarah had been especially close. They had shared their hardships and their secrets. Abe had told her his hopes and ambitions. When he cracked jokes, no one laughed more heartily than Sally. Quiet, industrious, deeply religious, unpretentious, Sally was much like their mother. Now that she was gone, Abe felt alone.

Neighbors dug a grave about fifty feet east of the Pigeon Creek Primitive Baptist meeting-house, and there the Grigsbys buried Sarah and her baby boy in the same coffin.[36]

Although Abe kept on good terms with Nattie and Jimmy, he nursed a resentment toward the elder Grigsbys. He seemed to blame them for Sarah's death. According to John W. Lamar, who talked to Lincoln, "Abe thought Sally's death was due to neglect." The Barkers said plainly, "They let her lay too long." [37]

Abe continued to go about his work at Jones' store and around the neighborhood. But, in addition to the occasional "fits of blues" described by James Grigsby, a cloud of darkest melancholy settled over Abe's usually sunny disposition. It was not lightened when, a few days later, he read in the Vincennes *Western Sun*, "We can learn nothing from the living which the dead don't teach. We must all come to the mournful and silent grave."

In a few weeks Abe heard that the Richardson family, including a son, Joe, and a daughter, Polly, had moved into the settlement. He sauntered over to their hurriedly thrown-up brush lean-to, rested his calloused hands on the muzzle of his long gun and said, "Ladies, I just dropped in to offer my services." The startled Mrs. Richardson and Polly apprehensively looked at the gun. A young giant with a rifle could make trouble. "Our men-folks have gone down to the river," said Mrs. Richardson, "to get another load off the boat. They'll be back any time. We won't need you."

Lincoln wasn't impressed: "They can't get back tonight for it's been raining too hard. So I'll just stay here with you." He walked over to a big tree, pulled the loose folds of his waumus about his lanky body and sat down, placing the gun across his sharp knees Long-Knife fashion. After listening for a while to the nervous chatter of the girl and her mother, he got up, dragged a huge dry limb near the lean-to and began building a brush heap. Excitedly, Mrs. Richardson asked, "Now what you fixing to do?" "Build a big fire," Abe answered. "These woods are plumb full of wolves. We got to have a big fire or the varmints might give us a heap of trouble." Mrs. Richardson: "I'm not afraid of wolves." Abe: "We'll see." After he had added more brush he kicked the leaves back from the pile and fired it.

Night shut in, black and dreary. Down in the low places jack o'lanterns bobbed along, rising and falling as if men were carrying them. Their bluish shapes conjured up wonder in Abe's mind. Like other people about him he did not understand the phenomenon and feared to investigate it.

Suddenly from deep in the woods came the howl of wolves. The women darted into the brush house. Timidly, Mrs. Richardson looked out and invited Abe in. "Much obliged," said Abe. "I'm all right. Just you step outside now and take a look at the green eyes." Polly looked out: "Why there must be a thousand of them!" Abe: "Oh, no. There're not more than a half-dozen of the varmints. And everyone of them is a coward. Just you watch and see." He grabbed a firebrand, ran toward the wolves waving it. Away they scampered. "See that? Now you folks go to sleep. I'll keep the fire going." So Polly and Mrs. Richardson slept in the lean-to and Abe Lincoln kept watch throughout the night. "I'll have to go home," he called to them at daybreak.[38]

Later that year James Gentry, Sr., asked Lincoln to ship as bow hand on a flatboat to New Orleans. "We need a big, stout feller to oar the boat. We'll pay you eight dollars a month," explained Gentry. Lincoln did not need to think it over. Here was a chance to get away from Pigeon Creek for a few weeks. Besides, several years before, while working for Isaac Bush, Tom Lincoln had flatboated to New Orleans. Ever since then Abe had wanted to see that city. "I'll go," he said. However, the trip had to be delayed; Allen, son of James Gentry, Sr., was going as captain of the boat and he did not want to leave until he knew whether he was father of a boy or a girl. Allen had married Anna Caroline Robey on March 20, 1828; and Katy, as she was known to everyone, figured the baby would arrive about Christmas Day.[39]

While Katy waited Allen and Abe worked at building the two-man flatboat on the south side of Spanker's Branch just below Rockport, right at the flatboat-steamboat landing and woodyard.⁴⁰ Except for danger of snowstorms and ice on the Ohio River, Abe's neighbors preferred to flatboat their farm produce south in late fall and early winter. Since they had little or no storage space, it was necessary to get rid of their surplus crops as quickly as possible after harvest. If they waited until spring the market would be closed; the sugar planters would again be raising food for their slaves, forage for their mules.⁴¹

In order to be near his job, Abe Lincoln boarded with Judge Daniel Grass, whose house overlooked the landing. On the first evening, as he swung up the steep path to the house, Abe saw a big sheep eyeing him. The instant Abe passed, the sheep charged. Abe turned and halted. He knew the sheep could butt him off the path, probably into the Ohio River. With his knees together, Abe stood waiting, hoping the trick would work. On charged the sheep. Just as it reached him, Lincoln whirled half way around and spread his knees apart, making an arched opening. As the animal passed under him, Abe sat down on its back and grabbed its horns. It bleated and tried to buck him off, but Abe held on with one hand and with the other began to scratch its neck and chin. That was too much for the sheep; it just gave up the fight and followed him to the house.

Abe found Daniel Grass about as interesting as William Jones. Grass had been Justice of the Peace, an Associate Judge of Warrick County, a member of the Indiana Constitutional Convention, and State Senator from Warrick, Spencer, and Posey counties in the first Indiana legislature. He had been so severely wounded by Indians at the Battle of Tippecanoe in upper Indiana, November 7, 1811, that he still walked with crutches.⁴² On the same day the judge was wounded, his friend Captain Spier Spencer had been killed; it was Grass who brought about naming the new county after Spencer.

In the Grass home Abe Lincoln had access to a small but well selected library. Suppers over with, he took down a book and read until the tallow-dipped candle burned out and the family had gone to bed. Then he poked up the fire, stretched out on his back with his head toward the flaming logs and read until midnight. Mrs. Grass said she was afraid the boy would "bake the top of his head or wear himself out for want of rest." ⁴³ But no matter how late he read Abe Lincoln worked as hard the next day as any man at building the Gentry flatboat. His great strength was always in demand when there was heavy lifting to be done. Long straight poplar logs, swung between high logging ox-cart wheels, were dragged to the river bank where the boat was being built bottom-side up. Abe framed the girders and gunwales, pinned sleepers into the cross sills, helped caulk seams with hemp. Launching day finally came. With one of the check lines made fast to the boat and oxen hitched to the other, the boat was turned top-side up and slid into the river. Built for crew and cargo, the boat was ready for loading.

As the time for Katy's confinement neared, James Gentry, Sr., ordered loading to begin. Having been a slave owner, he knew what sugar planters wanted most; so he ordered his hogs herded down from Gentryville, letting them feed on mast as they grunted their way through the woods. He stationed Abe Lincoln—recognized as an expert meat-cutter—on the landing to slaughter the hogs, pack the meat, and stow it aboard. Although Abe loathed that bloody job more than ever, he kept at it. Gentry added potatoes, kraut, hay, and ear corn to the cargo, but no hoop-poles or tobacco.[44]

On Sunday, December 28, 1828, Allen and Katy Gentry became the parents of a boy. They named the child James in honor of its sturdy grandfather. And now that the trip could get underway, James Gentry, Sr., ordered final preparations for it. A blizzard threatened. Already a strong northwest gale had blown a passing flatboat onto the Kentucky shore just opposite Rockport. Allen and Abe shook their heads as they anxiously watched the unfortunate crew push the boat off the bank, struggle back into the channel and go poling down the Ohio.

One of the last things Lincoln stowed on board was his own hand-made, hide-covered trunk with its bellows top and its side studded with brass-headed pegs. In it were his few belongings.[45] "Reckon you got your store clothes in there?" someone asked. "No," said Abe, "I got on the only pair of breeches to my back. And you can see they're buckskin."

Midway between Christmas Day and New Year the Gentry flatboat left Rockport landing, glided out onto the Ohio River and into a stinging winter blast.[46] With Captain Allen Gentry at the stern, handling the wide-bladed steering oar and Abe near the bow, working the forward sweeps, the flatboat headed for the sugar coast and New Orleans. Somewhere above Evansville, Lincoln and Gentry overtook the flatboat which they had seen opposite Rockport, blown onto the Kentucky shore. "Where you from?" Gentry hailed. "Concordia, Kentucky," came the reply.

Following the custom of flatboatmen who were neighbors of not more than fifty miles apart, the crews lashed their flatboats together. The Concordia boat, owned and commanded by Steve Birch, carried a cargo of pork, oats, corn and tobacco bound for the New Orleans market. Shipping as errand boy to Captain Birch was James H. Cunningham of Stephensport, Kentucky.[47] After giving an Indian war whoop, the two crews struck up the flatboatman's chanty: "Hard upon the beech oar!"

Every hour the December wind grew colder and growled louder. The near freezing river reached up and bit its icy dampness through the heaviest clothing. Night came early. Woodchoppers' fires outlined the banks. Here and there Abe saw a vessel wooding up. Not wanting to risk being iced in, Birch and Gentry ordered their flatboats to keep drifting. With bulls-eye lamps the crews picked out the channel and hoped to miss dangerous snags. It was hazardous business, drifting at night. In the small cabin on the Gentry boat Abe and Allen did their cooking. In there, also, they took turns sleeping. To raise the spirits of the Birch crew, Abe sometimes took out his Jews' harp— or band, as he now called it—and went over to their cabin. He clog-danced, and between performances he told the Concordians stories from *Aesop's Fables* and *Arabian Nights*. His new audience laughed, applauded, banged the table with anything at hand.

Around New Year's Day the two boats swung into the broad mouth of the Ohio, bore to the southwestward and entered the Mississippi River. They passed Reel Foot Lake and New Madrid. The cold northern winds slackened. The boats drifted past "Wappanocca," Ferguson's plantation on the Arkansas side. Memphis appeared on the left. And when, a few miles onward, the great world of the Deep South opened, Abraham Lincoln was as amazed as he had been in 1816 when he first saw the Ohio River. Mississippi River traffic churned in and out of bayous and small tributaries. White-columned mansions commanded busy plantations. Twisted liveoaks stood mute under veils of Spanish moss. Icy winds gave way to the cheerful songs of mocking birds.

At Vicksburg Captain Birch became so ill he was unable to continue the voyage. There he sold his boat to Allen Gentry and paid off all his crew except the youthful errand boy, whom he took back north with him. Lincoln, deciding he had better send his trunk back too, bundled his few things together and pointed to the empty trunk. "Please, Jimmy, put that off at Rockport," he said to Cunningham.[48] It is not known how soon or where Gentry disposed of the Birch crew and flatboat, but it is known that Captain Gentry and Bowhand

Lincoln continued their journey toward the sugar coast and New
Orleans, that Louisiana city which the Vincennes *Western Sun,* less
than two weeks before Christmas, had called "the wet grave where
the hopes of thousands are buried." [49]

By mid-March, 1829, Abe Lincoln and Allen Gentry were back in
Rockport.[50] Gentry had only a few rods to go to reach home and see
his three months old son, James; but Lincoln had seventeen miles to
walk to reach his cabin on the knoll. Arriving home, Lincoln turned
his flatboat earnings over to his father; then, becoming restless, he
went up to William Wood's place and stood around. Wood: "Abe,
what's your case?" Lincoln: "Uncle, I want you to go to the river
and give me a recommendation to some boat. I want a start." Wood
shook his head: "Abe, your age is against you. You're not twenty-
one. I won't do it for your own good." [51]

Three weeks later Tom Lincoln told Abe, "We been hearing from
John Hanks over in Illinois.[52] He says there's sod there that ain't never
had a plow point stuck in it. John says its the best land in the world
for all kinds of crop raising." Abe: "Reckon we might be pulling out
for it?" His father: "Well, it's mighty fine land over there."

Shortly, Abe learned that a big infare was planned to follow the announced Grigsby double-wedding. "All the neighbors except the
Lincoln family were invited," stated J. C. Richardson. "Abe undoubtedly felt miffed." [53]

Lincoln remembered helping his father do carpenter work on the
Grigsby house, such as making window shutters and the imposing
staircase. Up that stairway, Abe knew, the two brides would be led
by merrymakers and put to bed; that being what Pigeon Creek custom
dictated. He wondered what would happen if a mistake were made
and the bridegrooms went into the wrong rooms. The more he
thought about it the funnier it seemed; and, because of the fancied
slight, he decided to write a story about such a happening. To make
it appear more factual, he watched everything that took place at the
Grigsby home.

It was Good Friday, April 17, 1829, and Abraham Lincoln selected
a point in the woods from which he could watch the goings on. He
knew that yesterday Reuben, Jr., and Charles Grigsby, brothers of
Aaron, had married outsiders—that is, girls from other neighborhoods.
Reuben had married Elizabeth Ray whom Abe called Betsy. Miss
Ray lived on Crooked Hill, overlooking the Ohio River. Charles had
married Matilda Hawkins on Anderson River, near the Taylor ferry.
A little before noon Lincoln saw Reuben, Jr., and his bride, Betsy,

with eight guests, all on horseback, enter the Grigsby lane. A messenger on a white horse dashed past to greet them. The man was blowing a long tin trumpet. Then Lincoln saw Charles and his bride with twenty guests, also on horses, join Reuben's party.

"We formed a procession," Mrs. Reuben Grigsby, Jr., recalled later. "My husband and me and Charles and his wife in front. The messenger on the white horse led the way down the long lane, blowing all the time on his tin horn." [54] Such medieval pomp in the Indiana wilderness stirred Lincoln's imagination. He watched the gay procession move along under the arch of black walnuts and whiteoaks, over a carpet of saw briars and wood violets.

As the procession reached the house, "Old Man Reuben and his wife met and welcomed us," said Mrs. Reuben Grigsby, Jr. "Dinner was ready and we were invited out to eat. There was a big crowd and all the people did not finish eating until dark." [55] When the great feast ended and the contents of the Grigsby still-house liberally passed around, entertainment got underway. "We played all that evening Old Sister Phoebe and other kissing games," declared Mrs. Reuben Grigsby, Jr. "But there was no frolicing. Mrs. Grigsby (Mrs. Reuben, Sr.) would have run away from her own home if she had heard a fiddle. Good Baptist, you know." [56]

"After the infare was over," according to Joseph C. Richardson, "the two women were put to bed. The candles were blown out upstairs. The gentlemen—the two husbands—were invited and shown to bed." Then "by accident as it were," said Richardson, unexpected events happened. [57]

Lincoln wrote a piece about that accident. Unlike the "Adam and Eve's Wedding Song" he had composed for Sarah and Aaron, this piece was a satire on the Grigsby infare. I Chronicles, chapter 5, verse 1 of the Bible may have inspired him to do it in "scriptural style" as pioneers termed such writing. He made copies of his manuscript and dropped them where neighbors could easily find them. Mrs. Josiah Crawford called Abe's new work "First Chronicles of Reuben"; others called it the "Book of Chronicles." Mrs. Reuben Grigsby, Jr., memorized Abe's piece:

"Now there was a man whose name was Reuben, and the same was very great in substance; in horses and cattle and swine, and a very great household. It came to pass when the sons of Reuben grew up that they were desirous of taking to themselves wives, and being too well known as to honor in their own country they took a journey into a far country and there procured for themselves wives. It came to pass also that when they were about to make the return home they sent a messenger before them to bear the tidings to their parents. These, inquiring of the messengers what time their sons would come, made a great feast and called all their kinsmen and neighbors in and made great preparations. When the time drew nigh they sent out two men to meet the grooms and their brides with a trumpet to welcome them and accompany them. When they came near unto the house of Reuben, the father, the messenger came on before them and gave a shout, and the whole multitude ran out with shouts of joy and music, playing on all kinds of instruments. Some were playing on harps, some on viols, and some blowing on ram's horns. Some were also casting dust and ashes towards heaven, and chief among them was Josiah, blowing his bugle and making sound so great the neighboring hills and valleys echoed with the resounding acclamation. When they had played and their harps had sounded till the grooms and brides approached the gates, Reuben, the father, met them and welcomed them to his house. The wedding feast now being ready they were all invited to sit down to eat, placing the bridegrooms and their wives at each end of the table. Waiters were then appointed to serve and wait on the guests. When all had eaten and were full and merry they all went out again and played and sung till night, and when they had made an end of feasting and rejoicing the multitude dispersed, each going to his own home. The family then took seats with their waiters to converse while preparations were being made in an upper chamber for the brides and grooms to be conveyed to their beds. This being done the waiters took the two brides up-stairs, placing one in a room at the right hand of the stairs and the other on the left. The waiters then came down and Nancy, the mother, then gave directions to the waiters of the bridegrooms, and they took them up-stairs and placed them in the wrong rooms. The waiters then all came down stairs. But the mother, being fearful of a mistake, made enquiry of the waiters and learning the true facts took the light and sprang up-stairs It came to pass she ran to one of the rooms and exclaimed, 'O Lord, Reuben, you are in bed with the wrong wife.' The young men, alarmed at this, ran out with such violence against each other they came near knocking each other down. The tumult gave evidence to those below that the mistake was certain. At last they all came down and had a long conversation about who made the mistake, but it could not be decided. So endeth the chapter." [58]

"The Chronicles kicked up a big hullabaloo," said James Gentry.[59] The outraged Grigsbys got hold of Lincoln's original manuscript and hid it. Meanwhile, children memorized the copies and mouthed them up and down Buck Horn Valley, making women blush and men wink with each recitation. "It wasn't so my man got into the wrong room and Charles got into my room," insisted Mrs. Reuben Grigsby, Jr., "Lincoln just wrote that for mischief." [60] Nattie Grigsby said: "It hurt us." [61]

A terrific fist fight was expected; but Abe Lincoln did not appear to be worried as he strolled about Gentryville. After several weeks tempers cooled and the Grigsbys, seeing the funny side of Abe's lampooning, began laughing it off.

But soon Lincoln was again in an argument with one of the Grigsby boys. William, brother of Aaron, Nathaniel and Reuben, Jr., came to the Lincoln home to claim a spotted pup. Grigsby claimed a neighbor had given it to him. Abe claimed the same thing. Both boys started walking and had gone about one hundred and fifty yards west of the house, arguing all the time, when suddenly William shook his fist in Lincoln's face. "Let's fight it out to see who owns the pup!" Grigsby challenged.

"Bill," said Lincoln, "you know I can lick you, so what's the use of making such a proposition?" Recognized as one of the best rough-and-tumble fighters in Southern Indiana, Grigsby shot back: "Just the same I'll fight you for that dog!" Tipped off earlier by word flashed over the wilderness grapevine that a fist fight was brewing, "strong men and bullies" had come from several miles away. They followed along as the pup claimants edged toward Gentryville. Still not wanting to fight the smaller youth, Lincoln declared, "Tell you what I'll do, Bill. Although I know that pup belongs to me, and you know it, too, I'm willing to put up John Johnston here to fight in my place. He's more your size. And whoever whips gets the pup."

According to Nattie Grigsby, "Abe being larger and stronger than my brother turned over his stepbrother to do the fighting." Immediately spectators made a scuffle ground by kicking dry leaves into a big circle. John D. Johnston and William Grigsby stepped inside the ring, sized up the crowd and selected their seconds. Johnston chose Aaron Standage and James Taylor; Grigsby selected William Whitten and William Bolen. [62] The date of the fight was July 16, 1829. [63]

Almost from the start James Gentry, Redmond Grigsby, Wesley Hall, Joseph Gentry, Joseph Richardson and others, including Lincoln, saw that Billy was too much for the youngster, Johnston. The longer Lincoln watched the worse he felt. He saw Grigsby had Johnston staggering, which meant Grigsby was winning the fight and the pup.

A clout to the head sent John Johnston down with Grigsby on top of him. Spectators yelled and pressed in closer. Then William Bolen reached into the ring.

Yelling, "Bill Bolen shows foul play!" Abe Lincoln jumped inside the circle of leaves, grabbed Billy Grigsby by the seat of the pants and scruff of the neck and threw him into the air so hard Billy went sailing out of the ring over the heads of the spectators. The fall nearly killed Grigsby. Benjamin Hesson and some others picked him up and carried him to the Gentry-Romine store.

Abe Lincoln stood inside the scuffle ring and dared all Gentryville to step in and fight.[64] Not a person moved toward him. But a fight did break out between Grigsby's seconds. Whitten struck Bolen so hard he knocked Bolen's shoulder out of place. Still Lincoln stood in the center of the ring daring one and all to cross the leaves. He towered over that crowd as a giant whiteoak over a clump of scrub brush. "I'm the big buck of this lick!" he shouted. No one tried to prove he wasn't.

Convinced that neither the "strong men" nor the "bullies" present wanted to fight him, Lincoln walked out of that leafy circle the undisputed owner of the spotted pup.[65]

As soon as William Grigsby recuperated he challenged Abe to a duel. Replied Abe: "I'm not going to fool my life away with one shot." [66] However bad feelings between Abe and Billy did not last very long. A few weeks later Abe acted as second for Billy in a fight with Thomas Sumner. "We are going to fight to see who is the best

Interior of a log cabin. (Courtesy Indiana Historical Bureau).

man," Grigsby explained simply. This fight took place on Blue Bill Harris' hill, the drill-up grounds. For over three hours Grigsby and Sumner fought with bare fists. Finally, Sumner conceded: "Billy, I got enough." [67]

Feeling somewhat remorseful about the mischief he had done in writing the "Book of Chronicles," Lincoln tried to make amends by turning the grindstone at the home of Reuben Grigsby, Jr. The latter owned the only good grindstone in several miles around, and people brought their axes, hoes, scythes and other tools to sharpen them against the stone while Betsy, Reuben's bride, turned it. "Let me turn for you, Betsy," Lincoln offered. Pleased to get away from the drudgery, Betsy let Abe handle the job. Only when he sharpened his own tools did Abe allow Betsy Grigsby to turn. "Betsy," he said after he had ground one side of his axe, "I can turn this on the gee side but I want to grind on the haw side. I think you'll have to turn a little."

Betsy answered, "All right, Abe. I'll turn." [68] With such neighborly cooperation hard feelings between the Grigsby family and Abe melted away. "It's all over now," said Nattie Grigsby. [69]

CHAPTER FIVE

DESIGNS OF PROVIDENCE

At Pigeon Creek Abraham Lincoln grew up in an atmosphere of religious fervor. Night after night in his own home he heard his mother say, "Remember our God is a prayer-hearing God." He saw her kneel and heard her pray for divine guidance. Before meals, he heard his father intone, "Fit and prepare us for humble service, we beg for Christ's sake. Amen." The creed of his parents and many of his Hoosier neighbors was that of the Regular Primitive "feet washing" Baptist Church: "The doctrine of election by grace and that the elect were chosen in Christ Jesus before the world began." [1]

There being at first no meetinghouse in the community, the settlers worshipped in one another's homes, sometimes gathering in the Lincoln cabin. Sometimes when there were no services at all on the Sabbath, Abraham Lincoln said his mother spent "a portion of the day in reading the Scriptures aloud to her family." [2]

Reverently, Nancy Hanks Lincoln said, "I would rather Abraham would be able to read the Bible than to own a farm if he can't have but one." [3] So, encouraged by their mother, Abraham and his sister worked hard at learning to read. When they were able to stumble along over the pages, Mrs. Lincoln let the children share the duty of the Sunday reading. By the time he was nine years old, Abe Lincoln was well acquainted with the family Bible.

The Lincoln Bible, known as an Ostervald Bible, was printed in 1799. Bound in stiff board and calf-skin, part of its title page announces, "Arguments prefixed to the different books and moral theological Observations illustrating each chapter composed by the Reverend Mr. Ostervald." Those observations—footnotes or reflections—were in reality little sermons. Between the Old Testament and the New, young Lincoln found the Apocrypha. [4]

Some of the advice given by the Reverend Mr. Frederick Ostervald, a Swiss divine who lived from 1663 to 1747, profoundly impressed Abe. "It is a very great fault to neglect, as many do, the reading of the prophesies," wrote Mr. Ostervald. "If Christians would but read them they would find an astonishing light dart from them." Searching for the light Abraham learned whole chapters of Isaiah.

Lincoln thumbed and meditated over pages of Isaiah XLV until they became worn and stained. Ostervald declared, "This chapter containes one of the most remarkable prophesies in the Old Testament." He said it was prophesied that God would go before a king named Cyrus, who would grant the Jews leave to return to their country and cause them to rebuild Jerusalem and the temple. "These things," said Ostervald, "were foretold two hundred years before they happened. These predictions which were so exactly fulfilled, invincibly prove the divine origin of the Holy Scriptures. They prove, that there is a God who knows things to come, and who presides over all events and everything that happens in the world. They prove, in particular, that He disposes of things which depend upon the will of man without depriving him of his liberty; so that men, without knowing it, bring about the designs of Providence."

Selecting verse 23 as the climax to Genesis XLIII, Ostervald wrote, "What Joseph said to his brethren when they came again into Egypt and his manner of treating them, shewed his extreme tenderness . . . notwithstanding the injuries they had done him. This character of kindness and meekness is the sure mark of good men." Those words cut deeply into Lincoln's young mind. Joseph's interpretation of Pharaoh's dreams, and what Ostervald had to say about Jacob's dream as set forth in Genesis XXVIII, quickened Lincoln's interest in the Bible. Ostervald wrote that the vision of the ladder reaching up to heaven assured Jacob "that God would be with him wherever he went."

Lincoln thought it strange there was so much in the Bible about dreams. He said, "There are, I think, some sixteen chapters in the Old and four or five in the New Testament in which dreams are mentioned. If we believe the Bible, we must accept the fact that in the old days God and His angels came to men in their sleep and made themselves known in dreams." [5]

John XIII, describing the Lord's Supper, seemingly was read and re-read by the Lincoln household. Time and again in Primitive Baptist meetings, Abraham watched members of his family reverently carry out this admonition of Jesus, "Ye also ought to wash one another's feet." He saw them gird themselves with a towel, pick up a bucket of water, cross the floor, kneel down and wash a neighbor's feet.

In spite of the religious fervor of the Pigeon Creek neighborhood and the Lincoln household, when Nancy Hanks Lincoln died in October, 1818, there was neither funeral nor committal services. For one thing, there was no preacher in the community. The principal reason, however, for no service undoubtedly was the Primitive Baptist custom of setting aside the first Sunday in June for a mass funeral for all persons who had died during the preceding twelve months.⁶ So, at Abraham's request the Reverend David Elkin, or Elkins, arrived from Kentucky on the first Sunday in June, 1819, to preach funeral services for Nancy Hanks Lincoln and all the other milksick victims.⁷

Preacher Elkins entered the Pigeon Creek-Buck Horn Valley community riding a sorrel horse and smoking a pipe. He had ridden a hundred miles across Kentucky's open country and through Indiana's wilderness. Now past forty and weighing two hundred pounds, Dave Elkins didn't pay much attention to the appearance of his long, red hair and longer red whiskers. In his youth he was so wild he had been nicknamed Devil Dave. He had been a rip-roaring fiddler and a hearty whiskey drinker. People said he could lick his weight in wildcats and never bat an eye. He couldn't read, but recognized the letter "O" because it was round. At twenty-two he "got religion." Devil Dave took up preaching and you could hear him for a quarter of a mile, according to Dennis Hanks.⁸

In front of the Lincoln home that bright June day, two hundred people stood in hushed silence. They had come from twenty miles around to attend the mass funeral. Some had come in ox carts; some had ridden, two or three, on a horse; others had walked, carrying their shoes. Almost all of them knew David Elkins. To one and all it was a solemn day.⁹

As Preacher Elkins stepped out of the cabin door, followed by Thomas Lincoln, Sarah and Abraham, and Dennis Hanks, the people quietly opened up a lane before them. Slowly the minister and the Lincoln family started up the mudsled trail. A long and sorrowing procession followed them to the mound-dotted hilltop. Eyes grew moist and chins trembled as the grieving families looked at graves sunken by winter snows and spring rains. Reverend Elkins took his stand at the foot of Mrs. Lincoln's grave. Thomas, Sarah, Abraham and Dennis stood at the head. Peter Brooner, with his sons Allen and Henry, waited at the nearby grave of Mrs. Brooner. The other mourners went to the graves of their dead. There was a long silence.

Then Abe Lincoln heard the Reverend Mr. Elkins offer up a prayer and sing a hymn. He heard him say he had come because Nancy's little son, Abraham, had requested it.¹⁰ And he heard him say: "Nancy Hanks Lincoln was a precious Christian woman. She was an example of true womanhood." David Elkins also eulogized Uncle Tom and Aunt Betsy Sparrow and those others who had died during the milk-

sick terror.[11] When the mass funeral ended, the mourners quietly
shook hands all around. In silence all watched Devil Dave mount his
horse and ride away.

That fall of 1819 was the first anniversary of the milksick calamity.
With one accord the survivors said: "Let us build a house unto the
Lord. A meetinghouse will be an acceptable thanks offering for our
escape from death."

On June 8, 1816, states the deer-skin covered minute book, a congregation had been organized in Lincoln's community under the title
of "The Baptist Church of Christ Jesus known by the name of Pigeon
Creek Warrick County Indeanne Territory." Since March 13, 1819,
members had been seeking a church site. Late in December they
selected a spot on a gently rolling knoll across a brushy hollow five
hundred yards north of Noah Gordon's mill and between the forks of
Buck Horn Creek. Nearby was a pool of living water, a good place for
baptizing. John Romine donated land for the graveyard or God's
Acre, as the members called it.

Amidst this planning, returning flatboatmen brought to the Lincolns
and their neighbors terrifying news: "Yellow fever is worse in New
Orleans and Natchez than it has been for many years. Crews of
several boats have nearly all perished." [12] To this news, Abraham's
neighbors nodded their heads and repeated, "What is going to happen
is going to happen and it was so decreed before you were born."

But if all things were decreed beforehand, then why have a meetinghouse? Why not let Providence run its course? Lincoln heard many
answers to such questions. A meetinghouse, said his neighbors, would
be a proper place for the Pigeon Creek community to congregate; it
would be a proper place in which to hear the Scriptures explained
and in which to wash feet; it would be a temple in the wilderness where
it would be easier to praise the Lord and fight the devil. Here,
even as the Psalmist, they could exalt "our God and worship at His
footstool."

So work on the meetinghouse began. Having completely recovered
from the horse-kick received at Noah Gordon's mill, Abraham Lincoln swung an axe alongside his grown-up neighbors. The job of boss
carpenter was assigned by the elders to Thomas Lincoln who fashioned
a two-brick mold, which was used by David Turnham in making
bricks for the chimney. John Romine, Weldon Barker and others
operated the kiln. Reuben Grigsby, Sr., James Gentry, John Kitchens,
Jacob Oskins, William Stark, Owen R. Griffith, Robert Oskins, and
probably the Reverend Young Lamar, also, took turns at cutting logs

and riding the shaving-horse. Noah Gordon, considered an exception-
ally good hand with a foot-adz, was awarded the honor of hewing the
timbers.[13] With froe and maul still others split the clapboard shingles.

When completed, the meetinghouse was a one and a half story,
hewn-log building twenty-six feet wide and thirty feet long. The
long way set north and south. Outside brick chimneys hugged each
end. A planed battened church door faced the east. Two gaping
windows, twenty by thirty-six inches, let in daylight. Inside, the
meetinghouse appeared unusually roomy and cheery.[14] Heat from the
huge fireplaces warmed the worshippers as they faced the pulpit of
wild cherry which Thomas Lincoln had skillfully made. Fenced in,
it had a gate at one end. At its back a bench ran the full length and
could easily accommodate six preachers.[15]

Preachers were paid in corn, smoked meat and whiskey. Some
called this giving to the Lord, but one preacher explained, "This giving
to the Lord—as if He needed anything—is outside the teachings of
the Lord. You are giving to me, a man who has a wife and children to
feed."

On entering the meetinghouse, the saints of the Lord—as the more
pious members styled themselves—separated. Men saints went to
the benches on the men's side and women saints to those on the
women's side. The center benches, known as the sinners' seats,
were reserved for nonmembers. That was where Abe Lincoln sat;
he was neither a member nor a saint.

In almost every sermon Lincoln listened to, the Primitive Baptist
doctrine of predestination was mentioned. "A time was appointed for
you to be born into the world," the preacher would declare. "If it
wasn't so how would God know about you? God sets the bounds of
every man. God knows where you are at. If He didn't set out
bounds, how would He know where you are at? God knew you would
be here before you came to church today. If not, then it is an experiment with Him and this Scripture (pounding the Bible) is a farce!"

While Abe listened to the preachers, some of whom could hardly
read, he must have wondered if there were an all-knowing, Supernatural Power hovering over the speaker and congregation. He was
growing up among these people—his people. Plain people. They
believed in the moving power of dreams and visions. Eventually,
he ascribed that power "to the Almighty Intelligence that governs
the universe."[16]

As services drew to a close Abe heard the preacher ask, "Any inquiry after the peace and fellowship of the church?" If no one said

anything, the preacher next asked, "Nothing of that nature? How beautiful it is to dwell in peace and harmony. Any inquiry as to the sick and needy of the church?" [17] That answered, Thomas Lincoln and his brother saints got up from their benches and slowly filed past the pulpit, shaking hands with the minister. And as they walked they sang, their voices stirred by religious zeal. They turned from the pulpit to the women's side and shook hands with each sister. Then, as the singing died away, they moved to the center benches, solemnly clasped the hands of sinners, and returned to the men's side. Lining-out the closing hymn, the preacher read aloud each line of the verses. Finally the whole congregation, sinners included, joyously sang:

> "*There's room enough in paradise*
> "*For a shout in glory.*"

Pronouncement of the benediction freed them for socializing and visiting.

When his stepmother was unable to attend services in the meeting-house Abraham went, listened closely, came home and repeated the sermons almost word for word, even throwing in the preacher's gestures. According to Mrs. Lincoln he had a remarkable memory: "Abe could easily learn." He once astonished David Turnham and a gang of boys by mounting a log and repeating Reverend Jeremiah Cash's text and sermon. [18]

On those Sundays when his stepmother and Thomas Lincoln had gone to church, Matilda Johnston recalled, "Abe would take down the Bible, read a verse, give out a hymn and we would sing. He would preach and we would do the crying. Sometimes he would join in the chorus of tears." They used Watts' Hymns. [19]

A preacher came to the Lincoln cabin one day and got into an argument with Abe over Jonah and the whale. For an hour they argued. Suddenly Abe asked, "Who was the father of Zebedee's children?" That unexpected change of subject so bewildered the wrought-up preacher he could only answer, "I don't know." [20]

Even though Thomas Lincoln had served the congregation as boss carpenter in building the meetinghouse and Mrs. Lincoln had regularly attended services there for more than two years, neither joined Pigeon Creek Church until Saturday, June 7, 1823. That day, according to the minute book: "Opened a dore for the Reception for members. Received Brother Thomas Linkhon by letter. Received Brother John . . . by Relation and Sister Linkhon and Thomas Carter by Experience."

Next day being the second Sunday in June and baptizing day, Abraham stood on the cool, wooded banks of Buck Horn Creek—a branch of Pigeon Creek—and heard the church members singing hymns. He knew that Article 8 of their Articles of Faith declared: "We believe that baptism and the Lord's supper are ordinances of Jesus Christ and that true believers are the onely proper subjects and the onely proper mode of baptism is immersion." Abraham watched his stepmother calmly walk into the pool of living water and, as the singing stopped, saw the preacher "bury her with Jesus in baptism;" then saw her go "straightway out of the water" as the Saviour had done from the river Jordan.

Back in Kentucky Thomas Lincoln had been a member of the Freewill Baptists and had been baptized by the Reverend William Downs in Knob Creek.[21]

At sixteen, Abe Lincoln was given a job as sexton at the Pigeon Creek meetinghouse and his friend Jimmy Grigsby went with him to look it over. Observing that "this place needs cleaning up," Abe made a broom of small hazel-brush limbs tied together with skin stripped from the brush, and swept down cobwebs and cleared out cuttings left by squirrels.[22] And while he worked, little blue lizards snapped their shining tails over the puncheon floor and ran up and down the walls. Judging by a memorandum book notation, Abe probably brought some candles from home.[23]

One Sunday morning Lincoln sat on a sinners' seat, listening to the preacher—an old man, wearing a tow linen shirt held together by a single button at the collar, and barn-door pantaloons, the kind with the wide flap which lets down in front. Loudly the preacher announced his text: "I am the Christ whom I shall represent." Just then Abe saw a lizard jump onto the old man's foot and run up his leg underneath the pantaloons. Without pausing in his sermon, the preacher slapped at the lizard. But the lizard kept on climbing. Lincoln, watching the man slyly loosen the center button of his waistband, wondered what would happen. The pantaloons dropped and the old man stepped aside, left in his long tow shirt which hung down like a nightgown.

Abe squirmed on the bench and tried to figure out what the next move would be. He noted that the congregation was more interested in the lizard's progress than in the sermon. "Mr. Lizard passed the equatorial line of the waistband, and was calmly exploring that part of the preacher's anatomy which lay beneath the back of his shirt," said Lincoln.

The old man kept right on preaching until he was unable to stand it any longer. "With one sweep of his arm off came the tow linen shirt," said Lincoln. The congregation sat dazed. Standing in the pulpit was their pastor, naked as Adam on the day of his creation. Finally, in the back of the church, an old lady stood up and looked sternly at the preacher. "If you represent Christ then I am done with the Bible!" she shouted.[24]

When he was about eighteen Abe borrowed a most unusual book: Volume IV, Part II of "Practical Discourses upon all the Collects, Epistles and Gospels, to be us'd thro-out the year." It was written by Matthew Hole, DD., Rector of Exeter College in Oxford. Its title page states the book was printed in London in 1716 by "F.D. for T. Varnum in Lombard Street, W. Taylor, H. Clements at the Half-Moon in St. Paul's Church-yard and J. Bourne with-out Temple-bar." Abe borrowed this Church of England book from the parents of Elizabeth and John Tuley. He read it so carefully and made so much use of it as he preached from stumps that the Tuley family started calling it "Abe Lincolns book of sermons."[25]

Abe found that Dr. Hole was not always happy over world conditions in 1716. "It is a vicious world we live in," wrote Dr. Hole. "Always the more vice the more unbelief. Instead of building Men up in their holy Faith, and carrying on the work and Business of the Christian life, we are forced to combat the Atheists and the Deists who are still pecking at the foundation."

Set forth in detail on page 312-318, Abe found arguments and conclusions bearing directly on the Saviour's two Great Commandments. After repeating the parable of the Good Samaritan, Dr. Hole declares that Christ was intimating "that every one that is in want and stands in need of Relief, although he be as a Jew to a Samaritan, is yet to be looked upon as a Neighbor, and to be the Object of our Mercy and Pity."

Back on page 261, which shows considerable thumbing and treats of the Gospel for the Tenth Sunday after Trinity based on St. Luke XIX, 41-47, Lincoln learned from a few words much about the character of Jesus: "From the Saviour's weeping over Jerusalem we may observe his tender Sense and Concern for the Miseries and Calamities of other Men; and that may teach us to shew Pity and Compassion upon like occasions." Concern for the miseries of other men—in fact for all living creatures—was beginning to be firmly rooted in Abraham's own character.

If Lincoln had not before known why his parents and others knelt

to pray, he would have learned from Dr. Hole's *Practical Discourses*
on the Epistles for the 16th Sunday after Trinity, Ephesians III, 13
to end. "The humble posture us'd by St. Paul was kneeling," says
Hole. "For this cause I bow my knees. St. Paul did not, as too many
in our days do, sit at his Prayers, or present his Maker with a rude
unmannerly Devotion. No, he shew'd more Reverence and bowed the
knees before him. Sitting is a Posture of Ease and Sloth, and betokens
that Freedom and Familiarity which may well enough pass among
Equals but is never used in Gesture of Reverence or Respect to
Superiors." Dr. Hole pointed out that Daniel "kneeled upon his
knees three times a day." He described "our Blessed Saviour *upon
his knees* praying to his heavenly Father."

With Dr. Hole's *Practical Discourses* in mind, Lincoln mounted
stumps and competed with circuit-riding preachers who visited the
neighborhood. One of his victims was the Reverend Henry Hart,
pastor of both Pigeon Creek and of Little Zion over in Warrick County
where he lived. It was on a Sunday morning said the Reverend
Hart's daughter, Sarah Hart Gray, that "Abe Lincoln went down
below the church, got upon a stump and made a speech." Having
read widely and thoroughly, Abe's sermon contrasted sharply with
that being delivered in the meeting house. "It was not long before
he had as large a crowd as there was at the church," recalled Mrs.
Gray.[26]

In Dr. Hole's book Lincoln found such subjects as: Death and
Damnation; Signs and Wonders; No Man Can Serve Two Masters;
God is Their Belly; One Baptism; The Good Samaritan; Jesus Casting
Out Devils; The Blessed Trinity; Works of the Flesh; Wisdom of the
Serpent and Harmlessness of the Dove; and a hundred other subjects.
Abe memorized whole sermons, delivering them verbatim. He spoke in
parables. He propounded doctrines his unlettered listeners had never
dreamed were in existence.

Lincoln also had access to another book filled with items of religious
nature: Lindley Murray's *English Reader*. In it he found "The
Apostle Paul's Noble Defense Before Festus to Agrippa;" Colton's
"Religion and Death;" Milton's "Discourse between Adam and Eve;"
Thompson's "A Man Perishing in the Snow;" Horne's "On the Beau-
ties of the Psalms." Horne said the Psalms were "Calculated alike to
profit and to please. They inform the understanding, elevate the
affections and entertain the imagination." In Abe's judgment, Murray's *English Reader* was "the best school book ever put in the hands
of an American youth." [27]

Matilda Johnston, Lincoln's stepsister, said her brother, John D., one day caught a land terrapin and took it to where Abe, atop a stump, was preaching to several boys and girls, repeating the sermon which he had heard the Sunday before. After the choir had sung, she recalled, Abe's prayer had worked the children up to a high pitch of fervor. At that moment John, coming near Abe, hurled the terrapin against a tree so hard the reptile's shell was crushed. Lincoln looked down at the helpless creature writhing in agony at his feet. He looked at John; then at the Pigeon Creek youngsters. Obviously remembering Aesop's fable about the boys and the frogs, Abraham Lincoln preached a stinging sermon against cruelty to animals. He told those young Pigeon Creekers that "An ant's life is just as sweet to it as ours to us;" that "the little soul of that small terrapin is as great to it as the larger life to man." [28] He went home and wrote a piece which he called "Against Cruelty to Animals." His stepmother observed that Abe "loved animals generally and treated them kindly." According to Nathaniel Grigsby, Abe wrote "essays on being kind to animals and crawling insects." [29]

On another Sunday morning Lincoln was down by the meetinghouse sauntering around with some neighbor boys. A church member poked his head through an open window and yelled, "Abe, the devil will get you!" [30] Apparently Abe was considered to blame for the boys being outside.

Wandering alone in the dark woods the adolescent Lincoln thought over the simple faith of his people: God and the devil; heaven and hellfire. But surely there were other elements which should be emphasized in their spiritual labors, such as charity; or, as Dr. Hole had suggested in the *Practical Discourses,* pity and compassion. One day, in the silent Indiana forest, Abe heard a voice. "I turned. I saw no one. But the voice was there," he told Henry C. Whitney. [31] Over those woodlands now brooded a new force which Lincoln could feel, but could neither see nor explain.

In Indiana, also, Lincoln was introduced to religious form different from any taught in church or by the books he read. In its same dark forests Lincoln annually observed the Indian captors of Reuben Grigsby, Sr., perform their sun-worshipping rites. They flapped their arms and crowed like roosters in salute to what Lincoln called "the rising god of day." Some of Lincoln's neighbors—veterans of the Battle of Tippecanoe—retold the story of Chief Tecumseh scorning Governor William Henry Harrison's invitation to sit on the Governor's porch at Vincennes. It was claimed Tecumseh haughtily replied, "The sun is my father and the earth is my mother. On her bosom I will recline." [82]

Even if these Indians did not worship in the manner of Lincoln's parents, they did worship something supreme to themselves, which was more than Robert Owen and his Utopian Socialists and Scottish philanthropists were doing at the New Harmony communistic experiment on the Wabash, forty miles to the westward. Abe was reading, in the Vincennes *Western Sun*, Robert Owen's debate with the Reverend A. Campbell, what Owen termed The Four Grand Positions of Religion. Held in Cincinnati and widely reported in newspapers everywhere, that debate was proving to be the greatest religious debate ever held in America.[33] The *Western Sun* carried Owen's argument that all religions are: (a) founded on the ignorance of mankind; (b) are the real sources of vice, disunion and misery; (c) are the only real bar to the formation of a society of virtue, intelligence, sincerity, and benevolence; (d) are maintained only through the ignorance of the mass of the people and the tyranny of the few over the mass.

Prior to the debate the *Vincennes Sun* reported an interview which the Reverend Ely of Philadelphia had with Robert Owen in New York harbor. Lincoln read of Dr. Ely's shock on being told by Owen that after death he might "become a cabbage head, a cucumber, or an ass; that there is no other God but the universe; that the substance of his own beard and remarkable nose is a part of the Supreme Being; that all the evils which are supposed to result from those things which are called vices, really result from the religion of men and the priesthood of such gentlemen" as himself. Owen further shocked Ely by saying, "All our judgments and other mental actions are the result of fate, and we are not free agents in anything."

But what was fate? Lincoln's family and his Primitive Baptist neighbors came rather close to calling Owen's idea of fate, the designs of Providence: What is going to happen is going to happen and you cannot do anything about it. Hearing Baptist preachers at Pigeon Creek Church deliver sermons on these designs and reading about them in the Ostervald Bible, Abraham Lincoln early accepted the doctrine of fatalism. "All my life I have been a fatalist," he told Isaac Arnold.[34]

The debate and Owen's further statements added to the raging storm over the proof of a Deity—Theists claiming the eternal Being was a knowing immaterial substance; Atheists claiming the eternal Being was a senseless material substance. In the midst of it all, Lincoln's pious neighbors shook their heads and held fast to their belief in the God of Moses and of Jesus as set down in the Bible. Their meetinghouse at this time needed a new chimney. To build it, according to the minute book, Thomas Lincoln and others signed up to deliver at William Barker's place "good merchantile produce"—such items as "Corn, wheat, whiskey, soft Linnen wool or any other article to do the work with." The Lincolns donated "White Corn—manufactured pounds—24." [35]

Once a year churches belonging to the Regular Primitive Baptists held a great meeting of Corresponding Associations. Saints from Blue River to Pigeon Creek to Little Zion attended the meeting held in a big clearing. Men left their plows; women put away their spinning wheels. If roads and trails were muddy, the women walked barefooted, carrying their shoes and stockings. At the meetings Abe Lincoln heard emancipation preachers exhort the people; saints testify; backsliders renew their faith; and sinners beg for mercy. At one such meeting Lincoln heard an old man named Glenn testify, "When I do good, I feel good; when I do bad, I feel bad. And that's my religion." That old man could have been Samuel Glenn who lived on the banks of Blue River about ten miles northwest of the home of Abraham's uncle, Josiah Lincoln. [36]

In spite of saints and camp meetings, some of Lincoln's teenage companions ripped out long oaths. Not using profanity himself, Lincoln admonished them, "Swear off your boyish ways and be more like men." [37]

September, 1829, was an harassing month for the bodies and souls of Lincoln's more pious neighbors. Milksickness had showed up again. Yellow fever was killing forty people a day down in New Orleans and would likely be carried to Pigeon Creek by returning flatboatmen. [38] And, as if to further plague the people, a rebellious brother in the church bluntly declared he "believed that the doctrine of predestination came from hell and would go there and all who preached it." That declaration so angered the Salem Baptist Association that it sent a sharp message to the Pigeon Creek Baptists: unless they "relieved themselves of their disorder they would be dropped from the Union Association." [39]

A secret trial was held by the church. Not being a member, Abe was barred; but he could and did ask questions of those who attended. From their answers and reactions it was apparent to him that the trial was more concerned with sex problems than with the rebel's fight against the doctrine of predestination. Lincoln wrote a poem about that church trial, calling it "The Neighborhood Broil." It kicked up an even greater hullabaloo in Buck Horn valley than had his "Chronicles of Reuben." [40]

When Abe's family prepared to move from Indiana to Illinois, Thomas and Sarah Bush Lincoln asked for their church letters and were given them in November. Before they left, however, Sister Grigsby declared she was not satisfied that the letters should have been given to Sister Sarah and Brother Thomas. She demanded their recall. Shortly, all parties met in Brother William Hoskins' cabin and patched up their troubles. [41] At the time Abraham Lincoln reached the legal age of twenty-one and was ready to move from Indiana, he still had not joined any organized religious body. But his Indiana surroundings had filled him with the belief that a Supreme Being truly existed. "I know there is a God," he said. [42]

CHAPTER SIX

PERSEVERANCE

While working as a hired hand for Josiah Crawford in 1825, Abe resolved, "I will study and get ready and some day my chance will come." [1] Seven years prior to that he had been a pupil in an Indiana subscription school. "Abraham Lincoln and Sally (Abe's sister) and myself all went to school together," recalled Nathaniel Grigsby. "We went to Andy Crawford in the year 1818 in the winter, in the same year Mrs. Lincoln died." [2]

A paper had been passed around in the neighborhood and patrons "subscribed to get a school." Although money was very scarce with him that dreary winter, somehow Thomas Lincoln managed to scrape enough together to subscribe to Andrew Crawford's school. In that way he gave Abe and Sarah a chance to escape each day from their lonely, motherless cabin.

Before being hired to make up a subscription school in the Pigeon Creek-Buck Horn Valley community, a teacher must prove to the patrons that he could shape first class pens from a bundle of quills handed to him; that he could read, write, and cipher to the Rule of Three; that he could expertly handle a hickory limb on the backs of deserving children. "If a straggler supposed to understand Latin happened to sojourn in the neighborhood, he was looked upon as a wizard," Abe reminisced. [3]

The Crawford schoolhouse was almost a mile and a half south of the Lincoln home. To reach it Abe and Sarah followed the trail around their mother's hilltop grave, past their second cabin as well as the old pole-house, cut across the leased eight acre tract of land and continued two hundred yards farther southward. The schoolhouse stood on Reuben Grigsby's land and overlooked the wilderness trail which ran from the Pigeon Creek settlement to Grandview down on the Ohio River. Built of hewn logs, it was just high enough for an ordinary man to stand up in and was sixteen feet wide by twenty-five feet long. On its southeast side was a door. Close by was a cistern. Sunlight shining through the greased-paper window fell on the puncheon floor and split-log benches. A stick-and-mud chimney filled the north end. [4] Above the door and pegged to the wall was a very fine pair of buck antlers. Crotched over the teacher's chair was a long, slender hickory limb.

To keep their hands warm on bitter cold days Sarah and Abe—as well as the Grigsby, Gentry, Brooner, Oskins, Wood, Tuley, and Robey children—carried hot, baked potatoes in their mittens. At noon recess they ate the potatoes.

Since Andrew Crawford was both schoolmaster and Justice of the Peace of Carter township, he generally was addressed as Squire Crawford. The squire ran what was called a blab school: that is, all pupils studied aloud. It was said the rumble of his school could be heard away off in the wilderness.

Among the first things Crawford attempted to teach was good manners. He told Abe and the other pupils to imagine the interior of the schoolhouse to be the drawing-room of a grand lady of quality. "You girls are young ladies and you boys are young gentlemen," he said. He instructed Abe to leave the room and take a look at the paw-paw brush, sweet briars, persimmon trees and wild grapevines surrounding the schoolhouse. That dense thicket, Crawford insisted, was a formal garden about a mansion set in an imaginary world. Abe went out, looked, tried hard to see the mansion; then came back and knocked at the door.

A young gentleman of quality opened the door and with imagined dignity escorted Abe to the benches where sat Sally Lincoln, Elizabeth Wood, Katy Robey, Hannah Gentry, Betsy Tuley and other girls of the community. "Let me make you acquainted with Mr. Lincoln," said the escort solemnly.

Abe bowed low, his long, pipe-stem legs bending backward, his big ears flapping toward the very girls he had just been snowballing. Each girl tried hard not to break into a spasm of giggles as she replied, "I sure am proud to make your acquaintance, Mr. Lincoln." [5]

It was Friday afternoon and Squire Crawford had lined up a spelling class along the wall. He gave out the word *defied*. Back of him was Abe. Around the class went the word, each pupil spelling it with a *y* instead of an *i*. That nettled Crawford so much he cast off his justice-of-the-peace decorum. "I'll keep you here all night," he threatened, "if you don't spell that word correctly!"

Lincoln knew that if the pupils were late leaving school they would get whippings when they arrived home. Besides, panthers and bears sometimes attacked schoolhouses in broad daylight. What would they do to children on a trail at night?

Halfway around the spelling class *defied* had gone again when it reached Anna Caroline Robey, whom everyone called Katy. Abe liked her and it hurt him to hear her stumbling "d-e-f-." He winked and caught her attention; then he nodded and pointed at his eye. Katy began again, "d-e-f-." She looked at Abe's pointing finger: "i-e-d," she spurted.[6] The angry teacher was so relieved he dismissed school immediately. Out flew the pupils, jubilant over being freed. "We had spelling matches frequently," said Nathaniel Grigsby. "Abe was always ahead of all the classes."[7]

On another day a class was reading the Bible account of Nebuchadnezzar ordering the three Jews cast in the fiery furnace (Daniel III, 11-14). One dull little fellow stumbled along until he came to the three victims, Shadrach, Meshach, and Abed-nego. "He couldn't do anything with them. After the teacher slapped him, the boy tried again. But he could not pronounce the names," Lincoln related. "Skip them and go on," ordered the teacher. The boy sniffed and read a bit farther. Suddenly he stopped, dropped the Bible and burst out crying. "Now what's the matter?" shouted the teacher. The boy wailed: "Here's them same damn three fellers again!"[8]

Squire Crawford usually kept a very close eye on his pupils; but one day he had to leave the room and Abe Lincoln got up, grasped the buck antlers over the doorway and tried swinging on them. The pupils applauded Abe's antics for all knew how very proud the Squire was of those antlers and all secretly wanted to do what Abe was doing, but none dared. Then to the consternation of all a horn broke off and down Abe dropped. He went to his seat and began studying out loud.

In walked Crawford, saw the damaged antlers and demanded, "Who broke that horn?" Not a blab-pupil answered. Crawford took down the long hickory limb and looked around the room. Except for Abe's studying aloud, the room was absolutely silent. Crawford's gaze rested on Lincoln. Abe's big hands moved nervously in plain guilt. Out of the corner of one eye he saw Crawford's stern face purpling with rage. He heard Crawford thump the butt-end of the hickory persuader on the desk. "Do you know who broke that horn?" stormed the teacher. "Yes, sir," said Abe. "I did, sir, but I didn't mean to. I just hung on it and it broke." Crawford roared, "What did you hang on it for?" Meekly Abe replied, "I wouldn't have hung on it if I had known it was going to break."[9]

During the fall and winter of 1823, Lincoln attended Azel W. Dorsey's school.[10] Dorsey, a most versatile man, had served in the Third Kentucky Regiment under General William Henry Harrison of Vincennes, and had fought at Tippecanoe, November 7, 1811, when Har-

rison's victory over Chief Tecumseh's brother, The Prophet, destroyed
Tecumseh's hopes for an Indian Confederacy. During the War of 1812
Dorsey served in Captain Benjamin Shaklett's mounted Kentucky
Volunteers. After the war he became Commissioner of Revenue Tax
for Kentucky. In 1816 he moved to Indiana and two years later was
Coroner for Spencer County.[11] He cried the sale of town lots in Rock-
port, 1818, while free whiskey was passed around to open the hearts
of the bidders.

Tales of Coroner Dorsey's learning spread from the Ohio River to
the Ten O'clock Line, from Blue River to the Wabash. He was referred
to as The Wizard at Figures. Here was Lincoln's opportunity to learn
mathematics. "We had an old dog-eared arithmetic in our house.
And father was determined that somehow I would cipher clear through
that book," said Lincoln.[12]

According to Nathaniel Grigsby, Lincoln "used Pike's arithmetic."
This was Nicholas Pike's *New and Complete System of Arithmetic*.
While studying the book, Abe encountered simple addition, compound
subtraction, multiplication, division, vulgar fractions, coins, weights,
and measures. About one-fourth of the way through the volume he
ran into the "Single Rule of Three Direct." Although Pike included
chapters on geometry, trigonometry, algebra, and how to find the
"Proportion of Tonnage of Noah's Ark," parents of Abe's schoolmates
felt children were well educated when they could read, write and cipher
to the Rule of Three. Then they could correctly measure a field, a
haystack, a tree, or a crib of corn.[13]

"The Rule of Three Direct," Pike informed his readers, "teacheth
by having three numbers given to find the fourth, that shall have the
same proportion to the third as the second hath to the first. The rule
on account of its great and extensive usefulness is sometimes called
the Golden Rule of Proportion." Pike set forth problems. In working
those in dry measure Lincoln had to contend not only with pints,
gallons, pecks and bushels but with hottles, strikes, cooms, quarters,
chaldron, weys and lasts. Aside from barley corns, he found nothing
unusual among the inches, feet, yards, poles and acres of land measure.

To be prepared for Coroner Dorsey's arithmetic class next day, Abe
worked late by light from the fireplace or from the sputtering flame of
burning tow in a lard-filled scooped-out turnip. Sitting cross-legged
on the sandstone hearth, he solved, or tried to solve, Pike's problems.
He worked them on puncheons, on clapboards he had rived out on his
father's shaving-horse, on the wooden fireshovel. He charred a stick
in the fire and used it for a pencil. He went to the creek bank and dug

out a lump of red keel and used it for chalk. If he could find a piece
of paper he wrote on it with pens made of turkey quills, ink made from
blackberry briar roots. Anything he could lay his hands on that was
usable he used.

He took arithmetic seriously. On one page he set down, solved and
proved problems in compound subtraction. In the lower left corner of
the page he wrote:

> *"Abraham Lincoln*
> *"his hand and pen*
> *"he will be good but*
> *"God knows When."* [14]

No matter how busy he was with his studies and working for
neighbors, Abe found time to do some truck-patching for himself.
Judging by the way he handled watermelon thieves one night, truck-
patching helped keep mathematics on his mind. Quietly he investi-
gated and saw Joseph Richardson and others eating melons. After
watching them for a while, Abe decided to make things miserable for
them. "Now I've got you!" he growled as he sprang into their midst.
The startled boys stopping eating. Not one dared to run while Abe
stood looking at them. "What are you going to do?" he demanded.
Nervously Joe spoke for the group: "Abe, we just don't know what
to do. We sure don't." Lincoln let them squirm a moment: "Well, I
do. I'll let everyone off that can repeat the multiplication table!"
That was a bitter dose for the boys. Lined up, eyes on Lincoln, hands
opening and closing in anxiety, the boys did the best they could with
the table. "That shows the beat of Abe's mind. Always toward
learning something," said Richardson. [15]

In the fall of 1827 Abe began his last term of school with Dorsey
by tackling the "Directions for applying Superficies to Surveying" in
Pike's Arithmetic. There he discovered rules for measuring a tetrahe-
dron, an octahedron and "How to take the height of an Object standing on a hill which is inaccessible." On days he was not in school he
cut wood and split rails with a neighbor by the name of Simmons. According to the latter, "Abe Lincoln would work all day as hard as any
of us, and studied by firelight half the night. In this way he made
himself a thorough and practical surveyor." [16]

Isaac Arnold said: "Like Washington, Lincoln became in early
life a good practical surveyor. I have in my library the identical book
from which, at eighteen years of age, he studied the art of surveying." [17]

Lincoln's formal school training ended when Azel W. Dorsey moved from Indiana to a farm near Rushville, Illinois. There Dorsey began telling people, "Abraham Lincoln is not only one of the noblest boys I have ever known but he is certain to become noted if he lives." Soon, too, William Jones at Gentryville told friends that Lincoln "will make a great man one of these days." [18]

Already dreaming of the time when he would fulfill the prophesies of Dorsey and Jones, Abe wrote in Joe Richardson's copybook:

> "*Good boys who to their books apply*
> "*Will make great men by and by.*" [19]

With opportunity for classroom study over, Lincoln turned more and more to books for self-education. "What I want to know is in books," he told James Grigsby and others. William Jones gave him a copy of a history of the United States, evidently a popular work by William Grimshaw. "My best friends are those who give me books," said Lincoln.

About 1823 Nancy Hanks Hall with her husband, Levi Hall, moved from Kentucky to Indiana and brought along Bailey's *Etymological Dictionary*. Abe's uncle, Mordecai Lincoln, had bought it in 1793. By studying it Abe built up a good vocabulary. Not only did he stretch out on the sandstone hearth, his head toward a blazing fire of sassafras or hickory bark, but sometimes he assumed other postures while trying to find out what was in books. His mother's relative, John Hanks, who had lived in or near the Lincoln Pigeon Creek home four years, wrote: "When Abe and I returned to the house from work he would go to the cupboard, snatch a piece of cornbread, take down a book, sit in a chair, cock his legs up as high as his head, and read." According to Matilda Johnston, *Robinson Crusoe* was one of the books he read. [21]

During the winter of 1824-1825, when not reading at home, hanging around Jones' store, or doing odd jobs for Josiah Crawford, Abe cut cordwood for David Turnham. At the latter's home he found a new source of books. A single room eighteen by twenty feet, Turnham's house had a stone fireplace occupying almost one whole side. The ceiling was so low that when Abe stood up he bumped his head against it. One of the books he borrowed was *Sinbad the Sailor*. "Abe would lay on the floor with a chair under his head and laugh over them stories by the hour. I told him they was likely lies from end to end," said Dennis Hanks. [22]

Another Turnham book which appealed to Abe was William Scott's *Lessons in Elocution or a Selection of Pieces in Prose and Verse*. [23]

Abe's interest in this book probably had been whetted previously by his stepmother; her brother Isaac Bush had bought a copy of it in 1806 at the Bleakley and Montgomery Store in Elizabethtown, Kentucky.

In Scott's *Lessons* Lincoln read memorable passages from Shakespeare, for example the great soliloquy of King Claudius from *Hamlet*:

> "Oh! my offense is rank, it smells from heaven;
> "It hath the primal eldest curse upon't,
> "A brother's murder."

On the next page was Hamlet's soliloquy on death: "To be—or not to be." Commented Abe: "I think the soliloquy in Hamlet commencing 'Oh, my offense is rank' surpasses that commencing 'To be or not to be.' " [24] There was, too the soliloquy of *Richard III* beginning with:

> " 'Tis now the dead of night, and half the world
> "Is with lonely solemn darkness hung."

In the same book Lincoln probably met for the first time Shakespeare's charming liar—fat old Sir John Falstaff. Abe liked Sir John: "It is old Jack Falstaff who talks about villainy though of course Shakespeare is responsible." [25] Somewhere he found excerpts from *Othello, As You Like it, The Tempest, Henry V, Henry VIII, Romeo and Juliet.*

Scott quoted Socrates: "We should eat and drink in order to live instead of living, as many do, in order to eat and drink." Abe heeded that. Sarah Bush Lincoln tells us that "Abe was a moderate eater. He sat down and ate what was set before him, making no complaint." [26]

The lowly social position of Caius Marius, a Roman soldier who wanted to be a general, touched Abe. "I have since my youth been familiar with toils and dangers," Marius is quoted as saying in Scott's *Lessons.* "Want of birth and fortune is the objection against me. What if I can show no statues of my family? I can show the standards, the armour, which I have myself taken from the vanquished. I can show the scars of those wounds which I have received facing enemies of my country. Those are my statues."

In Scott's *Lessons,* too, was Gray's "Elegy Written in a Country Churchyard." Commented Abe: "My early history is perfectly characterized by a single line of Gray's Elegy: 'The short and simple annals of the poor.' "

Scott quoted Homer's "Parting of Hector and Andromache," Milton's "Lamentations for Loss of His Spirit," Dryden's "Alexander's Feast or the Power of Music." There were quotations from Hume's "Advantages of History," Atterbury's "On Doing as We Would Be Done By," Virgil's "Aneas and Queen Dido" giving an "Account of the Sack of Troy," Mark Anthony's funeral oration in *Julius Caesar*, and Cicero's oratory dealing with torture by red hot plates and the cross.

Scott explained how to express grief, penitence, fear, aversion, joy, and melancholy by posture; line-drawings provided illustrations. Lincoln tried out this newly acquired knowledge. He declaimed from stumptops and found he could easily move his fellow backwoodsmen. "Whatsoever you pursue be emulous to excell," counselled Scott. Lincoln wanted to excel in the pursuit of knowledge. His stepmother said that when there was no paper Abe "would jot things down in his mind, transferring them at times to boards, walls, anywhere he could stick them till he did get paper. Then he would look at it, think about it, repeat it to himself," at last saying, "Mother, I'll tell you what it means." He would then explain it "in simple words." [27]

As Lincoln's hunger for books mounted it was accompanied by increasing interest in Robert Burns' poems. Abe thought highly of the Scottish plowman's homey philosophy. Observed Isaac Arnold: "Burns he could quote from end to end." [28]

Word reached Lincoln that William B. Johnson, over on Blue Creek about fifty miles to the northeast, had a copy of John Bunyan's *Pilgrim's Progress*. Happily for Abe, Tom Lincoln needed another ox and Tom's brother, Josiah, near neighbor to Johnson, had one to spare. [29] Hours before daybreak Abe set out to get both ox and book. He swung into the peculiar gait some pioneers used when they had far distances to go, taking long strides, lifting his feet squarely from the ground and squarely setting them down hardly bending his toes and throwing little of the weight of his body on his heels. Being slightly pigeon-toed he stepped along as stealthily as an Indian and covered ground rapidly. He followed the Boonville-Corydon road—not much more than a trail through the unbroken Indiana forest—for about thirty miles, then veered northward and headed for the Blue Creek Primitive Baptist settlement. Soon he encountered big mud-holes that had been pawed out by bull buffaloes. Should he fall into one of them he would be in as bad a fix as Bunyan's Christian had been in the Slough of Despond. Wolves, panthers, bears, wildcats roaming the deep woods did not worry him, but denizens of the supernatural world did. "I can't help being this way," he said frankly.[30]

Every stream he crossed, every step taken brought the sixteen year old Lincoln closer to Indiana's cave stone country and the stamping ground of its legendary Headless Hermit of Locust Hill. A magic word was needed to get by this eccentric monster who carried his head under an arm while blood dripped on his white shirt and breeches. Woodchoppers swore that the head nodded and in guttural tones muttered: "Beneath that tree gold is buried in great piles." After that it gave the pass-word: "If you ever reveal this secret, death will wither the word on your lips!"

When Abe reached the cave stone country he saw funnel-shaped sink holes everywhere. He knew if he stepped into one of them he might fall into a cave where his Uncle Josiah's neighbors boiled bat guano in kettles and lixiviating troughs to get saltpeter for the manufacture of gunpowder.[31]

Rapidly Abe passed the village of Bib Spring (Marengo, Indiana), crossed Whiskey Run, Brandywine, and Cedar Fork. Safely beyond reach of the Headless Hermit, he was now in shouting distance of the homes of his Uncle Josiah and William B. Johnson. First he went to his uncle, got the ox Tom Lincoln wanted and rode it up the big road to the Johnson cabin. Through the darkness he yelled, "Hel-lo! [hel-lo!" The cabin door opened and a man's voice asked, "Who's here?" Response: "Tom Lincoln's Abe." Question: "What's wanting?" Response: "Want to borrow your *Pilgrim's Progress*, Mr. Johnson." Response: "Light and come in."

A local school teacher, William B. Johnson had moved from Kentucky to the Blue Creek neighborhood in 1821 and had married Miss Charlotte H. Pankey. Abe stayed all night with the Johnsons. Up early next morning, he went to the barnlot to get the ox. In spite of the horse-high, pig-tight, bull-strong rail fence around the barn, the ox had escaped; when it was finally found, Abe mounted and away the ox galloped. "Here we go!" shouted Abe, clutching *Pilgrim's Progress*.[32]

Even though he already had read Parson M. L. Weems' *Life of Washington*, when he heard Josiah Crawford had a copy of David Ramsay's book with the same title, Abe borrowed it. He credited Ramsay's book with providing a fuller and better account of Washington and the Revolution.[33] "Washington is the mightiest name on earth," declared Lincoln. "To add brightness to the sun or glory to the name of Washington is alike impossible." Ramsay's book helped

Abe learn much about Washington's standards. Patterning his own
after Washington's ideals he said, "I am nothing but truth is everything." [34]

Ramsay dramatically described battles. He quoted Washington's
address to the American Revolutionists as the British Army lay at
Staten Island: "The time is near at hand which must probably determine whether Americans are to be freemen or slaves." In April, 1793,
ten years after the war ended, M. Genet, the French minister to the
United States, began fitting out privateers to prey on British shipping.
War with France seemed imminent. In this connection Ramsay quoted President Washington: "There is but one straight course, and that
is to seek the truth, and preserve it steadily." Ramsey included
Washington's Farewell Address and told of his refusal of a third term
as President. Vividly Ramsay described Washington's death: after
getting wet in a December rain, the general was "seized with inflamma-
tory affection of the windpipe. He was bled in the night." Unable
to swallow "he undressed himself and went to bed to die." To Dr.
Craik he said, "I am dying, and have been dying for a long time. But
I am not afraid to die."

Late one evening Lincoln put Ramsay's book between the logs of the
cabin wall and went off to sleep in the loft. A rain storm hit and badly
damaged the book. He had no money to pay for it. Moreover, there
was not another copy in the region at that time. Very much depressed
he returned the book to Mr. Crawford. "I want to pay you for it,"
he offered earnestly. Crawford examined the book. Knowing Lincoln had no money, he replied, "If you think you ought to pay me for
it, and you choose to do so, you can top my field of corn." Lincoln
worked hard topping that six-acre field of corn. At the end of
three days Josiah Crawford dropped by. "Abe, that squares the
account with you," he said. [35]

Still another biography of an American Revolutionary War hero
fell into Lincoln's hands: Parson Weem's *Life of Francis Marion.*
Few books the adolescent Lincoln read contained more common sense,
fiery patriotism and practical religion; and few did more to shape
Lincoln's thinking. Known during the Revolution as South Carolina's
Swamp Fox, General Marion led a band of ragged, desperate men
armed with axes, clubs, guns, and swords made from handsaws. Marion
and his men dashed in and hacked to pieces both the king's soldiers and
those Americans who Weems considered "disaffected to the cause of
liberty and ready to join the British against their own countrymen."
As Marion lay dying, someone asked him what was the best religion.

Weems quoted the general: "I know of but one religion. And that is the hearty love of God and man. That is the only true religion." To his wife weeping at his bedside, Marion said, "I am not afraid to die; for, thank God, I can lay my hand on my heart and say that since I came to man's estate, I have never intentionally done harm to any man."

Lincoln found still another book in Josiah Crawford's home which commanded his attention—*Kentucky Preceptor,* published by Mc-Coun, Tilford & Company at Lexington, Kentucky, in 1812. On its inside cover is written: "Josiah Crawford reading Book, 1819." From it, according to Mrs. Crawford, "Abe learned his school orations, speeches, and pieces to write." [36] The preface by the book's compiler states: "Tales of love, or romantic fiction, or anything which might tend to instill false notions into minds of children have not gained admission." Among the pieces admitted Lincoln found the quarrel between Cassius and Brutus, Act IV, Scene 3, in Shakespeare's *Julius Caesar;* Goldsmith's "Deserted Village;" essays on the Scriptures and the discovery of America; the play "Eton Montem"; and "Selected Sentences." The last included items like these:

"Let not the sun go down on your wrath."

"A liar begins by making falsehood appear like truth, and ends by making truth appear like falsehood."

"From the creatures of God, let man learn wisdom; and let him apply himself to the lessons which they give."

"Harbour not revenge in thy heart; it will torment thy heart and prevent the best thoughts."

Having heard his father, mother and stepmother praise Thomas Jefferson as the mighty preacher of human liberty, Abe Lincoln now eagerly read Jefferson's First Inaugural Address: "What I deem the essential principles of our government are equal and exact justice to all men, of whatever state or persuasion, religious or political; peace, commerce, and honest friendship with all nations—entangling alliances with none; the support of the state governments in all their rights; the preservation of the general government in its whole constitutional vigor, as the sheet-anchor of our peace at home and abroad. These principles form the bright constellation which has gone before us, and guided our steps through an age of revolution and reformation. The wisdom of our sages and the blood of our heroes have been devoted to their attainment. Should we wander from them in moments of error or alarm, let us hasten to retrace our steps and to regain the road which alone leads to peace, liberty, and safety."

It is believed Lincoln read the *Columbian Class Book* while boarding in the home of Judge Daniel Grass at Rockport. At the time he
was helping to build the Gentry flatboat. A copy of the third edition
of the book, compiled by A. T. Lowe, and printed in 1827, has on its
left front inside cover the notation "Abe Lincoln 1828," in Lincoln's
handwriting. Below it is an amateurish drawing of an Indian labeled
Cornplant. Both autograph and drawing look as if they had been done
with a soft quill pen.[37]

Lowe's book opens with Kingston's "Biographical Sketch of Washington." This is followed by Chief Cornplant's speech to Washington;
Kingston's biographical sketches of Franklin, Hannibal, Isaac Newton
and Dr. Johnson; Chief Logan's famous speech to Lord Dunsmore;
Milton's "Lycidas"; Lord Byron's "The Corsair"; Josephus' "Destruc-
tion of Jerusalem"; Brewster's "Ancient Pompeii"; Goldsmith's essays
on Egypt, Holland, the ocean, and the universe; anecdotes of Alexander the Great; Pope's "Temple of Fame"; a detailed account of life
in Russia; Hill's "Sketch of the American Revolution," and other
items.

Lowe's story of Demosthenes stirred Lincoln. Demosthenes, Lowe
pointed out, "became a pupil of Isaeus and Plato, and applied himself
to the study of orations of Socrates" and overcame stammering by
speaking with pebbles in his mouth. By the time he was seventeen
he was a forceful orator. When the Macedonians demanded the surrender of the Athenians, Demosthenes reminded his countrymen of the
fable of sheep which delivered up their dogs to the wolves. Having
already met that fable in Aesop, Abe went on reading more books in
the Grass home by the light of flaming logs until midnight, reading
until Mrs. Grass expressed fear that Abe was not only going to
wear himself out from want of rest but was going to "bake the top of
his head." [38]

When Abe said, "My best friends are those who give me books," he
also intended to include newspapers and periodicals. Early in 1823, in
William Jones' store, he began to read the Vincennes *Western Sun
and General Advertiser,* a weekly newspaper. Three years later he was
borrowing and reading *The Telescope,* a weekly periodical.

William Wood, who lived on a ridge north of Lincoln's home, subscribed to *The Telescope* from about 1825 to 1830; Abe frequently
borrowed copies from Wood.[39] Edited by W. Beach in New York, *The
Telescope* carried at its masthead the words of Isaiah LVII, 14: "Cast
ye up, cast ye up; prepare the way, take up the stumbling block out
of the way of my people." An independent thinker, a liberal, and an

Abraham Lincoln lived in this hewn-log house 1818 to 1830,
age 9 to 21. His mother died in it in 1818. The foundation of
the house is now outlined by bronze logs. Lincoln City, Indiana.
(Sketch by John H. Rowbottom).

anti-slavery advocate, Beach devoted his life to taking up stumbling
blocks. Abe Lincoln became one of his disciples.

In the June 3, 1826, number of *The Telescope* Beach noted that
opposition to his paper was rising among "Bigots, Sectarians, the
Scribes and Pharisees." The July 15th issue told of the deaths of
John Adams and Thomas Jefferson. Both had died on July 4, 1826,
exactly fifty years from the day they signed the Declaration of Independence. Lincoln read, "The late President Adams departed this
life, age 92, on the evening of the 4th inst. as the bells were ringing for
the conclusion of the celebration. The venerable patriot rose on the
morning, in his usual good spirits, rejoicing that he had been spared
to witness the jubilee of his country's freedom. He became ill about
noon, grew gradually worse, and at six he fell asleep." When guns
firing a salute awoke him, he said, "It is a great and glorious day."
He never spoke again.

"Thomas Jefferson," wrote Editor Beach, "expired at Monticello at
ten minutes before one oclock on the Fourth of July within the same
hour at which the Declaration of Independence was promulgated in
the Hall of Congress fifty years ago. During his illness he constantly
expressed a wish to live to see another 4th of July . . . He was per-

fectly resigned to the will of Providence and declared he wished to
die in peace with all the world."

The Vincennes *Western Sun* for July 29 announced the deaths with
wide black mourning rules. Editor Elihu Stout called these events a
"Singular but felicitous coincidence." Like Beach, Stout, and others,
Abe Lincoln was profoundly moved by the concurrent deaths. "The
two men," said Lincoln, "most distinguished in the framing and
support of the Declaration were Thomas Jefferson and John Adams—
the one having penned it, and the other sustained it most forcibly in
debate—the only two of the fifty-five who signed it that were selected
President of the United States. Precisely fifty years after they put
their hands to the paper, it pleased Almighty God to take both from
this stage of action." [40]

Obviously mindful of the damage done to the book he had borrowed
from Crawford, Abe decided to make a bookcase to protect books,
papers, and periodicals. Since early youth he had been learning the use
of drawing-knife, jack-plane, brace-and-bit. At his father's workbench
he had helped make corner cupboards, desks, and coffins. Down at
river banks he had helped Tom Lincoln build overshot mill wheels.
He knew much about the art of wood working. Selecting well seasoned walnut and poplar clapboards, Abe smoothed them down, cut
them to desired lengths and pegged them together with wooden
pegs. When finished, his bookcase stood thirty inches high and eighteen inches wide. It had six drawers. Below these he put a shelf on
which to store papers and periodicals. The broad walnut top he used
for a study table. Somehow he managed to get candles now and
then. By candle light he often read until a puddle of sputtering tallow
burned holes in the table top. [41]

Lack of ambition, in anyone, to learn something new each day
seemed to annoy Lincoln. Once while passing the Lamar place he saw
young John W. Lamar and a group of boys watching John's father at
work riding a shaving-horse. "Well, boys, what have you learned
today?" Abe asked. When no one answered, he said emphatically,
"I wouldn't give a cent for a boy who doesn't know more today than he
knew yesterday." [42]

CHAPTER SEVEN

BRUSH COLLEGE DAYS

Denied the opportunity to attend an institution of learning higher than a subscription school, Abe Lincoln opened in the summer of 1827 what he called "Forest College." Soon his Pigeon Creek neighbors renamed it "Abe's Brush College."

In the course of frequent visits to his mother's grave during the previous nine years, Abe had worn a well defined path through the underbrush and sawbriars from his cabin to the lonely hilltop. Now he continued this path from the grave down a slope for about a quarter of a mile to the southwest, ending at a particularly big tree. He had taken James Grigsby with him. "Jimmy, we'll call this our Forest College. But I wish I could go to a real college for a year," he said.[1]

James, the thirteen year old son of Reuben Grigsby, Sr., was Abe's only fellow student. Small and frail, he had a defect in his speech; boys around Gentryville sometimes laughed at him. "Abe took me in charge," Jimmy recalled. "He showed them how wrong it was. Most of them quit. Abe would throw his long arm over my narrow shoulders and walk and talk with me. Why, Abe would even take me part of the way home." Jimmy's older brother noticed these things; Abe "was kind and clever to all. Indeed he appeared to cultivate it as a principle" wrote Nattie.[2]

Once Abe called Jimmy's attention to an uprooted, hollow sycamore a few rods from the big tree: "Jim, we need that to store our books in." With axes the boys chopped off roots and limbs and cut out a log about eight feet long. After rolling it under the tree they plugged the ends of the log with flat stones to keep out squirrels, raccoons, polecats and other forest animals. They put their almanacs and books in it. "Almanacs were not books", explained James Grigsby. "Real books had hard covers. Abe would go a long ways off to get real books."

The hollow log, the big tree and a nearby stump completed Abe's college equipment. His campus was an entanglement of blackberry vines, paw-paw, sumac, elbow-brush, wahoo, wild rose, honeysuckle and poison ivy. Overhead, mockingbirds sang Brush College songs. Mounting a stump, Abe looked northeastward at the hilltop where his mother was buried. Solemnly he opened each day's session with "Knowledge is power." After that he paraphrased a quotation: "There is no darkness but ignorance and, Jimmy, there is darkness in my soul." Remembering what he had read in Dr. Mathew Hole's *Practical Discourses,* he added: "Ignorance is to the mind what Blindness is to the Eye." Next he substituted Jimmy for Brutus and quoted from Act I, Scene 1 of Shakespeare's *Julius Caesar*:

> *"The fault, dear Jimmy, is not in our stars,*
> *"But in ourselves that we are underlings."*

Quotations out of the way, Lincoln followed the advice in his Dilworth *Speller*: "The heart of the prudent seeketh knowledge." He handed a book to Grigsby and pointed to a paragraph, maybe to a whole page. "Jimmy, see if I can repeat that," he said.

As Lincoln started talking, Jim, watching the page, walked slowly backward. Gradually Abe raised his voice. When no longer able to understand what Abe was saying, Jim called out, "Abe, I can't hear you!" Abe stopped his speech and shouted, "Come a little forward, Jimmy." Abe was learning voice control; he learned it so well his voice carried to people at great distances. But James Grigsby felt there was more to Lincoln's stump speaking than learning to speak clearly at long distances: "Abe seemed to think he had to learn by heart what smart men said to get smart himself. I held the Bible and Abe would tell what Solomon said. And tell what Christ said too. Sometimes Abe would get the blues. He wouldn't study for two or three days at a time."

When an attack of melancholy vanished, Abe usually returned to the *Farmer's Almanac.* Maybe the almanacs were not real books, not having hard covers; but they were good for Lincoln. According to James Grigsby: "There were lots of jokes in the almanacs. Some days Abe would go over them and twist and turn them into new ones till I would fall off a log and roll on the ground, laughing." [3]

If the *Farmer's Almanac* explanation of moon phases interested Abe, the signs of the Zodiac enchanted him. At night he would lie on his back and study the planets and constellations through treetops.

One night Jim told Abe he couldn't understand how there could be any signs of fish (Pisces) in the sky. Abe: "Don't rain come from the sky?" Jim: "Sure." Abe: "Dont rain make water for the fish to swim in?" Again Jimmy agreed. "Well," concluded Abe, "there's water in the sky for the fish up there." Jim: "I understand that now. But what about the feller a-shooting that arrow? And what about the billy goat up there, too?" With great firmness Abe answered, "Jimmy, heap smarter fellers than me link things together in the sky." [4]

In the face of taunts and jeers from his neighbors, it took a lot of courage for young Lincoln to continue with his "college" work. But standing on the stump under the big tree, in the shadow of his mother's hilltop grave, he showed the same courage he had shown on the scuffle-ground when he challenged all-comers. "The fault is in ourselves that we are underlings", he repeated to Jim Grigsby. He, Abe Lincoln, intended to be no underling, physically or mentally.

"Most men are cowards," Abe read in the June 23, 1827, *Telescope's* report of Dr. Lindsley's address to the graduating class of Cumberland College, Tennessee. "They are afraid to speak and to act when duty calls and as duty requires. Dare to do to others as you would have them do to you," Lindsley advised. "If you have learned how to study and have acquired a thirst for knowledge, you will continue to study and to learn while you live to be honest, just, magnanimous, true to your God, your country, to yourselves, and to the world."

Lincoln may already have felt as Dr. Lindsley did, that "most men are cowards." He examined himself in an effort to answer the question "What really lies behind man's actions and attitudes?" He sensed that man has values and strives in a worthwhile direction, that not always can one's aspirations be judged by one's outward appearance. Talking to Henry Brooner and others, Abe one time looked down at his own shabby breeches and remarked, "Boys, mind makes the man." [5] Later Jim Grigsby added: "Abe was just awful hungry to be somebody." When he stopped plowing to rest his old gray horse, "Abe had his pen and ink in the field," according to John W. Lamar; Abe "always put in the time to good advantage." [6]

Abe's Brush College was quite mobile. To conduct classes in its law and public speaking departments, Abe attended court in Boonville, county seat of Warrick County, and elsewhere. He heard many lawyers plead cases. But he never heard one with as great a reputation as had John A. Breckenridge. On both sides of the Ohio River, Breckenridge was renowned for his eloquent pleading. Admitted to practice law *ex gratia* in the Third Circuit Court at Indianapolis, this aristocratic Kentuckian had formed a partnership with C. Fletcher[7] and advertised: "C. Fletcher & J. A. Breckenridge as attorneys and councellors at Law will perform any business in that profession, even that which comes under the denomination of pettifogging if they are roundly paid for it." [8]

And now Breckenridge had been hired to defend Abe's neighbor, a

Mr. S., accused of murdering Mr. H., another Lincoln neighbor. Determined to learn how this forceful orator would plead a murder trial, Abe left long before daylight for Boonville, sixteen miles westward. Lately, every time Mr. H had called his hogs for a feed of corn, he had missed a few. After inquiring around, it was alleged, he had accused S of stealing them.⁹ Since many of Abe's neighbors considered hogs running wild in the woods as belonging in the same class with wild turkeys and deer, the charge of larceny was not considered serious. But early one morning Mr. H was called to his door. There was a shot. Mr. H fell dead. The murder inflamed the neighborhood.

At the *post mortem* a small piece of bullet patching (a bit of calico) was found in Mr. H's wound. That patching, some alleged, matched the pattern of Mrs. S's new calico dress. Friends of Mr. H angrily shouted, "S— killed him!" In the excitement some woman grabbed the patching and swallowed it. That eliminated the evidence pointing to Mr. S.

A change of venue was taken from Spencer County to Warrick County; so Abe Lincoln, coonskin cap pulled down tight against the cold, walked to Boonville and edged his way into the little courthouse. There women were smoking clay pipes; men, wearing deerskin suits, dangled side-knives at their belts. Abe found a place where he could hear every word Breckenridge spoke. He followed the famous lawyer's reasoning. He admired the man's gestures, oratory, and ability to think on his feet. He was impressed by the way Breckenridge threw back his shoulders and shook out his shirtfront ruffles. And as he listened to Breckenridge's final plea to the jury, Abe said to himself: "If I could make as good a speech as that my soul would be satisfied." ¹⁰

The jury acquitted Mr. S. As friends crowded up to congratulate his attorney on his victory, Abe, unknown to the great lawyer, offered his big, calloused hand. John A. Breckenridge looked him up and down. Ill at ease, bare shins showing, Abe stood first on one foot, then the other. Haughtily, Beckenridge turned and walked away. Dazed, humiliated, shame-faced, Abe stumbled from that Boonville courtroom. He went back to Gentryville and sought out James Grigsby. "Jimmy, I went to hear that feller speak and he wouldn't even shake hands with me," said Abe bitterly.¹¹

During the early fall of 1826, Abe Lincoln, operating the Taylor ferry across the mouth of Anderson River, stood looking at his own recently built flatboat. He was wondering how he could make it a little stronger when two men drove up in carriages. They got out and examined Abe's boat. One man asked, "Who owns that?" Lincoln replied: "I do" The man looked at the steamboat hove-to midstream in the Ohio River, and asked, "Will you take our trunks out to that steamer?" Assuming he would probably get a couple of bits for the job, Abe answered: "Sure, be glad to."

Abe loaded the trunks on his flatboat, and with the men sitting on them, he sculled out to the vessel, let the men jump on board and put their trunks on after them. As the engineer was turning on steam to start the paddlewheels churning, Abe yelled to the men, "You forgot to pay me!" The men leaned over the side and each tossed a silver half-dollar into Abe's boat. Abe couldn't believe his eyes; he had earned a dollar in less than a day. He pocketed the money, sculled back to the Indiana shore and tied up. He took out his two half-dollars, gazed at them, fingered them. He could do a lot with that dollar. Then one of the halves slipped out of his fingers and rolled in to the Ohio River. He sadly watched it go quivering into the current and out of sight forever.[12]

On the Kentucky side, opposite the Anderson River and the town of Troy lived the Dill brothers, John T. and Lin. Lincoln knew they were farmers and licensed ferrymen. Also he knew the Dills had arranged a bell, on each side of the Ohio River, to be rung by travelers wanting ferry service.

One day, the ferry bell on the Kentucky side rang and the Dills did not answer it. Maybe they were too busy with their farm work. The longer Abe listened to the bell the harder it was for him to keep from answering it. Here was a chance to add a little something to his lone fifty-cent piece. Finally unable longer to resist the jangling bell, Lincoln rowed across the Ohio. Just as he snubbed his boat into the mud bank, the Dill brothers leaped from a thicket, grabbed him and tried to duck him into the river. Lincoln smashed hard fists in their faces. John T. shouted: "You've violated the law of Kentucky." Abe: "How?" John T.: "By operating a ferry without a license. It's against the law. I'm the only person who has a license to operate a ferry back and forth across the river at this point."

Abe, then only seventeen years of age, looked across the river. It seemed a long, long way over to Indiana, longer than he had ever dreamed it could look. "Come on!" the brothers ordered. "You're going up before the Justice of the Peace, Squire Pate."

Between his accusers, Abe trudged through cornfields, tobacco patches, and an apple orchard; on past Squire Samuel Pate's slave quarters and up a little hill to the Pate plantation mansion. The Dills told their story to Mrs. Pate. While they guarded Abe on the veranda, Mrs. Pate sent a Negro servant to call his master in from the fields.

When the Justice of the Peace, still in his early thirties, arrived, he led the Dills and Lincoln into a low-ceilinged room in the east end of the house. Mrs. Pate's sixteen year old niece, Ann Meeker, along with some white neighbors, found seats in the rear of the room.[13] John T. Dill swore out a warrant against Abe, charging him with illegally operating a ferry across the Ohio River. Squire Pate rapped for order, opened magistrate's court, and the trial of the Commonwealth of Kentucky *vs.* Abraham Lincoln was underway.

Abe watched John T. Dill take the witness stand. Ferryman Dill swore he had seen the defendant pick up passengers on the Indiana side and carry them to steamers out in midstream. Dill swore his license gave him the exclusive right to set passengers across the Ohio River and that Lincoln was injuring the Dill ferry business. Lincoln could clearly see Dill's testimony was interesting Squire Pate. After all, the Dill brothers operated their ferry out from Pate's land. They paid the Squire rent for use of the landing. Suddenly, Abe realized he was in a pretty tight spot.

When Lin Dill took the witness stand he corroborated his brother's testimony. More neighbors entered the courtroom as Squire Pate asked "Any witnesses for the defense?" There were none. Abe Lincoln stood up: "Your Honor, I would like to say something." Squire Pate nodded. Abe admitted he had carried travelers to steamers hove-to off the Indiana shore. "But, Your Honor, I did not know that was against the law. I don't understand how it could be." Explained Squire Pate: "Mr. Lincoln, the northern boundary of Kentucky extends to the low-water mark on the Indiana side."

The Squire took down Volume I of Littell's *Statute Law of Kentucky,* turned to section 8 on page 363 and read aloud, "If any person whatsoever shall, for reward, set any person over any river or creek, whereupon public ferries are appointed, he or she so offending shall forfeit and pay five pounds current money for every such offense." According to Pike's *Arithmetic* Abe knew five pounds, based on the North Carolina table of exchange, amounted to $12.50. If he had to pay that much for each time he had violated the Kentucky law pertaining to the Indiana side of the river, it would come to more money than he could possibly raise. He would have to lay out his fine in jail. In that quiet courtroom he could already hear Kentucky prison doors clanging shut after him. He felt every one was watching him, including Ann Meeker. He wet his lips.

"Your Honor," Abe said earnestly, "I never meant to violate any law. And I never set any person over the Ohio River." The court-room was so quiet he heard only the shuffle of a foot here and there. "Sir, all I have ever done is to set passengers halfway across the river." He heard Squire Pate call for Dill's ferry license. And as he watched him read it, and heard him re-examine the Dill brothers' testimony, Abe wished he had learned something about law, especially the law which gave to Kentucky jurisdiction over the Ohio River along the Indiana shore.

Aloud Squire Pate reread Section 8. Noting that the law establish-ing ferries said nothing about carrying passengers for hire to the middle of any stream, he pointed out that the evidence presented by the plaintiff had failed to show that the defendant had at any time transported a passenger over a river or creek belonging to Kentucky. Therefore the case must be dismissed.

The Squire's words stunned Lincoln. He was free again. Although he could barely speak, he managed to thank the Squire and started to follow the Dill brothers from the room. But Squire Pate stopped Abe and invited him to sit for a while on the veranda overlooking the plantation and the Ohio River. As he sat there he heard Pate's slaves singing at their work in the tobacco barns and fields near the river.

Carefully Pate explained to Abe the pitfalls that lay in the path of anyone ignorant of the law. And while the Squire talked, his black servant, Harrison, hovered in the background. The Squire told Abe that the world would be a better place if all men had a general know-ledge of the law, that certainly all ferrymen should know the law per-taining to their ferry business. Abe listened so eagerly that Pate in-vited him to return and attend magistrate's court as a spectator.

Between his flatboat trip with Jefferson Ray to Arkansas, odd jobs around Jones' store and work on the Ohio, Abe somehow managed to find time to make a few visits to the court. Slave-holder Samuel Pate had aroused in him considerable interest in the law. Besides that, the Squire's attractive niece, Ann Meeker, had also aroused Abe's interest.[14]

When Abe's friend and neighbor, David Turnham, offered him the appointment of deputy constable, he promptly accepted, for here was an opportunity to see law in action. He was cutting cordwood and splitting rails for Turnham that fall of 1827, when David was sworn in as constable. To acquaint himself and Abe with the legal aspects of their offices, Turnham obtained a copy of *The Revised Laws of Indiana Adopted and Enacted by the General Assembly*, printed by

Carpenter and Douglas at Corydon, the state capital at that time. Turnham said, "When Abe and I were associated he would come to my house and sit and read it. He fairly devoured the book."

Although Abe had heard law quoted at Boonville and in Squire Pate's court, the *Statutes of Indiana* was the first law book he ever read.[15] The Turnham copy has 438 pages and a complete index. In addition to the laws and State Constitution it contains the Declaration of Independence, the Ordinance of 1787, and the Constitution of the United States.

The Indiana Constitution revealed to Lincoln the many general and special laws necessary to set up and govern a state. "The printing press," he read, "shall be free to every person who undertakes to examine the proceedings of the legislature or any branch of government. The free communication of thoughts and opinions is one of the inviolable rights of man." Branding slavery a tyranny, the state constitution forbade the "holding of any part of the human creation in slavery." But the constitution approved the system whereby any boy or girl under eighteen could be "bound by indenture of his or her free will and accord, or with the consent of his or her father." If such children, known as "bound out," ran away and were caught they were to be thrown into jail by order of the Justice of the Peace and returned to their masters or mistresses just as if they were Negro slaves! Abe Lincoln and his sister Sally were fortunate that when hiring them out to the Crawfords, their father did not bind them out.

The definition of a legal fence interested Abe. It had to be at least five feet, six inches high, and comprise "what is commonly called a stakeing and ridering fence." However, any fence was considered legal by Lincoln's neighbors when it was horse-high, pig-tight, and bull-strong.

Together, Lincoln and Turnham studied the laws governing the office of constable: "It shall be the duty of every constable to apprehend and bring to justice all felons, and disturbers of the peace, to suppress all riots and unlawful assemblies, and in other respects to keep the peace. To serve and execute all warrants, writs, precepts, and other processes to him directed."

Because in that rather rough-and-tumble Pigeon Creek-Buck Horn Valley community it was not easy to apprehend and bring to justice all felons, Constable Turnham needed the help of big fists; hence his appointment of Lincoln as his deputy. Since Thomas Lincoln had been constable in Cumberland County, Kentucky, 1802-1804, Abe already had heard something of the duties of the office.[16]

On his trips with David Turnham, Deputy Constable Lincoln saw how criminals, locally classed as bad medicine, acted when apprehended. At that time "There was more drunkenness and stealing on a small scale, more immorality, less religion, less well-placed confidence" in the community than could be found a few years later, wrote Turnham.[17] When one law violater objected to being arrested and drew back to strike Lincoln, Abe doubled his fists, eyed the man and warned, "Before you strike me you better stick your head in the fire."[18] The man went meekly with Officers Turnham and Lincoln.

Experiences with Turnham, in Squire Pate's court, and in the Boonville courthouse sharpened Abe's interest in the law so much that John Pitcher, Sheriff of Spencer County, stated: "Abe wanted to read law with me but his father was too poor to spare him from the farm and the mill. Tom Lincoln [had] built a horse mill for grinding corn," and "Abe used to bring me my meal regularly."[19] Sheriff Pitcher, influential politician, postmaster at Rockport, successful lawyer, was thirty-three years old, an alumnus of Yale and proud of his Connecticut ancestry. "His powers of sarcasm and ridicule were perhaps unequaled by any man in this section," one of his neighbors recalled. While Pitcher's little son, Thomas G., toddled about the place the sheriff tried to talk Lincoln out of thinking of a legal career: "Better give up the idea." Abe: "Can't do it." Pitcher did not reply but, as he later admitted, "I didn't think he had it in him."[20]

Prevented from reading law in Pitcher's office, Abe asked to borrow some law books to take home. Unable to dissuade him, John Pitcher handed him Sir William Blackstone's *Commentaries of the Laws of England,* Volume I of the fourteenth edition, edited by Edmund Christian and printed in London, 1803, by A. Strahan, Law-printer to his King's Most Excellent Majesty. Pitcher had bought the book in 1823.[21]

Lincoln tucked the volume under an arm and left for Pigeon Creek. Interested at finding the book dated Lincoln's Inn, London, May 1, 1803, he thoughtfully read editor Christian's statement that "The Commentaries form an essential part of every gentleman's library; the purity of the language, the classic elegance of the quotations and allusions, the clean and intelligable explanations of every subject, must always yield the reader as much pleasure as improvement." That statement led Abe to read late by the light of blazing sassafras brush in the fireplace.

Abe discovered Volume I of Blackstone's *Commentaries* was not only a 'gentleman's library' but almost a law school in itself. Its five hundred pages covered such topics as: The Nature of Laws in General, The Laws of England, The Rights of Persons, The Absolute Rights of Individuals, Parliament, The King and His Title, Subordinate Magistrates, The People Whether Alien Denizens or Natives, Master and Servant, Husband and Wife, Parent and Child, Guardian and Ward. Here also Abe had a fair view of the background of English statutory law, common law, and Roman law. Having read the Holy Bible, parts of Shakespeare's dramas, and now a volume of Blackstone's Commentaries, he had acquired the beginnings of a good literary education.

It was a warm summer day and Abe Lincoln was returning Blackstone's *Commentaries* to Sheriff Pitcher. He came to a shallow stream which had been sent to overflowing by a sudden heavy rain. Seeing that the footlog was out, he tossed two fence rails across the creek and walked onto them. Halfway across, one rail broke, tumbling Abe and Blackstone into the muddy, rushing water. Somehow he held onto the book, waded out and went on to John Pitcher's country home to face the Sheriff's powers of sarcasm. There he told Pitcher what had happened. "I have no money," he added, "but I will do anything to pay for the damage I have done to your book."

Sheriff Pitcher turned the soggy book over and examined it. Anyone could see it was almost ruined. As he looked out across his farm he told Abe: "I have a cornfield down there that has burrs and weeds in it. You can go down there and pull them." Abe went to work, pulling every cockleburr and weed he saw. He worked day after day, hard and long. Then one day John Pitcher came to the field. Abe waved a hand and kept right on pulling weeds. "Abe," said Pitcher, "you have pulled enough." Straightening up, Abe answered, "Sheriff, if I paid you for the good I got out of that book I would be here all summer." [22]

With an idea of the dignity of the law, Abe dipped his quill pen into his homemade ink and wrote: "The American Government is the best form of government in the world for an intelligent people. It ought to be kept sound, and preserved forever; that general education should be fostered and carried all over the country; that the Constitution should be sacred, the Union perpetuated, and the laws revered, respected and enforced." Not a word about slavery. Why? Was it because slavery was considered legalized by the Constitution? Or was it because slavery was such a controversial subject among his borderland acquaintances he wanted to avoid taking a definite stand on it at this time? Regardless of his reasons he turned the piece over to William Wood. The latter passed it on to Sheriff John Pitcher,

who read it, exclaimed "The world can't beat it!" and sent it off to
a paper that published it.[33]

Lincoln had his first opportunity to try out his legal knowledge
when one of his neighbors missed a gray goose, visited a suspected
neighbor. Pointing to a goose, he claimed that it was his. "No," insisted the neighbor, "That's my goose." They argued heatedly, almost
taking clubs to each other. Subsequently, they hired lawyers and the
Justice of the Peace set a day for the trial to be held in the log schoolhouse a mile west of Lincoln's home. Both men had such loyal friends
that their strife rocked the neighborhood. These settlers regarded
stealing as about the most serious offense anyone could commit; it
violated the frontier code: "A man has the right to do anything
but injure his neighbor." A man who would steal a goose might easily
slip into stealing horses or other possessions which Lincoln's neighbors
highly prized and needed for survival.

On the day of the trial Abe Lincoln and Joseph Gentry walked
through the woods to the schoolhouse. On opposite sides of the room
they found the litigants surrounded by friends and relatives. Abe
looked over the crowd and was pleased to find no lawyers had come yet.
This was just the opportunity he wanted. When he stepped out in
front of that angry, sullen crowd, all eyes turned on him. "Friends,
what means this great gathering of old neighbors?" he asked solemnly.
He waited for an answer but none came. He felt a silence as deep as
that of the surrounding forest. A grin began playing about the corners
of his wide mouth. His black eyebrows lifted. Again he asked, "What
brings us together?" But this time he did not wait for an answer.
"I'll tell you. Why—an—old—gray—goose!" he drawled.

Abe pointed to the claimant and said, "Mr. A has lost a goose. He
asserts that his neighbor, Mr. B here, has it." Lincoln pointed to the
defendant. "Mr. B disclaims having in his possession any goose not his
own. Not able or disposed to settle the difference between themselves
they have decided to go to law. And that is why we are all here."
Allowing the crowd only a moment to think that over, Lincoln went
on: "Mr. A, you say you have lost a gray goose and that you know
Mr. B has it. Rather than lose it you resolved to bring the matter into
court. Now you, Mr. A, and you, Mr. B," turning quickly from one
to the other, "after you have had your trial today—no matter which
way it goes—what has either of you gained?" He paused. "Well, if
you win, Mr. A, you'll get back your old gray goose worth about two
bits. And you, Mr. B, if you win today, you'll get to keep your old
gray goose—worth about two bits."

Laughter rippled through the crowd. "But I'll tell both of you," Lincoln added, "whichever one wins is going to lose! Lose what, you say. You have been neighbors. You will lose your friendship for one another. And it won't stop there." Waving his long arms at the crowd, he cried, "What means this array of witnesses?" His voice dropped: "It means your wives and families and friends will be at outs. You have set up a commotion in this entire neighborhood. And about what?" He paused and grinned. "Why all on account of an old gray goose." Even the litigants began to see the amusing side of the quarrel. "If I were in your place, I would stop all this hair pulling and wool gathering," said Lincoln. "I'd get together here and now and settle this thing. I'd make up and be friends." Grinning sheepishly, the two quarreling neighbors walked to the center of the room and shook hands. As the crowd applauded, two lawyers and the Justice of the Peace entered the room. It was too late; the gray goose case had just been settled.[24]

Young Lincoln, according to his stepmother's statement, "visited law trials and heard them with admiration."[25] Already there glowed in his adolescent mind the desire to be a lawyer. His long trips to the courthouse at Boonville and down to John Pitcher's law office at Rockport, his reading of the *Revised Laws of Indiana* and Blackstone's *Commentaries,* even his successes in Squire Pate's magistrate court and the handling of the gray goose case—all proved to be worthwhile experiences. All gave him a glimpse into the legal profession.

Abe's struggle for an education went on. When he became one of the best penmen in the Pigeon Creek community he wrote letters for his neighbors. According to his stepmother, he had "a copy book, a kind of scrap book in which he put down all things and thus preserved them. He ciphered on boards when he had no paper or no slate. And when the board would get black he would shave it off with a drawing knife and go on again."[26] By thinking over and repeating to himself the things he had heard, read or written down, Abe Lincoln, founder of Brush College, was steadily clearing away what he termed darkness in his soul. "There is no darkness but ignorance," he often told Jim Grigsby.

CHAPTER EIGHT

POLITICIANS

On January 10, 1818, when Abraham Lincoln was not quite nine, the Indiana legislature moved his father's whole farm over into a newly formed county merely by moving the boundary line of Warrick and Perry counties eastward from Pigeon Creek to Anderson River. In a twinkling the new county, named Spencer, was roaring with political skullduggery. That was the beginning of a training school in politics for Lincoln, who proved to be a close observer and apt pupil.

Alert and curious, the boy Lincoln found himself at once in the midst of ruthless politicians and scheming speculators who dickered for power and quick money. Since Thomas Lincoln had been a successful politician back in Cumberland County, Kentucky, and knew short cuts to the political pie-counter, the Lincoln home soon became a popular meeting place for office-seekers and political-fixers.[1]

"In Indiana," Abraham Lincoln related, "all the local politicians used to come to our cabin to discuss politics with my father. I used to sit by and listen to them, but father would not let me ask many questions. And there were a great many things I did not understand." After the men had left, Abe would climb to his place in the loft. "I'd sit down," he said, "or pace back and forth till I made out just what they meant. And then I'd lay awake for hours just a-putting their ideas into words that the boys around our way could understand."[2]

It may never be known how much of the dickering and scheming to create Spencer County took place in the Lincoln cabin, but certainly Abe heard enough to bewilder him. The big battle was between two able leaders: Ratcliff Boon and Daniel Grass. Grass wanted the county set up; Boon opposed it. Boon, Warrick County's first treasurer, had become so powerful politically in the county and beyond its borders as to be nicknamed King of Warrick. He objected to the formation of Spencer County on the grounds it would chip away Warrick. His townsite then would no longer be centrally located in his backwoods dominions. Somehow Boon had to be "sweetened." And the one to do the job was Joseph Lane, a young man living a few miles west of the Lincoln cabin. Lane, a North Carolinian, was a political mentor and an employee in the clerk's office at Darlington, county seat of Warrick. Also he cut and rafted saw logs for the famous ornithologist, John James Audubon, who lived a little farther down the Ohio River. Politically, Boon feared him. Whether Tom Lincoln suggested to Grass and other leaders that Lane should handle Boon is not known; but it is virtually quite certain that Tom Lincoln, as well as many of his neighbors, knew Lane had the King of Warrick so worried that the King planned to have the strip of land on which Lane lived transferred to Vandenburg County in order to move Joe politically out of Warrick. Boon did it, too.[3]

The scheme to handle Boon surely was talked over in the Lincoln cabin. The idea was for Joe Lane to persuade Boon to allow the new county to be set up in exchange for favors, such as Boon locating and naming the new county seat of Warrick. Lane talked to Boon about it, adding, "By doing so you will make many friends." More friends meant more votes to Boon who, already a member of the State Legislature, wanted to be State Senator. Boon agreed and Spencer County was created.[4] Warrick's county seat was moved from Darlington to a place near the site of Chief Set-te-down's old Shawnee village just east of Boon's big tract of land and was named Boonville. That year Boon was elected State Senator. No wonder Abraham Lincoln said, "There were a great many things I did not understand."

Reportedly a cousin of the wilderness trail blazer, Daniel Boone, Ratcliff Boon had dropped the "e" from the family name. Lincoln had probably heard the story that when Dennis Hanks had asked Nancy Hanks Lincoln what she was going to name her new baby, she replied, "Abraham, after his grandfather that come to Kaintucky with Dan'l Boone." [5]

Among Lincoln's Indiana neighbors Ratcliff Boon was as popular an Indian fighter as had been old Dan'l over in Kentucky. Right after Chief Set-te-down and his warriors killed the Meeks family on Pigeon Creek, "Boon figured conspicuously" in meting out justice to those Indian raiders.[6]

Soon the first great financial and industrial depression hit the country. But Abe Lincoln was too young to understand that the trouble was due to the backwash of the War of 1812 and the Napoleonic Wars in Europe. Prices soared. People less fortunate than the Lincolns clamored for food. Under the law, overseers of the poor grabbed up paupers and sold them at auction. Since the county had to pay the buyer for taking care of these unfortunates they were sold not to the highest but to the lowest bidders. Paupers not sold were thrown into debtors prisons like the ones at Vincennes and other county seats.[7] The state bank at Vincennes failed and pulled down its branch banks. Being the depository for United States land sale funds it took along in its crash the eighty dollars which Tom Lincoln had paid into it.

Desolation spread to every corner of the Union. There was no gold, no paper money; no market for the farmer's produce; no hire for the laborer's hands. In the Indiana wilderness Abe Lincoln could not hear people beating on the doors of State Legislatures, crying, "Relief! Relief! Give us relief!" But he could hear silver dollars being made into halves and quarters. Except for some bits—twelve-and-a-half cent pieces—the only hard money in circulation was Mexican silver dollars. To get a half-dollar or a quarter cut from one of these, Abe went with his father to the blacksmith shop. There he watched the blacksmith lay the dollar on an anvil and, using chisel and hammer, cut the coin into pieces called cut money. To combat speculators who connived with smiths to cut dollars into five pieces and pass them off as quarters, county commissioners made up diagrams of true cut-quarters. When Tom Lincoln paid his taxes amounting to seventy-five cents, he merely laid his Mexican dollar on the official diagram and a true quarter was cut out, leaving the rest for taxes.

Was there any hope for better times? "People must buy less than they sell," advised the *Western Sun* editor, adding, "They have tried too many experiments."[8]

Meanwhile the sweetening effect wore off Lincoln's fiery neighbor, State Senator Ratcliff Boon, who announced for Lieutenant Governor of Indiana. In the *Vincennes Sun* Boon set forth a homely creed designed to catch votes: "In presenting myself to you I have nothing to claim through my ancestors, nor former services; but alone depend on what may be thought I justly merit."[9] Not tall but standing very straight, forty-one year old Boon was credited by Lincoln and others with carrying a lot of knowledge under his receding forehead. He was a gunsmith by trade. He advocated a reasonably strong protective tariff. But it was his uncompromising opposition to slavery which automatically put him in the political camp of Governor Jonathan Jennings, candidate for reelection.

Jennings was popular in the Lincoln household. Ever since the Log Convention and his election as Indiana's Delegate to the Eleventh United States Congress, Jonathan Jennings had been running and being elected on the platform: "No slavery in Indiana." He had succeeded in labeling his pro-slavery opponents—Harrison-Randolph-Taylor forces—The Virginia Aristocrats. He modestly called his

followers The People. At log cabin raisings he carried up a corner
and thereby proved to all comers that he was not above doing manual
labor. That of course increased his popularity in Lincoln's neighborhood. There also voters never tired of retelling about the toast
drunk by General William Henry Harrison and others: "To Jonathan Jennings—the semblance of a Delegate—three groans." [10] That
toast got a vote-getting laugh for Jennings.

The Jennings-Boon fight against chattel slavery enraged anew the
Pocket Country pro-slavery people. Wealthy, prominent citizens from
Pigeon Creek to Vincennes held Negroes in slavery by declaring it was
indenture for only ninety-nine years' service. To aid the pro-slavery
people, the Vincennes *Sun* editor quoted President Monroe's maxim
"Principles not men" and scoffed, "Let the people of Indiana adopt
this maxim. And what becomes of Jonathan Jennings and his hireling
sycophants? Why they wither and fade like leaves of autumn."

On election day in August, 1819, Thomas Lincoln, Schoolmaster
Andrew Crawford, and other local citizens went to the Carter township polling place in Jonathan Greathouse's home and voted. [11] Instead
of fading away, Jennings and Boon were elected, giving Abraham
Lincoln a Lieutenant Governor for a neighbor. That election somewhat muted the cry for legalized slavery in Indiana.

Three years later, at the height of a "shaking ager" epidemic,
Governor Jennings resigned to accept a seat in Congress (September
12, 1822). And Ratcliff Boon became Governor. From that hour
onward, until long after William Hendricks had taken over the Governor's chair, everything the King of Warrick said or did greatly interested Lincoln and his fellow Pigeon Creekers. To get back and forth to
the State capital at Corydon, Governor Boon traveled the Boonville-
Corydon road right past Abe Lincoln's door. Whether it was the
sight of the Governor of Indiana and his retinue of political henchmen
riding by or just a chance to show off, Lincoln never did say, but
it was about that time Abe began carrying a knotted beech cane. [12]
Hooking a long leg over the top rail of a fence, he waved his cane and
shouted, "What's the news, Governor?"

Also riding by the Lincoln cabin was the political-fixer, Joseph
Lane, recently elected to the Indiana Legislature from Vandenburg
and Warrick counties. [13] He was a pro-slavery man. Although Ratcliff
Boon had succeeded in moving Lane and the Lane farm into Vandenburg County, the King had not been able to check young Joe's popularity with Warrick voters.

A little more than a year later, near the end of 1823, Abraham

Lincoln began reading the Vincennes *Western Sun* regularly each week in the William Jones' store.[14] In it, soon afterward, he read President Monroe's world startling message to Congress proclaiming the doctrine of the Americas for Americans. The Monroe Doctrine appears on page one of the *Western Sun* for January 3, 1824. Referring to the proposed invasion by the Holy Alliance to help the Spanish king put down the revolt of Spanish American colonies, President Monroe proclaimed, "The political systems of the Allied Powers is essentially different from that of America. We owe it to candor and to amicable relations existing between the U. States and these powers, to declare that we should consider any attempt on their part to extend their systems to any portion of this hemisphere as dangerous to our peace and safety."

In a few weeks the wild, free-for-all Presidential campaign opened. According to William Jones, "When the campaign of 1824 came on Abe [although only 15 years old] was prepared to watch the political movements intelligently." [15]

The Federalist Party had died. President Monroe's Era of Good Feelings had ended. The Whig Party had hardly been conceived. Thus the Jeffersonian Republican-Democratic Party held the field and about everybody belonged to it, including the Lincolns. Consequently, the campaign was not of parties but of men—four men: Andrew Jackson, Senator from Tennessee and known as Old Hickory, the Hero of New Orleans; Henry Clay, Speaker of the United States House of Representatives, affectionately called by frontiersmen The Mill Boy of the Slashes or Harry of the West; John Quincy Adams, Secretary of State from Massachusetts and suspected by Western backwoodsmen of being a pampered aristocrat; William H. Crawford, Secretary of the Treasury from Georgia, about whose head fluttered rumors of crooked doings in the Treasury Department. There being no political parties, followers of a candidate took the name of their favorite. They called themselves Jackson men, Clay men, Adams men, Crawford men. Lincoln was for Clay. William Jones said, "Anything about Henry Clay was eagerly read and digested by Abe." [16] At night in his loft Abe lay awake longer than ever, putting what he had read into words which the boys around his neighborhood could understand.

It was now that Abe Lincoln, Nattie Grigsby, and Joe Gentry carried their three-way friendship into the political field. Lincoln and the Grigsbys were solidly Clay men. The Gentrys were just as solidly Jackson men. The three boys met in one another's homes, listened to the political talk and studied the ways and methods of hopeful

politicians. They argued over the merits of their favorite candidates. They hung around Gentryville or went to cross-road stores
and listened to travelers and stump speakers. "We talked everything
over and over. In fact wore it out. We learned much in this way,"
stated Nathaniel Grigsby.[17]

The *Western Sun* editor bolstered Lincoln's sympathies for Clay by
publishing "Twelve Good and substantial reasons why Clay ought *not*
to be elected President." First, explained Editor Stout, because Clay
"is a plain old fashioned Republican and should he be made President
will furnish his house with articles purely American, and, not like his
illustrious predecessor, send to Europe for chairs, carpets, cut glass
&." The editor said Clay's dress and ease of manners "would ill accord
with the courtly apparel and lordly strut which many of our Senators
and Representatives have so happily acquired from their intercourse
with foreign ministers and noblemen. It serves to distinguish them
from the common people." Besides, went on Editor Stout, Henry
Clay "had the unparalelled impudence, in March, 1818, to introduce
into Congress a resolution for acknowledgement of the Independence
of the South American provinces then engaged in a most unholy war
against their parent country, Spain." [18]

But no matter how much about Henry Clay that Abe read and
digested, and tried out on Joe Gentry, he could not shake Joe from
Jackson. Even gentle-hearted Nattie Grigsby could not sway Joe.
The Gentrys were Jackson men and that was all there was to it.

By midsummer the four-cornered campaign reached extreme bitterness. Henry Clay's northern enemies accused him of being pro-
slavery because he came from the slave state of Kentucky. They said
slave state atmosphere disqualified a man for the Presidency. In
the July 19, 1824, *Western Sun* Lincoln read a reply to that charge:
"Washington, the illustrious Founder of our liberties, and the enlightened and patriotic Jefferson, were born and educated in a slave-
holding state; and it may be seriously doubted whether the uncon-
taminated air of the North will soon give birth to men more worthy
of the love and admiration of the American people. Henry Clay,
a young man just commencing his professional and political career,
unaided by wealth, an orphan boy, fought advocates of slavery
with all the power of his elocution talent and all the strength of his
reason. He joined a corps of gradual abolitionists in Lexington and
declaimed in favor of gradual emancipation." As a lawyer, said the
reply, Clay "has never been prevailed upon to appear against a slave
suing for his freedom. On the contrary Mr. Clay has *without fee or*

reward acted as counsel for a great number of slaves when suing for their freedom."

With mounting interest Lincoln read in the *Western Sun*, "Where are the proofs that Mr. Adams has changed his political principles? Has he ever avowed himself a democratic republican? No! In his 'Publicola' written in express opposition to Paine's 'Rights of Man' he contends for the same legitimate doctrine now held by the holy Allies that no people have a right to overthrow one constitution and establish another without the consent of the Government." [19] Lincoln knew a lot about Tom Paine's "Rights of Man" for he had heard his father, mother, and stepmother talk that for years. If Adams expressly opposed Paine's "Rights of Man" as charged, then he, Abe Lincoln, had no use for Adams. As a matter of fact John Quincy Adams had few, if any, friends in Lincoln's community. Almost everyone was either a Jackson man or a Clay man. Crawford was not even noticed.

A friend of Jackson broke into the columns of the Vincennes *Western Sun*, August 7, and gave Joe Gentry a big argument in favor of Old Hickory being President. Abe Lincoln and Nat Grigsby were stumped for an answer to what the friend wrote: "Look to the city of Washington and let the virtuous patriots of the country weep at the spectacle. There corruption is springing into existence, and fast flourishing. With the exception of this great man, the hero of Orleans, Andrew Jackson, all have toiled through the winter at Washington seeking every species of art & finesse to further their own views and press themselves into favor. Why is not Jackson there too? Because he has a soul that towers above intrigue."

By late September it had become clear to some Pigeon Creekers even if not to Abe, Nat and Joe, that not one of the Presidential candidates would receive a majority. In that event the election would be decided by the House of Representatives. Ratcliff Boon who had been reelected Lieutenant Governor of Indiana and had resigned from that office in January, 1824, and announced for Congress, now saw the political value of the snarled national situation to his own campaign. In the *Western Sun*, September 25, he promised, "Should I be elected and the choice of a President devolved upon Congress, I pledge myself to support for that station, the person who shall receive the majority of the votes of the state." Boon was running as a Jacksonian Democrat.

While Boon's campaign interested Lincoln, the plots against Clay worried him. A friend of Clay accused the Adams men, in the Vin-

cennes *Western Sun,* of trying "to detach our support from this true
champion of our interests by asking us to support General Jackson." Lincoln talked to William Jones about it. "I don't see how the
people can elect Jackson. But the majority must rule, and, I reckon
it is right," said Abe.[20]

Growing fearful that Clay would be elected, Indiana friends of both
Adams and Jackson decided to yoke Crawford to Clay. Stump
speakers resurrected the A.B.C. Plot which "charged illegalities and
misconduct on the part of the Secretary of the Treasury, Mr. William
H. Crawford." As soon as the Jackson strategists felt the yoke scheme
to be effective, they ran this story in the *Indiana Gazette* and had it
reprinted in the October 30th *Western Sun:* "The circumstances of so
many friends of Clay turning over to Jackson in this state may be
accounted for by the reason which we have heard some give, viz.: That
the electoral ticket got up for Clay is only a Crawford ticket in dis-
guise. The people would rather vote for Adams or Jackson. They
do not want to elevate Crawford over the shoulders of Clay."

The Jackson high command followed that blast with a break with
the Adams men. Lincoln read about this in the next week's *Sun:*
"The friends of Mr. Adams are proposing to abandon the ticket heretofore formed for him, and act in concert with the friends of Mr. Clay.
The object of this combination is to prevent the *Jackson* ticket from
succeeding in this state. But they will fail in their puny efforts. In
Indiana the Hero of Two wars is invincible." To the joy of Joe Gentry
and to the chagrin of Abe Lincoln and Nattie Grigsby, the Jackson
warriors concentrated their election eve fire on Henry Clay. They accused Clay of supporting the United States Bank, contending he was
under its influence. "Our Hero of Orleans is under no such influence,"
they asserted in the *Western Sun.* "He has nothing to do with banks.
He detests them all and he cannot be placed under their influence."

The election was held. Indiana's five electoral votes went to Andrew Jackson for President. The state supported John C. Calhoun of
South Carolina for Vice President. In the national totals Jackson
received 99 electoral votes; Adams 84; Crawford 41; Clay 37. No
candidate had received the majority necessary to be elected; therefore,
the election was thrown into the House of Representatives.[21] Since
only the three highest candidates were considered, Clay was eliminated. Lincoln and his friends could see that with a little judicious bargaining, Clay's 37 votes could elect either Adams or Jackson. Immediately supporters of the three top candidates began writing flat-
tering, affectionate letters to Clay, addressing him as "Dear Harry of

the West." Seeing through their hypocrisy, Clay wrote a friend, "I am enjoying, whilst alive, the posthumous honors which are usually awarded to the illustrious dead." [22]

For weeks Clay's refusal to make public comment on the three candidates kept Lincoln, Grigsby, and Gentry in a turmoil of expectancy. Then, without fanfare, January 8, 1825, Clay advised his friends in the House to vote for John Quincy Adams. Why? Because Adams favored Clay's policies: internal improvements, a reasonable protective tariff, closer association with Central and South America. The House of Representatives met. Four states voted for Crawford; seven (including Indiana) for Jackson; thirteen for Adams. That elected Adams by a majority of two.

On March 4, 1825, Lincoln's sturdy neighbor, Ratcliff Boon, was sworn in as a member of the Nineteenth Congress. That same day John Quincy Adams took the oath of President and John C. Calhoun the oath of Vice President, of the United States. President Adams promptly appointed Henry Clay Secretary of State. "It's a corrupt bargain!" friends of Jackson charged. Lincoln read in the Vincennes *Western Sun* Clay's reply to the charge: "I interrogated my conscience as to what I ought to do. And that faithful guide told me to vote for Mr. Adams. What is a public man worth if he will not expose himself on fit occasions, for the good of his country?" [23]

Having learned a great deal about the art of President making, sixteen year old Abe soon added more to his political knowledge when his own Congressman, Ratcliff Boon, began slugging voters. News of Boon's fight set more fists to flying up and down Buck Horn valley. The Congressman was indicted and tried in the Common Pleas Court at Boonville, September 7, 1825, charged with "rude insolence and with force and arms did unlawfully beat and wound Edward Beems." The jury, which included Lincoln's former school teacher, Andrew J. Crawford, returned the verdict: "Guilty and assess his fine to five dollars." [24] From Boon's act Abe learned that a politician sometimes indiscreetly uses his fists as well as his tongue.

It was not long thereafter that Lincoln read in the *Western Sun* that politicians also fight with pistols. His political idol, Secretary of State Henry Clay, had challenged Senator John Randolph of Virginia to a duel. Randolph had called the Adams-Clay affair "A coalition of Bilfil and Black George, a combination unheard of until now, of Puritan and blackleg." [25]

According to the *Western Sun*, Clay and Randolph had hardly met on the duelling ground before Randolph's pistol went off. Clay let it pass as an accident. Then Randolph's second supplied him with a hair-trigger pistol. At a given signal the men fired at one another. Each missed his target. Up rode Senator Benton of Missouri and shouted, "Gentlemen! Stop!" Clay ignored Benton and fired again. That time he shot Mr. Randolph in the coattail. Mr. Randolph pointed his pistol skyward and exclaimed, "Mr. Clay, I do not fire at you!" He fired into the air. Clay and Randolph eyed each other for a moment, walked to the center and shook hands. Senator Benton called the duel "among the highest toned I ever witnessed." [26]

Hardly was the duel over with when Abe Lincoln's interest was focused on the 1826 campaign. His Congressman, running for reelection as a Jacksonian Democrat, was having more trouble with the voters. On election day Ratcliff Boon polled 5202 votes to Thomas H. Blake's 5203. Beaten by just one vote! [27] Blake had run as an Adams Republican.

By the spring of 1827 Lincoln was reading in the *Western Sun* that it was believed General Jackson would carry Pennsylvania, Virginia, North and South Carolina, Louisiana, Mississippi and Missouri in the 1828 Presidential race. Jackson might even carry New York, Maryland, Kentucky, and again Indiana. Ohio and New Jersey were doubtful. Editor Stout of the *Sun* was sure President Adams could not be reelected unless he won New York's support. [28] That touched off hot debates between Adams and Jackson men in Jones' store, to the delight of Abraham Lincoln who enjoyed listening to political arguments. By fall the Jacksonian cry of "Clay and corruption" was ringing loudly in the ears of Lincoln and his fellow Hoosiers. To find out how effective it was, straw votes were taken at Indiana regimental musters as a sort of public opinion poll. The *Vincennes Sun* published the results. At New Albany there were 49 for Adams and 169 for Jackson; at Bedford 54 for Adams and 742 for Jackson. "These signs of the times must be very encouraging to the friends of Mr. Adams," the editor commented. [29] With a politician on every stump the 1828 Presidential campaign opened in Indiana. Lincoln heard Jackson men accuse President Adams and "King Caucus" of ruling democratic America through the succession of Cabinet members and manipulators in Congress. Speakers declared General Jackson would slay that ornery king.

Adams men fearing Jackson might do exactly that called attention to the case of The Six Militia Men. They accused Jackson of slaying those Tennessee militiamen during the War of 1812. An Adams man wrote in the March 8 *Sun*: "Those poor men were condemned by an illegal courtmartial, instituted by General Jackson, for no other offense than claiming and exercising the right to go home after their legal term of service had expired. The act was illegal, cruel and tyrannical. How can any humane man honestly support General Jackson?"

Under the headline "Hear the Witness" the *Western Sun* quoted Colonel G. C. Russell, U.S. Army, who "superintended the execution of the six militia men." Colonel Russell said the ringleader of the alleged deserters "was a sort of a preacher of that denomination called the Baptists. He was in profession a saint and in reality a mischievous man among people more ignorant than himself." Some of Lincoln's neighbors felt that the mention of Baptists was an intentional slur at their church. So while Abe did odd jobs at Jones' store he read aloud to customers and loafers the Adams-Jackson battle as it waxed hotter. Adams men called the execution outright murder. Jackson men replied, "No! Not murder but justice!" Lincoln had never had much use for John Quincy Adams; and his faith in Andrew Jackson was now shaken. Still he held to Henry Clay in spite of all the corrupt bargaining charges.

In the midst of the rising fury of the campaign Congress passed the Tariff Act of 1828. Southern planters called it a discrimination against unpaid labor—Negro slave labor—and a blow directed at planters. John C. Calhoun said the new tariff was an unconstitutional usurpation of powers by the Federal Government which violated the essential principles of states' rights. South Carolina held tariff meetings and threatened to secede from the Union unless that law were repealed.[30] Obviously impressed by the threats of South Carolina, Editor Stout, in the *Western Sun*, pointed out—to Lincoln's delight—that this was "the first tariff that ever promised any advantage to the West. This act has been passed by the present Jackson majority in Congress. Who are the real friends of the Manufacturer and the Farmer?"[31]

Protective tariff for manufacturers and farmers was part of Clay's American System. And since the Jackson majority in Congress was now for Clay's system, Abe Lincoln and Nat Grigsby joined with Joe Gentry in whooping it up for Jackson. Adams men made desperate efforts to hold onto the Clay men, telling them of their love for Harry of the West. Amused by the antics of the Adams people, Lincoln borrowed the first two lines from Robert Burns' *Auld Lang Syne* and wrote the following piece which Nattie, Joe and others around Gentryville lustily sang:

"Let auld acquaintance be forgot
"And never brought to mind,
"And Jackson be our President
"And Adams left behind." [32]

The Presidential campaign was claiming the attention of everyone in the Indiana Pocket Country. Everywhere politicians were heaping abuse or praise on Adams and Jackson. To get the most of the big political show, Abe Lincoln and other Hoosiers laid aside their work, met, formed processions and, led by an officer of the War of 1812, marched behind squealing fifes and thumping drums. Being Jackson men they set up stout hickory poles, dancing and whooping about them. A few hundred yards away Adams men likewise set up poles— maple poles—and tried to out-yell Old Hickory's followers. Meanwhile barbecued steers and sheep were passed out to all comers. Men and boys hunting trouble armed themselves with hickory and maple clubs and milled back and forth across the neutral ground between the poles. Every time a stump speaker called Adams a traitor or Jackson a murderer, clubs started swinging.

The women folk stayed at home. But whether in tiny one-room log cabins or in big two-story, double, hewnlog houses with airy dog-trots, family hearthstones flamed into political forums. At firesides mothers carefully explained to their children why the men were away to the political hustings. Quite likely it was at this time the legend sprouted: In Indiana children discuss politics by signs until they are old enough to talk. [33]

Probably during his youth, Abraham Lincoln never read a political article of greater value to him than "United States Political History Reviewed 1789-1828," which was published in the September 20th *Western Sun.* In it were described the administrations of Presidents Washington, John Adams, Jefferson, Madison, Monroe, and John Quincy Adams. The writer said that in Jefferson's administration "Benefits as well as monetary embarrassments & depressions were equally felt by the north, south, east and west. Yet not a whisper was heard about disunion from the great majority of the people. Not until the latter part of Mr. Monroe's administration, that seed of discord began to grow, and to acquire strength." But now, in 1828, the writer lamented, "Morality must have succumbed to an inordinate appetite for wealth and power."

As election day drew nearer the campaign grew hotter. Down on the Ohio River two men whom Lincoln must have met while attending ferry got into an argument in a skiff off shore. One hit the other over the head with an iron sheep's-foot and killed him.

Adams men pressed harder upon the story of Jackson shooting six militiamen. Nevertheless, Lincoln clung to Jackson. Undoubtedly a story offered in the *Western Sun,* October 18, 1828, to counter-balance the militia shooting, impressed Lincoln with Adams' unfitness for the Presidency: An eighty-two year old Revolutionary War veteran named Richard Nagle left his home in Cambria county, Pennsylvania, and went to Washington to see the President about getting a pension. In his affidavit, sworn to July 1, 1828, Nagle said a yellow man met him at the White House door and asked him what he wanted. Nagle showed the man three depositions sworn to by veterans who had served with him in the Revolutionary War. The affidavit further stated, according to the *Western Sun,* that President Adams ordered Nagle "to be gone for an imposter and a Dirty old Rascal or he, President Adams, would have him horsewhipped."

Naturally that alleged "base conduct of John Quincy Adams" to-ward war veterans intensified local hatred of Adams, for among Lincoln's neighbors were Revolutionary War veterans esteemed by everyone. Apparently expecting quick retaliation from Adams men, Editor Stout in the *Sun* warned friends of Old Hickory: "It is under-stood about the time of the election, or so near that the report cannot be contradicted, one simultaneous movement will be made throughout the United States. It will be that GENERAL JACKSON IS DEAD. Such rumors would promote John Quincy Adams to the presidential chair. We caution all our readers against this hellish project." [34]

With murder in the air and rumors of Old Hickory being dead, elec-tion day passed and Lincoln was happy to hear that the voters had "Let Jackson be our President and Adams left behind." Indiana had once more gone for Old Hickory. Jackson received a total of 178 elec-toral votes to Adams' 83. John Calhoun was re-elected Vice President by almost two to one over the combined votes of his two opponents. [35] In the race for Congress from Lincoln's district, Ratcliff Boon, still a Jacksonian Democrat, defeated the incumbent, Thomas H. Blake. "We were all Jackson boys and men at that time in Indiana," stated Nattie Grigsby in summing up the campaign. [36]

Right after the election, Editor Stout, in the *Western Sun,* showed Abe Lincoln that a victorious political strategist could have a con-science. Stout re-told the Nagle case and publicly apologized for the political trick by publishing the following affidavit:

"Now the said Richard Nagle, being duly sworn according to the law doth say the above is an entire fabrication—that he never saw the President of the United States to his knowledge, and consequently had no conversation with him. That at the time his deposition was taken before Squire Mageehan, said Mageehan omitted reading to him that part referred to; and that he was not aware of its being in the deposition." [37]

From that 1828 Presidential campaign Abraham Lincoln had seen how well-timed schemes, rumors and statements by stump speakers and the press could influence voters. By April, 1829, he also saw how opposition could quickly be built up against men recently elected to office. A widely distributed anti-Jackson circular showed a hickory broom captioned "Sweep, Ho! Sweep!" Below that ran:

> *"Turn out! turn out!*
> *"They are rogues no doubt;*
> *"And honest men and true are come*
> *"To put them all to rout!"* [38]

By listening to crossroads forums and reading newspapers Lincoln formed a picture of office-seekers scurrying to Washington and office-holders there, trembling at every swing of the hickory broom. President Jackson swept out a socially prominent postmaster and swept in a shoemaker. When a howl of protest went up, the *Western Sun* retorted: "It is monstrous to the ruffled shirt men that a mechanic should be appointed to office." [39]

By July 19, however, Editor Stout clearly was losing some of his pro-Jackson enthusiasm, for in that issue of the *Sun* he quoted Lincoln's favorite statesman, Henry Clay, as saying: "Now persons are dismissed not only without trial of any sort, but without charge, as if the intention were to defy opinion and give to the acts a higher degree of enormity." The following week Editor Stout even quoted the Fourth of July orator at Vincennes, E. H. Hannegan, who had declared that the triumphant party had adopted a "system of proscription" which "in our land had gone so far as to produce in some quarters the cry of DISUNION!"

In August Abe Lincoln attended a township election about four miles to the southeastward on the Troy-Vincennes trail. He climbed onto a rail fence alongside a slimy pond and listened to Hickory-broom Sweepers defend President Jackson by blaming King Caucus for the abuse of patronage. Soon a bully called Samson, from that area, swaggered up to the rail fence and stared at Lincoln. Abe ignored him and went on listening to the Sweepers argue. Samson, talking loudly about his horse, shouted, "I run him four miles this morning and he never fetched a long breath." Annoyed because he wanted to follow the political arguments, Abe said, "I presume he fetched a good many short ones." Arguments stopped. Everyone laughed. Red-faced and angry, Samson shook his fist at Lincoln and called him a name. "Hush up" said Abe calmly.

Mistaking the reply for a sign of weakness, Samson's abuse continued. Lincoln's hands gripped the top rail so hard his fingernails cut into the dry oak; he had reached the end of his patience. He pointed to the slimy pond: "Mr. Samson, if you don't shut up I'll take you by the neck and throw you into that water." Someone from Gentryville boomed, "Abe'll do it, too, and don't think he won't!"

The crowd moved in for a fight. Samson glanced around at them, then at Abe and at the pond. He muttered something to himself and sneaked off, leaving the disappointed voters with nothing to do but resume their arguments for and against President Jackson.[40]

"Abe went to all political gatherings and listened attentively to both sides of the question," according to his stepmother. "After hearing them through he could and did speak with more than substantial accuracy what both sides said. He was appealed to [to] know what was said."[41]

Across his years in Indiana, from the sweetening of Ratcliff Boon to the sweepings of the Hickory Broomers, Abe Lincoln picked up answers to some of the questions which his father would not allow him to ask of local politicians scheming in the Lincoln cabin. He had seen, heard and learned much about the art of politics. He wanted to be a politician.

CHAPTER NINE

ALL THINGS IN COMMON

Lincoln encountered a new sort of politics when his neighbors reported strange goings-on at Father George Rapp's Religio-Communistic society at Harmonie, a village fifty miles to the west on the Wabash River. These neighbors had taken their corn to Harmonie to be ground, and returned with fantastic tales of vineyards, orchards, a distillery, a labyrinth, huge community buildings where men and women lived separately, of an enormous church with a clock in its steeple. They described a limestone slab with the outline of a big foot in it, and they said the Rappites told them it was the Archangel Gabriel's footprint.

In the spring of 1815 George Rapp, leader of Pietism from Wurtemberg, Germany, stood on the bank of the Wabash, his seven hundred devoted followers, Wurtemberg peasants, kneeling all about him, and proclaimed the founding of Harmonie. Rapp ruled his flock by virtue of an allegedly divine call. He stretched forth his arm and said, "This is the arm of God." [1] Rapp preached and practiced both economy and industry. Basing his doctrine of the dual nature of Adam on Genesis I, 26-27, he declared Adam held within his body both sexual elements; therefore, celibacy was necessary for one's salvation.

In his oil mill, silk factory, brickyard, and gristmill, Father Rapp ordered vases of flowers to be put on or near each workbench and machine. To band music, Lincoln's neighbors reported, Rapp marched his people out of the village to till the rich Wabash land. Although envy plagued the hearts of many Pigeon Creekers as they listened to the wonders of Harmonie, not one was willing to exchange his individual freedom for Rappite serfdom.

When Abe Lincoln was sixteen word reached Gentryville that George Rapp had sold Harmonie and its surrounding farm of 30,000 acres for $150,000 to Robert Owen, Utopian Socialist, of New Lenark, Scotland. Also Rapp had sold his prosperous stores at Shawneetown and Vincennes. One Rappite, Brother Scheel, wrote in chalk under the stairway of No. 2 Community Building: "The twenty-fourth of May, 1824 we departed. Lord, with thy great help and goodness in body and soul protect us." Thus ended on the Wabash the State Sans Wedlock, as the poet Byron had called it.

Seldom was any frontier more excited over socialism than was Abe Lincoln's community. Robert Owen convinced many backwoodsmen that the Garden of Eden was at hand, a new day dawning for mankind right there in Indiana. "I reckon folks thought it was a new Jerusalem and nobody'd have to work," commented Dennis Hanks, who lived in the Lincoln home.[2]

Owen changed the name Harmonie to New Harmony. "Here, he announced, "is a village already built in a country where thought is free." Before he started his socialist experiment he went to Washington, where on February 25, 1825, he spoke in the United States House of Representatives before President Monroe, President-elect John Quincy Adams, President Monroe's Cabinet, and members of Congress. His subject, "On a New System of Society" aroused the entire nation.

Following President Adams' inauguration, Owen delivered a second address on the new day. This time, March 7, he had in his audience President Adams, ex-President Monroe, Adams' Cabinet and the new Congress. Said Dennis Hanks: "When this furrin feller spoke in Congress about the Garden of Eden he was going to fence in on the Wabash we soon heard about it. Boats brung news every week. There was scarcely anything else talked about for a spell." [3]

Owen astonished his distinguished listeners in Washington by telling them his new system of "Common property and co-operation will, from the soil, support in high comfort, double numbers, at the least, and hence its commercial superiority over the individual arrangement of society." Basing his doctrine on Acts II, 44-45, "And all that believed were together and had all things in common; and sold their possessions and goods, and parted them to all men, as every man had need," [4] Robert Owen declared that changes "are at hand greater than all the changes which have hitherto occurred in the affairs of mankind." In consequences "the degrading practice in which we are trained of buying cheap and selling dear will be rendered wholly unnecessary. The whole trading system is one of deception." He maintained that "the government and Congress of this new empire have only to will this change, and it will be at once effected. By such an act they give and secure liberty, affluence, and happiness to America and to the world." [5]

Lincoln saw the first public printing of Robert Owen's New Harmony Constitution in the May 28, 1825, Vincennes *Western Sun*: "The Society is instituted generally to promote the happiness of the world." It would prepare people "to become associates in independent communities, having common property. The members are all of the same rank, no artificial irregularity being acknowledged." Owen's plan was directed toward the permanent relief of the working classes and the blotting out of the profit motive. "I am come to this country to introduce an entire new state of society," Owen proclaimed, "to change it from the ignorant, selfish system, to the enlightened social system, which shall gradually unite all interests into one, and remove from all cause for contest between individuals." [6]

Lincoln and his neighbors were dumbfounded by Owen's plan to house those who accepted his doctrine of holding all things in common, in a building a thousand feet square. In it thousands of persons could live and have every domestic convenience. When completed, Owen's Community of Equality headquarters on the Wabash would resemble an ancient walled city. Each of its four corners would be bastioned with a tower. Sharp roofs would resemble battlements. Inside the great hollow square, buildings would serve as keeps and lookouts. A walled city to be built so close to his Indiana home greatly excited the adolescent Lincoln. But the promise of a free education to all those who held things in common excited him a great deal more, for Owen said he intended to establish "a complete school, academy, and university in which a superior education will be given from infancy to maturity." [7]

Lincoln's interest, as well as that of scores of his neighbors, was sharply increased when in January, 1826, news reached Gentryville that Owen's keelboat, *The Philanthropist*, had docked at New Harmony. It had passed down the Ohio and up the Wabash. Boarding it at Pittsburgh were artists, scientists, and teachers, who had come from Europe, assembled at Philadelphia under the leadership of the great American geologist, William McClure. In addition to McClure, that boat brought to New Harmony the greatest naturalist of the time, Thomas Say; Madam Marie D. Fretagoet, musician, kindergarten teacher and advocate of the Pestalozzian system in education; Dr. Gerard Troost, mineralogist; Samuel Chase, chemist; Phiquepal d' Arusmont, teacher of mathematics and music; Peter L. Duclos, scenic artist; Cornelius Tiebout, engraver and painter; Robert Dale Owen, age twenty-four, who, like his father, was an experimenter in Utopian Socialism and follower of Fanny Wright's radical ideas concerning Negro slave emancipation. Several students, and some capitalists, also, had come along to get a close up view of Robert Owen's New Jerusalem in Indiana.

Because *The Philanthropist* had carried so many people of learning,

Indiana backwoodsmen promptly nicknamed it *The Boatload of Knowledge*. About April, Lincoln and Jones' store loafers were given a new shock when word reached them that the Duke of Saxe-Weimar also had arrived at New Harmony.

On opening his schools, Robert Owen said, "If we cannot reconcile all opinions, let us endeavour to unite all hearts." [8] When the schools were underway, Albert Gallatin pronounced them the best in the world. Abe Lincoln told Dennis Hanks: "Denny, there's a school and thousands of books there, and fellers that know everything in creation." [9]

Whether Abraham Lincoln persuaded his father to try farming near Owen's New Social Order or whether he whetted Tom's appetite for land speculation may never be known; but the records of the General Land Office, Washington, D.C., do show that Thomas Lincoln bought eighty acres of land in Posey County, Indiana, just ten miles due east of New Harmony. [10] Back in December, 1818, Charles Whiting had entered that same tract of land. Soon the Whitings became prominent in close-by Cynthiana where they sold high grade whiskey and regularly attended the Baptist church. [11] By September, 1821, the Whiting farm was in the hands of the Memorial Forest heirs. A year later Forest's widow, Matilda, married James McCrary, the Reverend James Martin, a Baptist minister, solemnizing their wedding. [12] The next year the Posey county Probate Court, sitting at Mount Vernon, Indiana, "ordered that James McCrery [McCrary] be appointed guardian of Levicy Forest & Thomas Forest (and Sally Forest) minor heirs of Memorial Forest, deceased." Four years later the same court directed Guardian McCrary "to sell for the Best price he can get either at public or private sale" the west half of the 160.34 acres belonging to the minor heirs. [13]

On April 5, 1827, Thomas Lincoln appeared at Mount Vernon, Indiana. That day Guardian McCrary, for a valuable consideration assigned all rights and titles of the "heirs of Memorial Forest deceased to the W ½ NW ¼ 3.T5 S.R. 12W unto Thomas Lincoln, or Linkern and his heirs and assigns forever." [14] Thomas Lincoln now held rights to a land patent in Posey County and it probably had not cost him more than one hundred dollars. [15]

This new Lincoln farm lay mainly on an east and west ridge. Its northern boundary was a base line which ran straight west ten miles and just missed being New Harmony's main street, called Church Street. Its yellow clay soil was so fertile it sometimes yielded forty bushels of wheat to the acre. Parts of the farm were wooded with oak,

gum, walnut, poplar (tulip-tree) and sugar maple. Numerous springs
furnished abundant cold, pure water. Big Spring branch flows northward along the western edge of the farm and empties into Caney Creek
which flows southeastward. Caney Creek empties into Big Creek,
which flows southwestward. The three streams almost enclose the
Lincoln farm, making it into a triangular island.[16]

From the one-room, round-log cabin on the Posey County farm it
would have been a ten mile walk for Abe along the ridge to New
Harmony. In April, 1827, when he undoubtedly strolled its broad,
shady streets, the town was buzzing with applications for membership
in the Community of Equality. At that moment the New Harmony
Gazette was hailing 1827 as the "Fifty-first year of Political Independence" and the "First year of Mental Independence." Already, according to the paper, "several new cottages have been erected by
Communities No. 3 and 4." [17]

New Harmony contrasted sharply with what Lincoln was used to
back in Gentryville. Here he saw a town exactly one-half mile square.
Here stood on that flat bottom-land a brick and stone granary, five
stories high with a tile roof; a red brick tavern with a wing front; the
three-story dormer windowed Community House No. 2, used for a
school; the enormous Rappite church with its roof supported by
twenty-eight pillars of walnut and cherry. The cottages were set in
botanical gardens. Here was the Rappite labyrinth with its thorn
and flowering shrubbery lined paths symbolizing man's varied journey
through life.

Here all members of the experiment were expected to dress alike,
eat similar foods, live in similar houses. No one was to be held in
higher or lower esteem because of his occupation.[18] The community
disclaimed "all restraints of religion, marriage, or any other tie, but
what is purely voluntary." Moreover, "Children are taught in community, and like the Spartan children are not under the weak and
partial control of their parents. The Pestalozzi mode of instruction
is adopted. Instead of theories and doctrines they are taught facts." [19]

Children belonged to the community from their second year. Their
school life differed strongly from Abe Lincoln's blab-school training.
New Harmony children attended classes at four o'clock in the morning
in schoolrooms bristling with arithmometers and human skeletons.[20]
Joseph Neef, disciple of Pestalozzi; Constantine Rafinesque, the
pioneer ichthyologist; Robert Dale Owen and others taught the children. There, too, since early 1826, the first infant school, or kindergarten, in America had been functioning. William McClure attempted

to have the New Harmony Educational Society incorporated, but the Indiana State Senate rejected the bill on account of the popular belief that atheism flourished in the New Order's schools.[21] Possibly the Senators were remembering the Owen-Campbell debate and Owen's remark to the Reverend Mr. Ely that "there is no other God but the universe" and that "after death he himself may become a cucumber or an ass."

For a while Thomas Lincoln owned the fertile, rolling Posey County farm. Then there appeared in the *Vincennes Sun* this notice: "Important to U.S. Land debtors." Lands which had been forfeited since July, 1820, but not sold could be redeemed: "Payments for the land may be completed any time before the fourth of July by relinquishing any legal subdivision or by cash, allowing a reduction of 37½ per cent —or by both."

Again Thomas Lincoln went to the Vincennes District Land Office. And there, April 30, 1827, he relinquished both his eighty acre Posey County farm and eighty acres—the east half—of his Spencer County farm to the United States Government.[22] By relinquishing those two tracts he got enough money, or credit, to be entitled to a patent to the remaining eighty acres of his Pigeon Creek land, described as W½ SW ¼ 32. T4 SR5W. On June 6, 1827, President John Quincy Adams issued to "Thomas Linkern alias Lincoln" a land patent "as it appears full payment has been made."[23] In this way Tom Lincoln had adroitly traded himself out of debt and into full ownership of a Spencer County farm, and his son Abraham had lost forever the opportunity to attend the New Harmony schools.

While old Tom may have felt a little sadness at young Abe's pathetic efforts to obtain a higher education by setting up Brush College, the chances are the father was not displeased at his son's losing out on New Harmony. Wise old Tom probably already had detected weeds of disharmony sprouting in Robert Owen's Garden of Eden on the Wabash. Surely, he was not surprised when the news leaked out that the more industrious, progressive Owenites were growing tired of sharing the fruits of their labors equally with fellow members who were little more than panhandlers, sharpers, or lazy theorists. One Owenite, William Creese Pelham, thoroughly disillusioned, wrote, "We go on changing everything sometimes before we have an opportunity to find out its benefits." He added: "The women sometimes cannot agree among themselves who is the cook."[24]

Thomas Lincoln was undoubtedly much less surprised than the less experienced Abraham when, late in 1829, the Vincennes *Western Sun* reported that Robert Owen, arriving in Liverpool, England, had publicly stated, "The Americans are not capable of governing themselves; consequently, I abandon all idea of reforming them."

That gloomy pronouncement ended the social architect's experiments at New Harmony and blasted forever the bright hopes of Lincoln's neighbors for a New Jerusalem where, as Dennis Hanks said, "nobody'd have to work."

CHAPTER TEN

ROMANCE

Abraham Lincoln's interest in love began when the wagon of a family of movers broke down near his Pigeon Creek home. "I took a great fancy to one of the girls," he said. He was eight years old at the time.

While the mother and her two daughters cooked in Nancy Hanks Lincoln's pole kitchen and Tom Lincoln repaired the wagon, Abe stood around and watched the girl. After the movers left he thought so much about her that he wrote an imaginative story: "I thought I took my father's horse and followed the wagon. Finally I found it. They were surprised to see me. I talked with the girl and persuaded her to elope with me." When night came on, the story relates, Abe put the girl on his horse and they rode away. Several hours later they came to a camp only to find it was the same one they had left. The next night they tried it again. But the same thing happened: right back to the same place. "We concluded we ought not to elope. I stayed until I persuaded her father to give her to me. I think that was the beginning of love with me," Abe confessed.[1]

That mild beginning was quickened when Anna Carolina Robey was stumped during a quiz in Squire Crawford's blab-school spelling class in the winter of 1818-1819. Abe demonstrated his affection for Katy by helping her to spell "defied." He pointed to his eye and winked at her.[2]

Neither Katy nor any other girl interested Abe very much after that until he was seventeen. Then, on a balmy spring day he rode up to Benny Lamar's grist mill and found Betsy Ray there waiting her turn. He jumped off his horse, threw his sack of shelled corn onto the grinding floor near where Betsy sat curled up on her own sack of corn. Betsy, pretty and bashful, was barefooted. Abe was not barefooted but he did have a big hole in the knee of his pants and, as usual, his long shin bone showed. He sat down on his sack of corn, put a big hand over his knee, trying to cover the hole. Betsy drew her bare feet under her dress and shyly glanced at Abe. Both were embarrassed. They listened to the millstones whirr, grinding out meal

for customers who had come earlier. After a while Betsy broke the
tension. "Abe, I'm powerful glad to see you," she murmured.

Parrot-like Abe replied, "Betsy, I'm powerful glad to see you." He
could not think of another word to say, so he listened some more to
the whirring stones and wondered why it was much easier to talk with
men and boys than with girls. He shuffled his big feet. "What you
folks been doing?" he blurted. Betsy: "Nothing but working." As
she twisted around a bit on her sack she added: "What you folks
been doing?" Abe coughed nervously and examined his calloused
hands: "Just like you folks. Just working."

After a pause Betsy continued: "Abe, we're having a pound party
to our house and we want you to bring a lot of young folks from down
your way, will you?" Abe: "If some other feller don't beat my time."
Betsy was reassuring: "They'll never do that." By now her bare feet
had crept out from under her dress and Abe had forgotten the hole in
his pants. Betsy: "Everybody has to bring a pound of something
to eat. You can bring molasses candy or a cake or just anything to
eat." Abe: "What will you do if I don't bring anything?" Betsy:
"Fine you two cents for every inch you are tall." She eyed him
speculatively as if figuring that his six feet four inches would net her
quite a bit.

Two weeks later when Lincoln and his Gentryville crowd entered the
Ray's big, double, hewn-log house on Crooked Hill overlooking the
Ohio River, they found the tables loaded with pounds of food brought
by early arriving guests. Already the fiddlers had started playing and
the caller was clapping his hands. Out on the puncheon floor couples,
old and young, were hoeing it down to the popular tune of "Leather
Breeches Full of Stitches." Abe flexed his knees to the rhythm of the
caller's chant:

> *"You go round and I'll go through*
> *"I love to dance and so do you.*
> *"Home-made sugar on a puncheon floor*
> *"I'll dance this time and I'll dance no more!"*

Time came to unwrap the pound packages. Lincoln smiled at Betsy
and she smiled back at him. Nonchalantly he unwrapped his package
and revealed a pound of green persimmons. "Abe Lincoln!" scolded
Betsy, "I told you to bring something to eat!"

Abe nodded. "You sure did. But you didn't say anything about
whether it was to be cooked or ripe. Green persimmons're sure
something to eat."

Betsy laughed and pronounced sentence: "You'll have to pay a fine." Lincoln flung his arms about her: "Sure. I'll pay it right now." [3]

Less than a month later barefooted Abe was driving an ox-cart load of hoop-poles to the Ohio River. He had reached Crooked Hill and, as he rode along he gaily played his Jews'-harp, serenading Betsy. Just as he came in front of the Ray home a swarm of bees passed overhead. The rising and falling drone of Abe's harp must have attracted them for they wheeled and settled on him and his oxen. Away loped the team, down the hillside, piling Abe and his cart into a briar patch. Wildly he flailed his arms. The more he struck at the bees and the more the oxen kicked at them, the more they stung him and the oxen. He yelled for help. Betsy and her sister, Sally, ran to him, Betsy carrying a hoe. Never before had Abe been so glad to see that tool. With it he chopped his way out of the brambles and threw dirt at the bees. As they retreated he drove his oxen back onto the road and down to the river. He rode past the Ray home again that evening and again he was playing his Jews'-harp. "Abe's all right now for I hear his band," said Betsy to Sally.[4]

Abe forgot all about Betsy the moment Ann Meeker took a rear seat in the room of Squire Pate's Magistrate Court of Kentucky where the Dill brothers had arraigned him for operating a ferry on the Ohio River without a license. Ann was Squire Pate's sixteen year old niece. Following the dismissal of his case, Abe had remained, at Pate's invitation, to talk about law. Afterward he crossed the river several times to attend the Squire's court, but he found that strolling with Ann through the apple orchard was much more appealing than listening to legal discussions. One tree was Ann's favorite. From it she plucked a big, red apple and, Eve-like, gave it to Abe. When he bit into it and looked at her he thought it was the sweetest apple he had ever tasted.

Unluckily for Abe Lincoln, Mrs. Pate was anxious for Ann to marry William Thresher, a cousin. Quietly she began calling Ann's attention to Abe's shabbiness and uncouth bearing. Ann's eyes were opened; the orchard strolls ended.[5]

Not long after this Lincoln discovered a very attractive girl in Buck Horn Valley. However, before he could make any headway with her Nathaniel Grigsby also discovered her. Nattie made headway fast. One frosty night, hearing that Nattie was visiting the girl, Abe went to her cabin home and looked in at the window. By the firelight he could see Nattie's successes. Jealousy rose. Knowing the door had a latch on the outside, Abe crept around and fastened it securely, then went over to a log, sat down and waited. About midnight he heard Nattie try to open the door. Then he watched Nattie try to crawl through the window; it was too small. "Try the chimney, Nattie," Abe called roguishly. "The fire died down a long time ago." Nattie yelled back: "Unfasten that door!" Abe: "Go on, Nattie, try the chimney." With much grunting and clawing Grigsby climbed up inside, the hot stick-and-mud chimney and out onto the clapboard roof.

Soot-covered, sweaty and very angry Nattie shook a fist at Abe: "I got a notion to take a club to you!" Abe ignored the threat: "The only chance you got now is to try to get even with me sometime." Nattie Grigsby swung down off the roof and unfastened the latch. The two boys walked home together.[6]

That frosty night had long since melted into summer heat and on a broiling August afternoon in 1827 Abe Lincoln, astride a gray mare, a sack of wool tied on behind his saddle, rode into Princeton, Indiana, never suspecting that any girls lurked in the hot shadows of the town. He had ridden forty miles through the timber-wolf and panther infested Buckskin Country and his mind had not been on girls. He was looking for James Evans' carding machine to have some wool carded for his stepmother's spinning wheel. He rode past a general merchandise store, stared up at its big gilt sign, continued a block westward to the machine where he met John M. Lockwood, the apprentice boy.

Abe pointed to his sack: "I want this wool carded." Two months younger than Lincoln, Lockwood replied, "This is like going to mill. People take turns. Where you from?" Abe: "Spencer County." Lockwood: "Oh, you're from a considerable distance. I'll card it directly. What's your name?"

"A. Lincoln." Carefully Abe spelled *Lincoln*. Lockwood: "How do you want to pay—money or take toll out?" Abe replied "Take toll out," and walked away, heading eastward down the middle of the street.

Some distance beyond the carding machine Abe saw a young woman, possibly seventeen years old, approaching. His wide mouth flew open. Never before had he realized so much beauty existed in the world. The girl seemed more of a vision than a reality. As she passed him she said pleasantly, "Good evening," and walked right on. Abe gazed after her . . . For two hours he walked aimlessly, mooning over the vision. Above all else Abe wanted an introduction to the girl, but he wondered what she would think of him. His suit

Pole-house or half-faced shelter built by Indiana settlers.

of jeans was worn threadbare; his shin bones showed blue and briar
scratched.

Upon returning to the carding machine he found that his wool was
ready, carded into rolls and pinned up with thorns. Lockwood:
"You had eighteen pounds of wool. I tolled it three pounds." Abe
wasn't interested. Slowly he picked up the bundle and tied it on behind his saddle. "Good evening," he said dreamily and rode away on
his horse, unaware that the apprentice boy could have told him the
girl was Julia Evans, the carding machine owner's niece.

All the way home and for a long time afterward he thought of the
girl. "For two years scarcely a day passed that she was out of my
mind," he admitted to Dr. Lewis of Princeton. "She was the most
beautiful young lady I ever saw." He had determined to return to the
wool carding town and get an introduction to her but "Sad to relate,
some little bird six months after this whispered in my ear that she
was married to Silas Stephens and moved to Evansville," he said.

Gradually the vision of Julia dimmed in Lincoln's mind and his
thoughts turned to Elizabeth Tuley. Betsy, as he called her, was the
sister of John Tuley with whom he trapped wild turkeys. Upon
Abe's return from Arkansas three years before, Betsy had asked him
to her Valentine party. She lived in a rambling, hewn-log house a mile
north of Gentryville. Abe went to her party and danced two or three
sets with her. Even though men and boys considered him the best
clog-dancer there, Betsy expressed the opinion of the Pigeon Creek
girls: "Abe was big and awkward and couldn't dance much." However, he could read; he borrowed her father's copy of Dr. Hole's
Practical Discourses on the Gospels.

"Abe didn't try to go with me until I was eighteen," Betsy recalled. It happened right after church one Sunday morning. "Betsy, can I see you home?" Abe asked. Betsy hesitated a moment: "If you want to." She and Abe walked along a ridge through the woods to her house. He stayed for dinner, sat around all afternoon and late into the evening, talking and joking. "After that Abe came to see me several times," said Betsy.[8] John Tuley remembered: "Abe used to come to spark my sister. Sometimes his stepbrother, John Johnston, came with him."[9]

Betsy's family and even her neighbors started to tease her about Lincoln. They laughed about his coatsleeves and pant-legs being too short for him. Betsy didn't mind. She didn't mind anything until nattily dressed Benjamin Hesson showed up. Benny had moved in from Kentucky. The newcomer's interest in Betsy alarmed Abe. He knew how to knock a bully cold but he didn't know how to halt Benny's advances toward Betsy. Scared of losing her, Abe began to hint strongly that he was very fond of her. "I could tell by his chat that he wanted to marry me," said Betsy. Abe handled his chats so skillfully that it looked as if he had slowed down Benny's progress and might even halt it entirely. Jauntily, he went about the neighborhood, sure of winning. Then hard luck struck. "Abe got too much applejack," explained Betsy. "I never heard of him doing it again but father was very strict about such things."[10] So Betsy and Benny were married. And that ended Lincoln's interest in Indiana girls.

CHAPTER ELEVEN

SLAVERY

At almost the very moment seven year old Abe Lincoln was seeing his Indiana home on Pigeon Creek for the first time, either by coincidence or by the designs of Providence, a Negro slave named Frisby was escaping from an Ohio River boat at the mouth of that same creek. Frisby was being taken to New Orleans by his owners, who described him as "stout made, very large eyes, and a carpenter by trade."[1] While Abe may have had no personal contact with this runaway slave, the Negro's escape was the subject of discussions on both sides of the Ohio. Tom Lincoln probably pointed out to Abe that Frisby, in escaping into Indiana, had rightfully sought refuge in a free state. Tom may have reminded Abe that the Lincolns had left Kentucky partly to get away from slave soil.

In 1816 Indiana had entered the Union as a free state, but in 1817 it looked as if it would become the testing ground for strength between the anti-slavery and pro-slavery forces. Like many of their neighbors, the Lincolns had expected to find strict adherence to the Northwest Ordinance of 1787 and the State Constitution, both of which forbade slavery in Indiana. But soon they were aware that slave-holders on both sides of the Ohio River were conniving for legalized slavery in the new state. They heard it argued that the Northwest Ordinance was only an act of the old Congress, unconstitutional because it deprived owners of their slave property when those slaves were moved into the territory north of the Ohio; and that the Act of 1807, passed in defiance of that Ordinance by the Indiana Territorial Legislature, made it "lawful for any person the owner or possessor of any negroes or mulattoes of and above the age of fifteen years to bring said negroes or mulattoes into this territory."[2]

Born in an all-slavery atmosphere, Lincoln was growing up in a border country torn apart by the issue of slavery. Here his neighbors spied on one another to discover who was harboring fugitives. Pro-slavery neighbors began catching runaway Negroes, holding them in jails, chaining them in hogpens, advertising their capture. Those who engaged in this cruel but lucrative business were locally called "nigger-ketchers."

The conflict between slavery and free soil touched close to the Lincolns when the "nigger-ketchers" found Yellow Joel, a mulatto who, like Frisby, had escaped from his owner and hidden in the Pigeon Creek neighborhood. Since the Federal Fugitive Slave Law made Yellow Joel the property of his Natchez, Mississippi, master, local "ketchers" clapped him in the Perry County jail and held him for a fat reward.[3] Next they got wind of a slave from Tennessee hiding in an anti-slavery sympathizer's home near the jail. This Negro had a gun and when the Sheriff of Perry County, assisted by Joshua Wright, attempted to capture him, the Negro shot Wright in the belly.[4]

Slave-hunters coming into Lincoln's neighborhood looking for fugitives were called "patter-rollers." These men scoured the Indiana country-side trying to locate runaways. When they teamed up with tricky "ketchers" it was well nigh impossible for any fugitive slave to avoid being captured and returned to his owner.

One of Lincoln's close neighbors, James Cooper, paid taxes on 102 acres of land and "1 black," a legally recognized slave.[5] How did Cooper and others like him, get around the state law? One common method was to persuade or threaten Negro boys and girls of sixteen to sign contracts in court to serve an employer and his assignees for a term of ninety years. Negroes unable to write their names made marks. If these boys or girls ran away and were caught they were returned to their employers who were obliged to pay cash rewards to the "ketchers." From Troy, Indiana, right through Lincoln's neighborhood to Vincennes on the Wabash, there were in 1820 about 190 Negroes toiling in actual bondage.[6] Even Judge Henry Vanderburgh of the Territorial Supreme Court held slaves. And when the Judge died some time after Indiana had become a state, his Negro woman and child were auctioned off to the highest bidder at Esquire Justice Peter Jones' tavern door in Vincennes.[7]

Like Vanderburgh, Judge Jones, father of Abraham Lincoln's friend and benefactor, William Jones of Gentryville, owned slaves. In 1819, Jones' Negro Jonathan was appraised at $400, Jack at $300, Lette at $300, Ebby at $250, Jesse at $100, Maria at $100 and Maria's husband, Phillip, at $25.[8]

The Lincolns and others like them must have wondered how judges could hold slaves on Indiana's free soil. Why didn't federal agents do something to stop it? Some social reformers did try. But slave-holders blocked their efforts by the farcial procedure called "setting foot on slave soil." Hoosier slave-holders bull-tongued loads of Kentucky red clay to their Indiana homes and dumped it into boxes ten feet long, six feet wide and one foot high. When federal agents asked questions concerning the presence of Negroes, the slave-owner merely cracked his blacksnake whip and the Negroes scurried to the boxes. As long as they stood on that "slave soil" no one dared to touch them. So slavery continued.

Slave dealer W. Lagow of Vincennes advertised a Negro woman and boy for sale or hire. Thomas E. DuBois placed on sale "a likely Negro woman." [9] And all the time the story of the bitter quarrel between Judge Vanderburgh and Judge Turner at Vincennes in 1794 was kept alive by the pro-slavery people. Two of Vanderburgh's slaves, a Negro man and his wife, applied to Turner's court for emancipation by a writ of *habeas corpus*. Before the case came to trial the Negroes were kidnapped and carried away. Turner had the kidnappers arrested. He declared that the slaves were "free by the Constitution of the Territory," meaning the Ordinance of 1787. Complaints were made at once to Governor St. Clair, who opposed Turner's views. [10] St. Clair wrote Turner: "The declaration in our Constitution that there shall be no slavery nor involuntary servitude in the [Northwest] Territory applies to those slaves who may have been imported since the establishment of that Constitution. So far as it respects the past, it can have no operation, and must be construed to intend that, from and after the publication of said Constitution, slaves imported into the Territory should immediately become free." [11]

The old inhabitants, especially the French settlers, held slaves and had seen themselves in danger of losing their property under strict adherence to the Ordinance. But St. Clair's ruling eased the tension and the older families went on holding slaves just as they had done before the Ordinance was passed. [12]

The non-slavery-holding class resented slavery in Indiana. So bitter continued the feeling over slavery that in 1819 Abe Lincoln's neighbor, Ratcliff Boon, ran for Lieutenant Governor on Governor Jonathan Jennings' platform of "No slavery in Indiana" and was elected. But while the Jennings-Boon election muted the clamor for legalized slavery in the Hoosier State, the loathsome business of stealing free Negroes went steadily on. Steve Hardin, a free Negro, living a little way northwest of Lincoln's cabin, was stolen. With the help of Indiana "nigger-ketchers," a Kentucky "patter-roller" named J. Teal trailed Hardin to where he was visiting a farmer south of Vincennes. Word came back, "They've toted Stevey down to New Orleans and sold him." [13]

A few miles west of Abe Lincoln's home, towards Princeton, two free Negroes lived in a cabin. "Ketchers" broke into the cabin, handcuffed the freedmen, took them to Kentucky and turned them over to "patter-rollers," who took them on down south and sold them into New Orleans slavery.[14] John Hinton of Petersburg, northwest of Lincoln's home, caught a free, eighteen year old mulatto boy and sold him to Thomas Terrel of Clarksville, Tennessee. Either the boy ran away or was re-stolen, for Terrel advertised for him in Vincennes' *Western Sun*, offering a big reward.[15] Stealing free Negroes and selling them into slavery aroused abolitionists and emancipating preachers all the way from Lincoln's Buck Horn Valley community to the Wabash River.

No one whom Abraham heard speak was more determined to destroy the traffic in human beings than the Reverend Adam Shoemaker, a feet-washing Baptist preacher. Abe Lincoln saw the Reverend Shoemaker stand in the wild-cherry pulpit Thomas Lincoln had built and pound the Bible while he exhorted the Pigeon Creekers to stamp out slavery in Indiana. Since 1806 the battle cry of his Baptist brothers and sisters had been "Equal rights for all men: Emancipation! Let every man work for a living!" Adam Shoemaker carried that cry up and down the frontier.

Shoemaker earned the title of The Emancipation Preacher because he "exposed the horrors of slavery and awoke the people from their stupor." [16] Abe heard him lambast both the Northern slave-traders and the Southern slave-breeders. The minister denounced such hypocrites as the New England ship owner who, after his vessel had disposed of its human cargo in Southern markets, piously gave thanks on the following Sabbath that "an over-ruling Providence had been pleased to bring to this land of freedom another cargo of benighted heathen to enjoy the blessing of a Gospel dispensation." [17] Shoemaker denounced the contention of Southern planters that it was morally all right to breed Negroes and sell their offspring as you would breed and sell hogs and cattle. According to the Reverend's lights, slave-traders, slave-breeders, slave-owners, man-stealers were all the henchmen of the devil, for they violated God's commandments by trafficking in human souls. Preacher Shoemaker's sermons, delivered from 1822 to 1827, were building up in Abe Lincoln's impressionable mind an abiding hatred for human slavery.[18]

Abe had passed his fourteenth birthday only a few weeks before Thomas Clay, a Davies County, Kentucky, slave-holder, created a furor in the Pocket Country by deliberately bringing his slaves across

the Ohio River into Indiana. Clay led his slaves directly to the
Spencer County courthouse at Rockport and, on April 18, 1823, emancipated them. With this act Thomas Clay familiarized Abraham
Lincoln with emancipation and added more bitterness to the slavery
question raging in Southern Indiana.

Thomas Clay's recorded deed of manumission, on file in the courthouse at Rockport, reads: "I have and do hereby Emancipate
Liberate and Set Free the negro Slaves herein named to wit Old
Samuel and his wife Biddy. Betty Rachel and her children Henry and
Juliette the last two being under age I reserve to myself or agent the
management of them until the first day of June in the year 1827 when
they will be of lawful age to act for themselves (as well as the others
herein named) as free born people of colour and the clerk is required
to give them a certificate of their freedom on presentment." [19]

With slave-holders beginning to cross the Ohio to emancipate their
slaves, while "nigger-ketchers" and "patter-rollers" plied their man-
stealing trade in the Indiana border country, it was only natural
that the slavery issue should be intensified during the 1824 Presidential campaign, absorbing the attention of Lincoln and his fellow
Pigeon Creekers.

Another Clay added interest to this bitter issue. Henry Clay,
Speaker of the House of Representatives, who was admiringly called
by Western backwoodsmen the "Mill Boy of the Slashes," was one of
the four Presidential candidates. Abe Lincoln's interest in Clay
was intense at this time. "Anything about Henry Clay was eagerly
read by Abe," according to William Jones.[20] It was in the Jones' store
at Gentryville that the fifteen year old Lincoln read in the July 19,
1824, Vincennes *Western Sun* what the elder Gentrys, Grigsbys, and
Lincolns had long known: that during the Kentucky Constitutional
Convention of 1793, Henry Clay had vigorously tried "to have a
clause inserted for the gradual abolition of slavery." The *Western Sun*
went on to say that in the critical moment only four years ago "when
the north and south had almost assumed the armour and attitude of
defiance (over the Missouri question); when the slave-holding and
non-slave-holding states arrayed in bitter enmity and hostile phalanx
against each other; when a dissolution of the Union appeared almost
inevitable" Clay began "marking out the course of reconciliation
allaying the heart burnings and sectional feelings of the belligerent
parties" which led those "jarring interests . . . to a happy and amicable adjustment."

From stump speakers, political discussions in Jones' store and in

the Lincoln, Gentry, and Grigsby homes, Abe and his friends Joe
and Nattie acquired a good understanding of Clay's compromise of
1820, which let Missouri enter the Union a slave state and Maine
enter free, thus balancing a slave state against a free state. Henry
Clay's having "declaimed in favour of gradual emancipation," as
reported by the *Western Sun,* weakened his political standing with pro-
slavery sympathizers such as the Gentrys while it strengthened him
with the Lincolns and Grigsbys.[21] "Mr. Clay has *without fee or
reward* acted as counsel for a great number of slaves when suing for
their freedom," declared the *Sun.* Clay's fight against slavery increased Lincoln's admiration for him: "I can express all my views on
the slavery question by quotations from Henry Clay." [22]

About this time Abe obtained one of the most widely discussed
slavery books ever circulated in Indiana: Captain James Riley's
Authentic Narrative.[23] A trader and master of the American brig,
Commerce, Riley was shipwrecked on the west coast of Africa in
August, 1815. After his escape from cannibalistic natives he fell into
the hands of Arabs, who enslaved him. Two old women stripped him
and forced him and his shipmates to walk naked and drive camels
into the blazing Sahara Desert. Captain Riley wrote that a Negro
slave "would poke our sore flesh with a sharp stick to show the Arabs
what miserable beings we were." When one of Riley's shipmates
protested, Riley advised to "Let the Negro laugh if he can take
pleasure in it. He is merely a poor slave himself, and is only trying to
gain favour of his masters and mistresses."

Put up for sale in a slave market, Riley related, buyers "found
fault with my shins which had been a long time sore." Finally, Sidi
Hamet bought the captain for two blankets and a bundle of ostrich
feathers; subsequently he threatened to cut Riley's throat unless an
American at Swearah paid ransom money. Riley concluded his *Narrative*: "I have learned to look with compassion on my enslaved and
oppressed fellow-creatures. I will exert all my remaining faculties in
endeavours to redeem the enslaved and to shiver the road of oppres-
sion." He appealed to the United States Government to devise a
plan of gradual emancipation which would "wither and extirpate the
accursed tree of slavery."

And even as young Lincoln read about the terrors of Arabian slavery,
"patter-rollers" again invaded Indiana, looking for an attractive
colored girl. Local "nigger-ketchers" knew exactly where to fill their
order. Mathias Mount, living only a few miles from Lincoln's home,
had a free Negro girl working for his family. Not aware that "patter-

rollers" were around, the Mounts sent the girl on an errand to a neighbor's house. She never returned.[24] The next victims were an aged couple living west of the Lincolns. The old man worked for the Sawyer family and his wife worked for the Montgomerys. On his way to mill, the old Negro was waylaid by "ketchers," taken to Natchez, Mississippi, and sold back into bondage.[25]

Such stealing and selling of free Negroes was instilling in the adolescent Lincoln an intense hatred for slavery.[26] And while he gaily learned clog-dancing from Negro slaves down at Troy, it must have occurred to him that some of the blacks belonged to the river town's leading citizen and taxpayer, James McDaniel, a slave-holder who openly operated on Indiana's free soil.[27]

As July 4, 1826, approached a cry went up everywhere for fitting celebration of the fiftieth anniversary of the Declaration of Independence. In William Wood's copy of *The Telescope*, Lincoln read Editor Beach's attack on slavery: "If we make no efforts on this day of our celebrations to emancipate the slave population and abolish the foreign and domestic slave trade, shame must cover us. Shall a slave trade of 250,000 annually continue which had but 80,000 when prohibited?"[28] Three weeks later, Editor Beach quoted a British subject, Mr. O'Connel: "I have come now to the boasted land of freedom. You threw off the allegiance you owed us because you thought we were oppressing you with the Stamp Act. You boasted your deliverance from slavery. On what principle do you now continue your fellow-men in bondage, and render that bondage even more galling by ringing in the ears of the sufferers from your tyranny what you have suffered for freedom?"

In the August 26 issue of *The Telescope* Abe read about a freeborn Negro of New York being picked up in Washington, D.C., and thrown in jail. If his owners did not call for him soon he would be sold for jail fees. "He has no owners but God!" cried Editor Beach. "And yet 'We hold these truths to be self-evident that all men are created equal.' The inconsistency is too glaring—the blot upon our escutcheon too deep—to leave any patience. And yet we talk of European tyranny and despotism."

From travelers coming into Gentryville Abe got the news that Miss Frances Wright, using Robert Owen's Utopian Socialistic Colony at New Harmony for her headquarters, was working out a self-emancipation plan. Miss Wright's scheme called for a slave to work out his freedom through credit for his labor, less the cost of his food, clothing, and shelter. With $10,000 General Lafayette had advanced her,

Fanny Wright had bought a 2,000 acre place on the Wolf River near Memphis, Tennessee, and named it Nashoba.[20] George Flower, leader of the English settlement at Albion, Illinois, assisted her. From one end of Buck Horn Valley to the other, Abe Lincoln heard his neighbors jubilantly praise or angrily denounce Fanny Wright's efforts to free slaves and pay their owners.

Perhaps at no time between the Missouri Compromise and the outbreak of the Civil War, did Abe Lincoln hear a greater tumult over the slavery issue than in 1827 and 1828. In the fall of 1826, about the time he and Jefferson Ray flatboated down the Ohio and Mississippi Rivers, peddling their cargoes to planters along the Tennessee and Arkansas shores, Mexico suddenly freed all slaves in Texas. According to the Little Rock *Arkansas Gazette,* October 10, 1826, slave-holders had emigrated to Texas "under an assurance, we are informed, from local authorities of Texas, that they could hold their slaves." Mexico's action, said the *Gazette,* has "produced the greatest of consternation among slave holders" and they are "hurrying off their slaves in great numbers into Louisiana and Arkansas."

After settling with Ray, Lincoln got a job cutting firewood on Sheriff William D. (Wappanocca) Ferguson's plantation in Crittenden County, Arkansas Territory. There he observed at close range a Southern planter who treated his slaves with consideration. There, also, while cutting tupelo gum alongside Negro slaves, he was right across the Mississippi and a little way above the mouth of Wolf River where Miss Frances Wright's self-emancipation experiment at Nashoba was going full tilt. It can only be surmised that the Ferguson slaves told Lincoln what they knew about the experiment and Lincoln told them what he had heard at Gentryville and elsewhere in the Indiana Pocket Country about Miss Wright's association with the Owen New Harmony movement. Surely here Lincoln was seeing a different side of the slavery issue. This must have brought more forcefully to his attention the idea that slaves were property; that freeing them without compensation to their owners was not consistent with justice or property rights under the Constitution.

On his return home Abe Lincoln found many of his fellow Pigeon Creekers as firm as ever in their belief that Congress had authority to abolish slavery in the District of Columbia and should do so at once. In the March 10, 1827, copy of *The Telescope,* Lincoln read Editor Beach's obvious attempt to arouse widespread interest in the idea: "Hail Columbia! Happy Land! A Regular Market for Men unblushingly advertized within sight of the capital of this land of liberty."

And this is but one of the many such establishments under the very
eyes of Congress. What say you, Americans?"

As if to answer Editor Beach, some slaves banded together and
began plundering Southern plantations. Pro-slavery sympathizers in
both North and South, fearing a general uprising, armed themselves
and went out to put down the rebellion. Lincoln read in *The Telescope:* "A nest of runaway negroes was discovered in the fork of the
Alabama and Tombeck rivers. The negroes were attacked and after a
severe action were conquered. Three negroes were shot, viz.: Bust,
Hector, and Hal. Several were taken prisoners and others escaped
They had two cabins and were about to build a fort. They fought
desperately." [30]

To the exasperation of slave-holders and slave-traders, New York
freed her slaves. In the Vincennes *Western Sun,* August 4, 1827,
Lincoln read, "On July 4th instant Slavery ceased in the state of New
York. The event was celebrated on the 5th by the colored population
of the city in a very orderly manner. It is said that more than three
thousand joined in the procession." By freeing her slaves, New York
had condemned the slave system and offended Southern planters who
needed more slave labor in order to work their vast plantations. The
planters retaliated by calling for free trade with Great Britain, their
best market for cotton, hemp, and tobacco. "A tax on imports was in
incidence a tax on exports," they argued. [31]

In spite of increased activity by Northern slave-runners, Lincoln and
his anti-slavery neighbors learned from news and rumors reaching
Gentryville that the demand for slaves far exceeded the supply. To
meet that demand the more Northerly slave-holders bought virile
Negro men and fecund women and bred them like cattle. One breeder
advertised in the *Western Sun* a Negro woman he owned who "is in
her 42nd year and has had 41 children, and at this time is pregnant
with her 42nd child and possibly with her 43rd as she has frequently
had doublets." [32] The courts held that the breeders who owned the
mothers also owned the offspring "just like that of other animals." [33]

Standing on the north bank of the Ohio River, Abe Lincoln often
watched boats going down stream loaded with Negro field hands, house
servants, and wornout breeders. He saw them sitting chained together;
saw them rocking back and forth in misery; heard them singing,
praying, weeping. Such scenes must have disturbed him deeply. In
his ears dinned the propaganda for and against the slavery system.
Many slave-holders south of the Mason-Dixon Line said they were
not responsible for the introduction of the institution into America.

They pointed out they were not even engaged in the profitable business of running in slaves from Africa. They had left that job to the Northerners.

Some argued that "Slavery, as it exists in the United States, is the Providentially-arranged means whereby Africa is to be lifted from her deep degradation to a state of civil and religious liberty." [34] They contended that according to the Bible slavery was established "as a punishment of sin upon Ham's posterity." They cited Genesis IX, 22-27. They claimed that the natives in Africa had no temples, no priests, no legends, no history, no sacred grove; "all is one unbroken night of palpable darkness; no other people ever departed so far from God. Satan has employed his sagacity with fatal success in erasing every vestige of religious impressions from their minds." They further argued that "The African was not reduced to slavery by being brought to the United States." He was already "a slave in his own country—subject to much more severe bondage there than it is possible for him ever to experience here" [35]

Others declared: "Slavery is an evil; but under the wise direction of God it will become a blessing to the Negroes. The whites who have enslaved them will make them compensation for the sufferings through the gift of Christianity, the instructing them in agriculture and handicraft arts . . . thus they may be first instructed, and then gradually emancipated, and colonized in Africa . . . the heathen nations being finally Christianized and civilized through the Christianized and emancipated slaves of America." [36]

In addition to hearing Scriptural arguments favoring slavery, Abe saw favorable living conditions on the Pate and Ferguson plantations. There were no indications of cruelty at either place. Following his ferryman's trial in Squire Samuel Pate's Kentucky magistrate court, Abe crossed the Ohio River a number of times and visited the court. Pate held fifty-three slaves. Many of the men were clog-dancers, preachers. The women were excellent singers. From tobacco barns on the high ground to fields near the river the Negroes sang as they worked. At noon when Aunt Sarah, the head cook, blew on the big conch shell the slaves came laughing and joking. Harrison Pate, the Squire's body servant, showed genuine affection for his master. [37]

On the Pate plantation, as on others south of the Mason-Dixon Line, there were aged Negroes who had to be fed, clothed, sheltered, doctored. Few of them were able to do anything but shell a bit of corn or other light work. Some spent their last days resting in the sun. Children had to be taken care of until old enough to carry water to field hands or to bring up the cows at milking time. Yet old and young were treated the same as able bodied slaves. One planter, in 1827, expressed the feelings of many of his fellow-planters: "We are the slaves; not the blacks. They hang about us and grow up increasing and multiplying all our curses." Declared Bishop James O. Andrew: "I am a slave-holder for conscience sake. How am I to free them? Some of them are too old to work and are an expense to me. Some are little children. Where shall I send them? Many of them would not go. I believe that the providence of God has thrown these creatures into my hands and holds me responsible for their treatment." [38]

Abe heard, too, that slave-holders suffered economically when slaves died or were stolen. To pick up easy money Southern men kidnapped their neighbors slaves, ran them into an adjoining slave state and sold them. Handsome Negro sailors enticed slave girls on board vessels and took them up North. Abolitionists helped Negroes flee from plantations. To an owner the disappearance of a slave meant the loss of property. Since the slaves who disappeared usually were in their prime, the owner felt their loss very keenly; in many cases he had raised the slaves from infancy. Hearing these sides of the slavery problem, Abe was becoming convinced that slave-holders should be paid for their slaves before being required to free them.

Meanwhile in Lincoln's Indiana pocket country leaders of the American Colonization Society increased their efforts to free slaves in proportion to the efforts of Southern breeders and Northern importers to supply the heavy demand for slave labor. Replying to enemies of colonization, Henry Clay, a vice president of the Society, explained that the establishment of a colony on the coast of Africa was for American slaves already free or those whose freedom was to be purchased. The Charleston, South Carolina, *Mercury*, spokesman for the pro-slavery forces, countered with: "How dare the people of this society, the men of Ohio and the Wabash, presume to discuss a subject of which they know nothing, when their discussion can produce no other fruit than the bitter apple of disunion." [39]

The Telescope, September 15, 1827, lashed back with a quotation from the *Genius of Universal Emancipation*. "Man has no property in man," Abe read. "Neither has one generation a property in the generations that follow." To this the *Mercury* responded by accusing the Colonization Society of raising false hopes in the slaves "that Congress may adopt some measure to mitigate their condition. It will be a declaration of WAR and MUST be treated and resisted as such.

There must be no discussion. Discussion will bring on us one and all complete ruin if we are weak enough not to check it at the outset, and at every hazard, aye, at the hazard of DISSOLVING THE UNION!"

Listening to American Colonization Society leaders, and to others who feared a break-up of the Union over slavery, added no comfort to teen-age Lincoln's disturbed feelings. "I used to wander out in the woods all by myself," he told Henry C. Whitney. "I knew I was not alone just as well as I know that you are here now. Still I could see nothing and no one. But I heard voices. Once I heard a voice right at my elbow—heard it distinctly and plainly. I turned around, expecting to see someone. No one was there. But the voice was there." [40] Whitney: "What did it say?" Lincoln did not reply. Gloom and a look of pain settled on his lean face. In his family Bible was Ostervald's footnote to Exodus III: "Reflection upon this chapter regards the manner of God's calling Moses and revealing His design to make him the deliverer of his people Israel." Did Abraham Lincoln, alone in the silent Indiana forest, believe he had heard a voice calling him even as Moses had heard God's voice in the burning bush on the mountainside?

By the middle of February, 1828, every crossroads and trail-fork in Lincoln's border country sizzled over the justice or injustice of Congress' refusal to pay a Louisiana slave-holder for a Negro who had been wounded in the military service of the United States. During the Battle of New Orleans one of Marigny D'Auterive's slaves, a cart and a horse were pressed into service under General Jackson. The cart was wrecked, the horse killed, and the slave wounded in an eye and an arm. Congress paid D'Auterive for the cart and horse, but would not pay a penny for the disabled Negro.

The Committee on Claims reported to the House "that the United States is not bound in any case to pay for slaves injured or lost because they are not considered property." Representative Livingston of Louisiana leaped to his feet and shouted, "Slaves not property! What are they then? If they are not property the whole foundation on which the Constitution of this Union rests is shaken!" To this Representative Clark of New York retorted, "The honorable gentleman from Louisiana seems to think that to deny the right of compensation in this case would be to sap the foundations of the Constitution and dissolve the Union!"

Representative Drayton of South Carolina got the floor. "Much as we value this Union," he warned solemnly, "we would rather see it dissolved than yield to such violations of our rights. We would rather see our cities in flames, our plains drenched in blood—rather endure all the calamities of civil war, than parley for an instant upon the right of any power other than our own to interfere with the regulation of our slaves." [a]

Amid alarming threats of civil war and dissolving the Union the country moved into the tempestuous Jackson-Adams campaign of 1828 just as Lincoln reached his nineteenth birthday. Less than two months after Jackson was elected President of the United States, Allen Gentry and Abe Lincoln shoved off on their flatboat from Rockport, Indiana, headed for New Orleans. It was late January, 1829, when Captain Gentry and Bowhand Lincoln reached the Louisiana sugar coast. Plowing had begun for the new planting. From the fields came the slave-drivers' singsong to their plowgangs: "Put them plows in the ground and drive them mules!" Slaves put out for breaking were being flogged by professional breakers. Women with nursing children were in the suckers gang up by the cane mills. Other women hoed in the fields.

Gentry and Lincoln snubbed their boat into the soft Mississippi River bank and began peddling the cargo to planters. Foremen drove their slaves on board. After picking up their masters' purchases, the slaves coonjined down the gangplank to the crack of drivers' whips, swaying to the rhythm of jungle songs. As Abe Lincoln watched them sway away to the warehouses, he fully comprehended at last his Scotch Pigeon Creek neighbors' quotation from Robert Burns:

> *"Man's inhumanity to man*
> *"Makes countless thousands mourn."*

Six miles below Baton Rouge where long, narrow plantations radiated back from the curving Mississippi like spokes in a wheel, Gentry and Lincoln anchored their flatboat for the night at Madam Dunchene's plantation. Hardly had they dropped off to sleep when Lincoln was aroused by a suspicious noise on the river bank. He sat up and, Hoosier fashion, called out, "Who's here?" Receiving no reply, he jumped to his feet and through the partial darkness saw seven Negroes coming at him. Gentry yelled, "Get the guns! Shoot 'em!"

Abe and Allen suspected that the Negroes were runaway slaves turned bandits. No telling how many more would swarm in from the swamps and bayous. They might be killers from the runaway slave nest armed pro-slavery people had broken up eighteen months

A flatboat on the Wabash River.

before at the fork of the Alabama and Tombeck rivers. Again Gentry yelled, "Shoot 'em!" Lincoln grabbed a handspike and knocked one big Negro into the river. Three others leaped on board. Gentry rushed in, swinging a club. More Negroes boarded the boat. One husky black hit Abe on the head with a heavy stick of timber. Blood oozed from above his right eye. Luckily, the club was so long it reached beyond Lincoln and its end struck the deck, easing the blow. Up and down the deck, slippery with blood, whites and blacks fought savagely. At last Gentry and Lincoln drove the bandits off the boat, cut cable and left.[42]

After a few days the men sold their cargo and caught a cotton boat for New Orleans.[43] Such boats had low, broad decks for carrying baled cotton. They drew very little water and so were able to put into shallow tributaries and bayous. Sometimes their decks were piled with cotton bales almost to the tops of the smokestacks. And from high on the bales, Abe Lincoln soon was seeing for the first time the great Southern metropolis, the city of New Orleans. Its half-moon shaped harbor was matted with ships' masts. Riding at anchor, according to New Orleans newspapers for February 14 to 20, 1829, were 11 sloops, 18 schooners, 66 brigs, and 58 full rigged ships. All were being made ready to sail for the great ports of the world. Two weeks before Lincoln left Rockport, the Vincennes *Western Sun* described this Louisiana seaport as a city of "airy mansions of wealthy planters surrounded with orange, banana, lime and fig trees."

Abraham Lincoln reached his twentieth birthday just about the time his boat docked at New Orleans. Cotton boats regularly tied up at the open space at Esplanade Avenue and the levee. He and Gentry walked down the gangplank and sauntered up the levee to a crowd around a raised platform where Negroes, wearing hipclouts, stood. Due to his height Lincoln could see over the crowd and what he saw angered him. For probably the first time in his life he was witnessing the scene he had heard discussed so often—people selling people. He doubled his fists tightly; his knuckles went white. He watched men wearing big white hats and long black coats buy field hands and house servants. Black and ugly, such Negroes sold for $500 to $800 dollars each. The sale of "fancy girls" began. Bids started at $1500 or almost twice the top sale price for field hands. Bidding continued until some of the girls were knocked off at $2500 apiece. Unable to stand it any longer, Lincoln muttered to Gentry: "Allen, that's a disgrace! If I ever get a lick at that thing I'll hit it hard." Gentry: "We'd better get out of here, Abe." [44]

The two Hoosiers left the slave market and entered the Vieux Carre, gay section of New Orleans. On all sides they heard Negroes speaking French, whalemen swearing in Kanaka, pirates grunting words with double meanings. They saw river bullies fighting underworld ruffians for the favors of women. Wealthy Creole ladies jolted by in horse-drawn, silver-mounted barouches. People chatted on balconies of lacy ironwork. Strumpets flung open window shutters and invited passing men to drop in for a spell. Abe and Allen kept right on moseying along.

Beyond Royal and Bourbon Streets and about halfway to Dauphine, on the downtown side of Saint Ann Street, stood a story-and-a-half brick home, plastered on the outside. Here, it is believed, Lincoln and Gentry rented a room. From its dormer windows one could see the triple spires of Saint Louis Cathedral. [45]

For hours the two flatboatmen went sight-seeing. Because part of the city was almost as low as the riverbed, the only natural drainage was away from the river and towards the swamps and Lake Pontchartrain; thus water stood in the streets, garbage rotted in the gutters, and cesspools sent up stifling odors. Footpads added to the city's troubles by lurking in dark corners, dashing out and stabbing law-abiding people. The situation was so bad the Louisiana *Courier* demanded, "What is the city guard about? Do they merely receive the money of the citizens to vex them, and to run with drawn swords into the private yards in pursuit of negro boys for having fired a few squibs?" [46]

There were other people who vexed citizens, too. They were emancipated slaves. Abe and Allen watched them strut along. Freed by their white masters, many of these Negroes had acquired enough money to buy black slaves for themselves. Some even owned plantations where they cruelly worked their colored fellowmen. Slaves feared and hated them. "Dey is bad masters. If I was sold to a black man I'd drown myself. I would dat. I'd drown myself!" declared one old New Orleans slave.[47]

At the American Theatre, Lincoln saw billed for February 19th "that justly celebrated tragedian, Mr. Booth. He will make his first appearance in his own peculiar character of Richard III." [48] The tragedian was the very popular Shakespearean actor, Junius Brutus Booth, father of John Wilkes Booth. *Richard III* was one of Lincoln's favorite plays.

After three days in New Orleans, Lincoln and Gentry boarded a steamboat for Cincinnati and other Ohio River landings.[49] Whenever it pulled into shore at night to wood-up, an iron stove filled with fire was hoisted high on a rod. By the stove's red glow Lincoln watched slaves coonjine loads of cypress and cotton wood onto the steamer's deck. Listening closely he may have heard the low humming of slaves' forbidden song of spiritual freedom:

> "*My Mother! how long? Mother,*
> "*How long? Mother, how long?*
> "*Will sinners suffer here?*
> "*We'll soon be free! We'll soon*
> "*Be free! We'll soon be free!*

Any slave caught singing that song was given thirty-nine lashes.[50]

By the middle of March, 1829, Abe Lincoln was home again east of Gentryville. He showed the big scar over his right eye to John Romine and explained how a Negro bandit had made it with a club.[51] Restless and unable to find steady work on the Ohio River, Abe lit out for Louisville, Kentucky. Two years before he had worked near there on the Portland Canal and had been paid off in silver dollars.[52] This time he got a job in a tobacco warehouse at Fifth and Main Streets where he worked beside Negro slaves, handling heavy casks of tobacco in the rear of the long building.

At the entrance to the warehouse on the Fifth Street side a pitcher of drinking water stood on a shelf. Accidentally, a white boy knocked the pitcher off and broke it. The noise attracted the owner's son, who stepped to the door, looked in and, without a word, ran to the office, returned with a blacksnake whip and started flogging a nearby slave. Keyed up over the injustice, Lincoln said sharply, "Don't do that! A boy came in here and broke your pitcher." The owner's son growled, "Keep out of this or I'll give you some of it!" Lincoln glared.

The man lashed Abe Lincoln twice. The sting of that whip detonated in Lincoln's mind an accumulation of explosive resentments against slavery. He knocked the man to the ground and smashed hard fists into his bleeding face. Some white Kentuckians who also hated slavery advised Lincoln to run to the ferry and escape across the Ohio to Indiana.

Abe saw a mob forming up the street and knew if he ran bareheaded he would easily be detected: "But I don't have a hat!" Someone tapped him on the shoulder. He whirled around and saw a white man grinning at him: "I've got a hat." Abe snatched the hat and, with slave-holder's blood on his hands, fled toward the river. A ferryman overtook him. "This way!" the man yelled. As they ran along Main Street, Abe looked back and saw the mob gaining on them. His long legs carried him faster than they ever had before. He made it to the river, jumped into a skiff and rowed away from the bank.

When the mob of men arrived at the shore they threw rocks at him. He dodged as best he could and rowed in close to Punkin Patch Island. Then he shot across the Ohio River and landed on the Indiana side near the head of the falls, not far from where Henry Clay had fought a duel in 1809 with Humphrey Marshall.

Lincoln darted into the thick woods, heading northwestward. As he pushed his way through briars and tangled grapevines he began to realize the enormity of his act. He had defended a Negro slave. He had struck a Kentucky slave-holder's son. Slavery sympathizers, especially "patter-rollers," would surely cross the river and try to catch him. To throw pursuers off his trail, he avoided well-traveled paths and highways such as the Louisville-Vincennes-St. Louis stagecoach road and the Louisville-Corydon-Boonville road. Abe Lincoln skulked through the Indiana wilderness, living on roots, dry berries, acorns, beechnuts, wild honey—anything he could find that was edible. Finally, he reached Terre Haute on the Wabash. Fox-like he circled back, throwing real and imagined pursuers off his trail, and arrived home.[53]

This probably was one of Lincoln's last contacts with slavery during his formative years in the Indiana border country. And it helped him shape his total impressions of this controversial institution. He had seen slavery and had taken part in discussions concerning it. But like the nation itself, he was no doubt still confused over the problems— and their solutions—relating to man's ownership of man.

He had grown to hate slavery; he had promised himself that if he ever got a lick at the evil he would hit it hard. Yet he realized that there was a wide, deep gulf separating the viewpoints of pro-slavery and anti-slavery people. He could see that for some Americans the slave was not really a human being at all, but, rather, a farm animal similar to a horse or an ox that worked in the fields. He knew that for them the slave, just as the horse or ox, was property which had been bought at great cost or raised at considerable expense to the owner, through several non-productive years. Furthermore, he had seen that with some slave-holders the institution was a comparatively benevolent one, giving to some Negroes greater security and more personal comforts than they might have been able to procure for themselvs in the open labor market. Still it was interminable bondage.

Perhaps, and most important of all, Abe Lincoln had seen that many of the people who took violent stands on the controversy were so irrational about the subject that they were on the one side willing to deprive slave-holders of their property without recompense; or, on the other side, to sacrifice even the Union in order to maintain their property rights.

Lincoln's own strong belief in the necessity of preserving the Union and his adherence to the views of Henry Clay and Frances Wright, undoubtedly were shaping his personal feelings into a middle-of-the-road stand. He would compensate the "property owners" and preserve the Union; but he would work toward the eventual abolition of slavery. Back of this resolve was the memory of a New Orleans where he had seen mankind sold on the auction block. It remained with him as a goad. "There I saw slavery and slave markets as I had never seen them in Kentucky," he wrote.[54]

CHAPTER TWELVE

PARTING DAY

By the late summer of 1829 the Lincoln household experienced a new fear. During the recent hot, steamy days and nights "milksick" and malaria had again invaded Buck Horn Valley. The Lincolns could fight malaria, or buck-ager, as it was locally called, by just hanging on and shaking it out; or by following the suggestions carried by the Vincennes *Western Sun*: "When the fit is on take a new laid egg in a glass of brandy and go to bed immediately." But the milksickness which had killed Nancy Hanks Lincoln, Uncle Tom and Aunt Betsy Sparrow, and scores of others in 1818, was truly a formidable specter. Dennis Hanks probably expressed the family's attitude: "I was determined to leave and hunt a country where the milksick is not. Liked to have lossed my own life with it." [1]

Besides the fear of another epidemic, word kept coming from John Hanks over in Illinois that where he was there was plenty of new sod which had never had a plow point stuck into it. John's descriptions had aroused Tom Lincoln's restless, pioneer spirit. And Abe must have noticed it. "Pap, reckon we'll be pulling out?" he asked. "We're pulling out," said Tom.

Before leaving Indiana, the Lincolns had a number of affairs to take care of. Paying debts, for one thing. When Tom and Abe went to mill they usually paid for their grinding in toll. Not only did they take corn to the Gordon mill and Little Joe Phillips mill, but also to the Huffman mill six miles eastward on the Anderson River, and to the Enlow mill seventeen miles northward. Tom Lincoln owed Thomas Enlow for corn grinding. To pay up the old score, Tom made a lift-top desk of wild cherry and presented it to Enlow. [2] That out of the way, Thomas and Sarah Bush Lincoln asked for and received their church letters from the Pigeon Creek congregation. On the 26th of November Tom gave a bond of agreement to sell his farm to Charles Grigsby, one of the double-wedding bridegrooms. [3]

In the meanwhile Abe's stepbrother, John D. Johnston, had found an opportunity for him and Abe to make some cash money by operating a whiskey still for John Dutton. Articles of agreement, apparently drawn up by Abe, were signed by Dutton and Johnston. Abe

left the paper with Henry Brooner for safekeeping.⁴ Dutton's still,
classed as a "short-worm" type, was on his farm just north of the
Henry Brooner place on the Holland-Princeton road. Around it grew
an excellent stand of hickory and sassafras with which to fire the still.
Nearby gurgled a big spring of very hard water. Lincoln described
it to Stephen A. Douglas as "a little still-house up at the head of a
hollow." ⁵ Lincoln received $18 a month for working in it.⁶

With his little feist dog, Honey, at his heels, Abe labored over the
bubbling swill. Never a man to do things by half, he burned into
each run a bouquet highly pleasing to Dutton's customers. The making
of whiskey, Lincoln later pointed out, was "regarded as an honorable
livelihood and he who could make the most of it was the most enterprising and respectable" for "when all such of us first opened our
eyes upon the stage of existence, we found intoxicating liquor recognized by everybody, used by everybody, repudiated by nobody." ⁷
The full gesture of hospitality in a frontier cabin was a pitcher of
water, a lump of sugar and a jug of whiskey available to preachers and
sinners alike.

With the pungent fumes of Dutton's mash-filled retort clouding
about him, Abe Lincoln reached the legal age of 21 on February 12,
1830. He now was a free man and no longer bound to hand over his
earnings to his father.

To help with the final preparations for pulling out of Indiana he and
his stepbrother returned home. By selling to Henry Brooner his
half-interest in the rifle-gun, he added to the ready cash fund.⁸ He
visited Jones' store: "I want some goods to peddle along the road
to Illinois." Jones made up a pack-peddler's kit of needles, thread,
knives, forks, necklaces, breastpins, and pocketbooks.⁹ The bill came
to $36 dollars. Since Abe was unable to pay it all Jones extended
him credit. Meanwhile, an unusually large pair of shoes had caught
Abe's eye. He asked if he might try them on. Jones nodded. The
shoes fit all right but there still was the money question. Understanding Abe's problem, Jones told him to take them, too. Store
loafers hinted that trusting the lanky peddler for all that merchandise
was risky business. "I am satisfied," replied Jones, "Abe is honest.
He'll make a great man one of these days." ¹⁰

February 20 was a very busy day for Thomas Lincoln. That day
the Pigeon Creek church elected him moderator to settle "the difficulty
between Sister Grigsby & Sister Crafford." On that same day he and
his wife appeared before Justice of the Peace William Starke and
deeded their 80-acre farm to Charles Grigsby for the "sum of

One hundred and twenty-five dollars to them in hand." The deed, formally recorded in the Spencer County Deed Record Book-B, pages 63-64, states that this "is the same tract or parcel of land which the said Charles Grigsby holds a bond on the said Thomas Lincoln, dated November 26th, 1829." Tom signed it Lincoln, not "Linkern alias Lincoln" as he had signed less than two years before. Neighbors said Abe had "remodelled the spelling and corrected the pronounciation." [11] Sarah Bush Lincoln signed the deed by making her mark, an indication that she could write no better than Abe's mother.

Abe and his dog Honey went about the neighborhood paying final visits. They dropped into Joseph Richardson's place where some men were making handspikes. "What are you going to do with them?" Abe asked. "Carry that chickenhouse on them," a man replied pointing to a shed made of poles pinned together. After looking at the chickenhouse a moment Abe asked "is it heavy?"

Richardson: "Heavy enough, probably about 600 pounds. It'll make three ordinary men grunt and swear." Abe: "I reckon I can shoulder and carry it. Where do you want it put?"

Richardson indicated the spot. And, while he and the men watched in astonishment, Abe stepped into the center of the chickenhouse, grasped the handspikes run under it, slowly straightened up—and carried the building to its new location. [12]

In the midst of the preparations for moving to Illinois, Abe found time to read the *Western Sun* in Jones' store. The great Webster-Haynes debate was on, "arraying one portion of the Union against another." Webster was accused of attempting to "defeat the alliance between the South and the West by creating dissention between them." [13] By following the *Western Sun's* analysis of the speeches, Abe learned about the art of debate and political strategy. In one speech Daniel Webster said: "It is, sir, the people's Constitution, the people's government, made for the people, made by the people and answerable to the people."

The three covered wagons which Tom and Abe had been working on were finished. All had solid wheels made from boles of gum trees. About one wagon which had no iron parts at all, Abe commented: "I'm sure proud of this job." On that wagon they put the heaviest load. [14] By Sunday evening, February 28, three beds, the bureau, a table, a set of chairs, a clothes closet, cooking utensils, a pair of andirons, axes, carpenter's tools and some other things, were packed into the wagons. Then the three families—Lincolns, Hankses, Halls —went to the big two-story house of hewn-logs owned by James

Gentry, Sr., just east of Gentry's store. There they spent their last night on Spencer County soil. Next morning they returned to the Lincoln cabin.[15]

With the oxen hitched to the wagons and Abe's horse, Bulger, tied to the tail gate, everything was in readiness that first day of March 1830. Again, as in Kentucky, neighbors stood around talking; they didn't like to see the Lincolns leave.

Tom joked for a while, then glanced at the eastern horizon, "Folks, the sun is a-rising high in the sky. We got to be getting along." But Abe was missing. Looking in all directions, squinting his one good eye, Tom growled, "Where's that tarnal Abe?" No one answered. After a while someone said: "More'n likely he's off somewhere with a book." Bending an index finger in his mouth, Tom blew a shrill blast.

Down the hillside from Nancy Hanks Lincoln's grave, they saw Abraham coming, stumbling, rubbing his cheeks.

Tom Lincoln, with an ox-whip in his hand, showed impatience to be off to Illinois. But as he watched Abe he perhaps recalled the time back in December, 1816, when moving from Kentucky to Indiana, Nancy had come down with Sarah and Abraham from the Redmond graveyard on Muldraugh's stony hilltop.

Jimmy Grigsby whispered to someone in the crowd, "Watch old Tom flail him." Abe came up and stopped in front of his father. Neighbors craned their necks, eager to see what might happen. "Here, take this," said Tom matter of factly. He handed the whip to Abe, then waved an arm and shouted, "Start on!" [16] Abe stepped to the head of the column and cracked the whip in the frosty air.

The oxen leaned hard against their heavy yokes, stiffened their tails and pulled. Slowly the thick, solid wheels began rolling westward, creaking in the half-frozen mud. Tar buckets began swinging. Honey barked excitedly and jumped ahead of the oxen. Neighbors trudged alongside the wagons. The Lincolns were pulling out. In a poem Abe later wrote he called the event "that parting day." [17]

Three families, totaling 13 people, made up the caravan: Thomas Lincoln, 54; Sarah Bush Lincoln, 41; Abraham, 21; John D. Johnston, 14; Dennis Hanks, 31; his wife, Elizabeth Johnston Hanks, 23; their four children, Sarah Jane, Nancy Ann, Harriet and John Talbott, all under 9; Squire Hall and his wife, Matilda Johnston Hall, 19; and their 3 year old son, John.[18]

The movers followed the ridge road which walled out Pigeon Creek swamplands to the northward. Due to freezing and thawing, the road-bottom had dropped out, letting the wheels sink almost hub-deep into the stiff yellow mud; consequently, the stolid oxen drawing the heavily loaded wagons made barely two miles an hour.

When the movers reached Jones' store a shout went up from the men, women and children gathered there from miles around to say good-bye. "You're late," said William Jones. "Yes," Tom Lincoln answered, "one of my oxen strayed off last night and I had to hunt him. Found him up at Dave Turnham's." Tom had just sold about a hundred head of hogs and 450 bushels of corn to Turnham.[19]

In accordance with the early Indiana custom, as many neighbors as could leave their work went a Biblical day's journey with departing friends. So, on that parting day, the Lincolns were accompanied westward on the Corydon-Gentryville-Boonville road by men and boys: James Gentry, Sr., Joseph Gentry, John Romine, William Jones, James Grigsby, Nathaniel Grigsby, Redmond Grigsby, Hezekiah Harris, William Mason, Uriah Hartley, Jesse Isaacs, Robert Craig, William Roberts, John Kelly, and William Whittinghill. It is believed that John Tuley, Henry Brooner, John W. Lamar, and David Turnham also went a piece with the Lincolns. Turnham, who for 11 years had known Abe Lincoln intimately, wrote, "I never knew anything dishonorable of him." [20]

About a mile west of Jones' store and near the home of The Miracle Woman, the movers forded Pigeon Creek. The water was so high there that, "on account of the low wheels of the wagons, Mrs. Lincoln was taken across Pigeon Creek on a horse behind one of the neighbors." [21]

The Lincolns had now left Spencer County and entered Warrick. Mass Clark, with several Warrick County neighbors, greeted them on the creek's west bank.[22] "What road you going to take?" a Spencer County friend asked. "Were going by way of Boonville," Abe answered. "It is the only way we can go." [23]

Two miles farther westward the movers reached Pokeberry Creek. A temporary corduroy road of birch poles had to be built so the oxen could pull the wagons across. After helping the Lincolns to ford the stream, Mass Clark bade them farewell.

As darkness closed in on the mud-splattered travelers a wet, cold wind hummed through the leafless trees. But they kept on going. They passed through Lickskillet and Loafer's Station. Then their wagons mired down and had to be pried out. They struggled over Dividing Ridge. Just beyond Little Zion, sister church of Pigeon Creek, Brother Thomas Lincoln led his people off the road, halted and prepared to make camp for the night on Brother John Phillips' farm.

Edmund, Brother Phillips' son, ran out and accompanied them to the house.[24]

When no one was noticing Abe whispered to Nathaniel and Redmond Grigsby: "Boys, don't let anyone see this." He handed them a diary he had been keeping lately. "There are some things in there," he confided, "I would not want anyone to see." Possibly Abe was remorseful about some of his writings and was taking this means of explaining to the Grigsbys that he was sorry. Redmond Grigsby promised, "We'll take care of it." [25]

While the Lincoln-Hall-Hanks families were bedding down for the night at the Phillips house, Joseph Gentry, Hezekiah Harris and the three Grigsby boys, having gone the full Biblical day's journey, shook hands all around and started back toward their Pigeon Creek homes. Abe was reluctant to let them go; he walked between Nattie Grigsby and Joe Gentry far into the dark wilderness. Finally, Lincoln bade Nattie and Joe farewell, thus ending the three-way friendship which, begun in boyhood, had lasted through youth and into manhood.

Early Tuesday morning, March 2nd, the Lincoln caravan again was on the road. This time the movers must travel alone. Their groaning wagons broke through ice-crusted mudholes and made it hard going for the oxen. Swinging rhythmically back and forth like pendulums, slowly the tar-buckets ticked off Abe Lincoln's march toward greatness.

In the afternoon the movers reached Boonville, turned northward and followed the well-traveled state road which connected Newburgh on the Ohio with Vincennes on the Wabash. This highway bisected the Pocket Country. Mile posts and cheerful taverns lined its sides; road supervisors kept its corduroy sections in passable condition. Like the Lincolns, other movers were traveling its length, seeking new homes. Stage coaches lumbered by, spattering everybody with half-frozen mud. Mail coaches required 18 hours to travel from Boonville to Vincennes, a distance of only 62 miles.[26]

About dark the Lincolns made camp on Brother Joseph Langford's farm, three miles north of Boonville. Brother Langford and Brother Thomas Lincoln were close friends as well as fellow members of the Regular Baptist Association.[27]

On Wednesday Abe began peddling the notions he had brought along from Jones' store. "I didn't have a large stock, but I charged large prices. I made money," he said.[28] He sold a pocket-book and some tableware to Solomon Turpen who lived three miles north of the

Langford farm. In the pocket-book was pasted a piece of paper bearing the words: "A. Lincoln, Agent." [29]

Eight miles farther north, after crossing bridges over Otter and Big Creeks, the Lincolns halted for a brief visit with Nicholas Anderson Hanks, a cousin of Abraham's mother. [30] Again the movers pushed on. To their left lay Indiana's wild Buckskin country. Over-flow land sheeted with ice made traveling exceedingly hard for the weary oxen. To make the pulling easier, the men-folk scooped tar out of the buckets and greased the wooden axles. Evening found the Lincoln-Hall-Hanks caravan ten miles farther northward and camped at Millseat, a Patoka River crossing. There Abe tried to sell something to visitors— Benjamin Ashby, a 35 year old man, and Arthur Thompson, a 14 year old boy, but neither one had any money; Abe traded a pocket-knife to Thompson for some hides. [31]

Because of the treacherous condition of the road between the Patoka and White Rivers, the Lincolns traveled barely ten miles on Thursday. Since it was very hazardous to try to ford streams after dark, Tom Lincoln decided to leave the state road and make camp at White Oak Spring Fort. Here Abe saw a blockhouse built to shelter travelers and others fleeing from troublesome Indians. A family living near the fort brought a pone of cornbread to the Lincolns.

Friday was a very trying day for the movers until they crossed the broad, swollen White River at Rocky Ford near Petersburg. Then they followed the winding ridge road up one hill and down another. [32] Late in the afternoon they came to a small farmhouse. While the oxen rested Abe took his peddler's kit to the door and was met by a red-faced woman carrying a whip. Behind her stood her husband, a mild-looking, tow-headed man. Abe saw the place was full of children ranging in age from 17 months to 17 years. Almost all seemed to be crying. The woman barked, "What do you want?" "Nothing, madam," said Lincoln. "I merely dropped by to see how things were going." "Well, you needn't wait!" she snapped. "There's trouble here and lots of it, but I can manage my own affairs without the help of outsiders." "I can see that," said Abe. "This is just a friendly row," she raced on. "But I'll teach these brats their place if I have to lick the hide off of every one of them!" Abe nodded and stepped back out of range of the whip. "I don't do much talking," she claimed, "but I run this house. And I don't want no sneaking around a-trying to find out how I do it, either!" [33]

Again Lincoln nodded and walked back to the covered wagons. The movers pulled away from the warring cabin and struck the cres-

cent hills walling in part of Vincennes. To their left was the great,
flat-topped mound which Indians had used in their sun-worshipping
rites. They descended the long slope, entered the old town and halted
on the banks of the Wabash.

Since tires of one wagon needed setting, Tom Lincoln camped near
Slawson's blacksmith shop and the printing office of the Vincennes
Western Sun. Back of their camp loomed Vincennes University which
Abe's friend, William Jones, had attended. Up the river a few rods
was Governor William Henry Harrison's mansion where, Abe had been
told, Chief Tecumseh's quarrel with Harrison over the Ten O'Clock
Line Treaty had brought on the Battle of Tippecanoe, and destroyed
forever the hopes of any successful Indian confederacy.

On Saturday morning Tom and Abe rolled their wagon wheels into
the blacksmith's shop. There Jesse Slawson, a native of Maine, known
as "the old man of them all," ran his tire-measuring wheel around the
outside and inside the rims to determine the amount of iron to be cut
out. After the tires had been heated glowing hot in the forge Slawson
placed them on the hardy of his anvil and let Tom and Abe take turns
at swinging the hand-hammer.[34] That job done Abe strolled over to
the *Western Sun* office where for the first time he saw a printing
press. The editor, Elihu Stout, was setting type. Abe watched him
lock the forms with wooden wedges, pat down the ink with balls and
start printing the newspaper.

Since 1823 Abe had been reading Stout's paper in Jones' store at
Gentryville. It was the only newspaper Abe had regularly read.[35]
From Jones, Lincoln had heard much about Stout, who, perhaps more
than any other man, molded public opinion in Indiana. Heavy
shouldered, stern faced, courageous Elihu Stout, born fifty-eight years
before in Newark, New Jersey, was a friend to both Henry Clay and
Andrew Jackson. He had begun editing the *Indiana Gazette* at Vincennes, July 31, 1804; had been burned out; and had resumed publication under the name of *Western Sun & General Advertizer*, July 4,
1807.

With growing interest Lincoln watched Stout operate the Adam
Ramage hand press. Made of Honduras mahogany, the press had an
iron screw and wooden platen faced with brass. Two pulls of the big
lever and two turns of the bed crank were required to print one
side of the soft, moist paper.[36] The longer Abe watched the more
he hankered to experience the feel of printing words. He moved in
a little closer and offered to help; the editor stepped aside.

Lincoln grasped the lever and began working the press on which

Stout had printed the Statutes of Indiana Territory. That Saturday, March 6, 1830, issue of the *Western Sun* Abe helped print contained sixteen columns of advertisement, poetry, news, philosophy, and laws of the State of Indiana. Page one devoted three columns to a recent act of the Indiana legislature concerning the building of the Wabash and Erie Canal. There was a news story about a farmer who had just been scalped by the Indians. A brief history of Indiana closed column four. Page two carried a news story of great local interest: "Gen. Wm. H. Harrison, late minister to Columbia, had arrived at New York"; President Jackson's hickory broom had swept Old Tip out of office.

Page three disclosed that a tall, slim young woman with dark eyes and very black hair had been left in Vincennes "by an elderly man and his son because their carriage had broken down." Since the young lady was "totally deranged" hope was expressed that friends or relatives reading the story would do something about "this unfortunate female."

Under the heading "Poetical Asylum," on page four, was an original poem of seventeen stanzas satirizing "Them Yankys the bane of the nashun" who were bound for Texas "jist like Old Eden." The arrival and departure of the mails was also noted on page four. Mail was due from Louisville on Tuesday, Thursday, and Saturday; from St. Louis on Wednesday, Friday, and Sunday. An essay on seven as a significant number reminded readers that Hippocrates, like Shakespeare, divided the life of man into seven ages. While working for David Turnham, Abe Lincoln had read in *As You Like It* Jaques' whole speech on man's seven ages. Did the *Western Sun* essay set Abe to speculating on the number seven in his own life? His given and surnames each contained seven letters. He had entered Indiana at the age of seven and was leaving at 21 (three 7's). His sister, Sarah, had died at 21; his mother at 35 (five 7's).[37]

After helping to print the paper and after talking with the editor, Abe had a better understanding of a statement by Stout in the *Sun* a few months before: "Every man should have a newspaper in his family if he justly values his rights as a citizen of a free republic."[38]

The Lincolns soon discovered that Sunday in Vincennes was a noisy, carefree day. From the five thousand acre common field, bordering the town and cultivated after old French custom, farmers trooped in to mingle hilariously with travelers, *coureurs de bois,* gamblers, and cutthroats. They walked the wide streets, sometimes making passes at black eyed Creole girls. They fired guns. They crowded into taverns, drank wine and danced with gay women while fiddlers scraped out

*Albert T. Reid's conception of Lincoln
in the Vincennes Western Sun office.*

merry tunes. Blacksmiths blew and hammered—all making the Lord's Day close kin to a witch's sabbath.[39]

In spite of the biting cold, Tom Lincoln broke camp on Monday morning, March 8, 1830, and headed his people for Haines' ferry. They passed Captain Peter Jones' tavern, at whose door Negro slaves were illegally sold; passed Territorial Hall from which the Old Northwest and Louisiana Territories had been governed. They took a good look at the abandoned bank which had swallowed up Tom Lincoln's deposits. Before them rose Saint Xavier's Cathedral, set against the wide, sweeping bend of the Wabash River.[40] They gazed at the ruins of the old fort George Rogers Clark and his American Long Knives had wrested from British General "Hair Buyer" Hamilton's Red Coats in February, 1779.

The Lincoln-Hall-Hanks caravan drove down onto the ferry and crossed the Wabash from Indiana into Illinois. The river was so high that water covered the road and the low prairie. Abe picked up his little dog, Honey, and climbed into one of the wagons, but Honey jumped out, fell on a thin sheet of ice, broke through and was drowning. Abe leaped into the waist-deep water and seized the feist. "I saved him," he said.[41] The oxen, breasting the icy flood waters, leaned hard against their yokes, and resumed pulling the Lincolns towards John Hanks and the Promised Land.

Abe Lincoln's life in Indiana had drawn to a close. He had entered the state when only a child, passed through adolescence and, several weeks before, had reached the legal age of 21. During that character-forming period he had experienced great sorrows and some joys. Back on Pigeon Creek he had seen his mother and sister buried. Here he had gone to subscription schools and had read widely. He had become familiar with what some people considered a complete library: the Bible, Blackstone's Commentaries, and Shakespeare's plays.[42] He had been news commentator for the Jones' store customers. He had composed poetry, prose, and a song. He had seen some of his writings in print. He had mounted stumps and out-preached preachers. He had been in and out of puppy love. He had heard prominent lawyers plead cases; he had been hauled into court as defendant; he had read some law; and he had won the "gray goose" case. He had been a deputy constable, militiaman, ferryman, flatboatman, farm hand, church sexton, carpenter's helper, whiskey-still worker, hog butcher, and rail splitter. Yet "When I became of age I did not know much," he said.[43]

He had been recognized as the undisputed champion fist-fighter in a rough locality. He had been mistakenly considered dead. He had learned to clog-dance. He had observed at close range successful office-seekers and had been Hoosierized in politics. He had become a follower of Henry Clay. He had listened to Utopian socialistic discussions. He had been to New Orleans. He had worked along-side black men in Arkansas and in Kentucky. He had seen slavery at its best and at its worst. For the past six years he had repeatedly heard the slavery issue advanced as a reason for dissolving the Union. He had helped print an issue of the Vincennes *Western Sun.* He had heard voices. And he had vowed, "I will study and get ready and some day my chance will come."

CHAPTER THIRTEEN

LASTING IMPRESSIONS

Abe Lincoln lost the last of his baby teeth, passed through chaotic adolescence, and entered manhood while living in the Pigeon Creek community of Spencer County, Indiana. Those were his formative years; they were from late seven to early twenty-one, the period which psychologists and psychiatrists recognize as the time when much of man's basic personality is formed, the time when man's faculties for reasoning and analyzing mature.[1] Lincoln himself seems to have recognized this as a particularly important period of his life. Speaking at Trenton, as President-elect, he told the New Jersey Senate: "You all know, for you all have been boys, how those early impressions last longer than any others." The same idea cropped out when, as President, he told the 140th Indiana Volunteer Regiment: "I was born in Kentucky, raised in Indiana, lived in Illinois." From all these places came experiences which influenced his later life.

Lincoln's sorrows, pleasures and pains, loves and hates, observations of people, the schools he attended and the books he read, the arguments he listened to over slavery and the threats to the Union, the religious rites he watched, the neighborhood superstitions he encountered, the dreams he heard repeated, the sounds he heard in the dark woods—these fragments of his daily life in the Hoosier State buried themselves deep in his youthful mind; in his Presidential years they bobbed to the surface and influenced his behavior and speech. As President, for example, he called deserter cases his "leg cases." A deserter had legged it safely off to Mexico; when the President approved his courtmartial sentence he observed: "We will condemn him as they sell hogs in Indiana, 'as they run.'"[2] He picked up his fellow backwoodsman's notions of freedom and property rights: "A man has the right to do anything but injure his neighbor." William Jones, storekeeper at Gentryville, had watched Lincoln grow up and had chatted with him in the White House. "Mr. Lincoln," Jones boasted proudly, "laid the foundation of his character in Spencer County, Indiana."[3]

During his Presidential years Lincoln often needed courage to withstand bickering friends and scheming enemies. Some of that courage came from memories of the scene in the log cabin on Pigeon Creek, when his mother lay dying on the cornshuck tick in the corner. "I am going away, Abraham, and I shall not return," he heard her say. "Live as I have taught you. Love your heavenly Father." He saw lines of pain cut across her tired face, but he saw no hint of fear in her gray eyes. It may have been the memory of his mother's courage as she faced death that helped him to declare, "When the time comes for dealing with slavery, I trust I shall be willing to act though it cost my life." [4]

*   *   *

Memories of Lincoln's Indiana days were as much a part of him as his long shin bones and his quiet humor. How tenaciously he clung to those memories was demonstrated on the eve of his fifty-second birthday when, as President-elect, he was on his way to Washington, D.C. Upon entering Indiana he spoke of his early residence in Spencer County. At Lafayette he talked of the great changes in the state since his boyhood. At Thornton he was telling a tale when his train began pulling out and people ran alongside to hear him end the story. At Indianapolis, after telling a crowd of 20,000 people, "I grew to my present enormous height in this state," he urged: "Constantly bear in mind that not with Presidents not with office-seekers, but with you is the question: Shall the liberties of this country be preserved to the latest generations?" [5]

A forty-three year old man pushed through the crowd, waved a hat and yelled: "Abe Lincoln! The flatboat trip! Cunningham!" Police grabbed him. "Abe! The trunk! The trunk!" the man shouted.

"That's Jimmy Cunningham!" the President-elect called to the policemen. "Let him through!"

"Abe, I still got your trunk. Couldn't put off at Rockport. What you want me to do with it?" Jimmy had kept it since 1829.

"Keep it, Jimmy," said Lincoln. "Keep it until I call for it." [6]

The next day—his fifty-second birthday—Lincoln spent traveling across southern Indiana. The February sun shone brilliantly on his special train all the way. At Greensburg, John Doakes handed him a big red apple. A while later he passed a little east of Blue Creek where members of Uncle Josiah Lincoln's family still lived. There he had borrowed William B. Johnson's copy of *Pilgrim's Progress*.

Lincoln's train stopped briefly at Lawrenceburg. Again in his old boyhood environment and feeling very much at home, the President-elect looked across the slow-moving Ohio River to Kentucky and promised a tumultuous audience, "The power entrusted to me shall be exercised as perfectly to protect the rights of your neighbors across the river as to protect yours on this side. My power is temporary and fleeting. Yours is as eternal as the principles of liberty." [7] Those were the last words he spoke on Hoosier soil.

Following the inaugural ceremonies in Washington, people lined up at the White House to shake President Lincoln's hand. Among them were five of Lincoln's former Gentryville neighbors, including William Jones. Cordially Lincoln greeted the first four men by name and asked how the folks were back at Pigeon Creek. But when Jones came up the President decided to have a little fun. Casually he took the storekeeper's hand and pretended not to know him. Disturbed by this Jones exclaimed, "Mr. President, I'm from Gentryville! My name is Jones. Reckon you don't remember me." Lincoln grinned: "Oh, yes, Mr. Jones, I remember you very well." Then he bent down and whispered, "And I remember that shoe transaction." [8]

After Fort Sumter had been fired upon and the country was greatly excited, William Jones wrote to the President: "Sir, a number of the sons of your old friends have formed themselves into a volunteer company and selected their officers and have been using every effort to get into the U.S. Service but have failed. They urge that your old resident County should be represented in the Army and swear that death or victory is their motto. And ask through you an entrance into the Army. They are willing to March to any point to be received. Three of them are my sons. Annexed you have their appeal."

Calling themselves the Spencer Legion, the boys, in their appeal, told the President that they wanted "to get into the U.S. Service either 3 years or during the war and feel that we have been wronged by our Adjutant Gen'l." They concluded with: "Any place you may assign us in the Union we will never dishonor your early residence in Old Spencer." [9] Among the names signed to the letter were, besides those of Jones' three sons, some which Lincoln recalled as those of Pigeon Creek families: Grigsby, Richardson, Crawford, Turnham, Blackford, Clark, Taylor, Ray.

Touched by this eagerness of sons of his former neighbors to help him preserve the Union, President Lincoln requested the Secretary of War to accept four additional Indiana regiments. "Probably they should come from the triangular region between the Ohio & Wabash rivers, including my old boyhood home," he wrote on June 17th. [10]

The regiments were accepted. William Jones, then past sixty, served as Lieutenant Colonel of the 53rd Indiana Volunteers.[11]

But not all appeals to President Lincoln were calculated to help him, as is shown by that of a committee of reformers who, ranting against General Grant's liquor drinking, urged that he be recalled from command. Lincoln good-naturedly asked, "Gentlemen, can you tell me where General Grant procures his whiskey? If I can find out I will send every general in the field a barrel of it!" [12]

As a boy Lincoln had spent his first winter in Indiana under the eves of the Grigsby still-house; the youthful Lincoln, just turned twenty-one, used part of his last winter in the state firing John Dutton's whiskey still, a little way north up a hollow. The intervening years he had spent among sturdy Hoosier pioneers who were by necessity tolerant of drinking. So, although Lincoln was not a drinking man, he was quite able to assess Grant's military worth without being alarmed about the General's drinking habits.

One Sunday morning Senator Charles Sumner roamed the White House looking for the President. When he found him he was outraged at what he saw. "Why, Mr. President!" he exploded. "Do you black your own boots?" Responded Lincoln: "Senator, whose boots do you think I black?" [13] The self-reliant Lincoln who mended his own footgear with the Widow McFarland's cobbler tools back on Pigeon Creek had remained the same unassuming Lincoln in the White House.

While he was being reared in Indiana, Lincoln rubbed shoulders with the great and small of the frontier. Of all those whom he encountered, perhaps none had more to do with forming his character than the Grigsby family and William Jones. Of course, there were the Gentrys, Turnhams, Oskins, Romines, Brooners, Halls, Crawfords, Richardsons, Lamars, Azel W. Dorsey, William Wood, John Pitcher, Ratcliff Boon, Squire Pate, Joseph Lane, Daniel Grass, and others who influenced him. But it was the Grigsbys whom Abe met first when he arrived at Pigeon Creek. It was Aaron, eldest of the houseful of Grigsby children, who chose Abe's only sister, Sarah, for his wife. It was the Lincoln-Grigsby contact, running all the way from friendship to fist-fights and back again to solid friendship, that inspired Lincoln to make the most successful of his early literary efforts. When the Civil War broke out the Grigsbys, to a man, joined or tried to join the Northern Army to help "Abe Linkern," save the Union.

William Jones, too, proved himself a stanch Union man by disregarding his personal feelings toward slavery as an institution and aligning himself with Lincoln the moment war began. How much the suave, friendly, sensible Jones influenced Lincoln's opinions regarding the rising problems of slavery and preservation of the Union probably cannot be overestimated. Son of a well-to-do Vincennes slave-holder, Jones had been educated at Vincennes University with proceeds derived from slave-labor. At his store in Gentryville, beginning in 1823, he regularly supplied Lincoln with newspapers to read and an audience to whom Lincoln could tell what he had read. Conceivably, however, the same basic Hoosier training which persuaded William Jones to place the value of the Union above his personal gain planted in Abraham Lincoln's mind the conviction that at whatever cost to himself and to the American people, the Union must be preserved.

That man is controlled by the designs of Providence, the doctrine of Abe's parents and neighbors along Pigeon Creek, had abided with Lincoln the President. "I hold myself as an instrument of Providence," he declared in 1862. "I am conscious every moment that all I have is subject to the control of a Higher Power." [14] As the war wore on he more and more felt himself selected by that Higher Power to save the nation. "God selects His own instruments, and sometimes they are queer ones; for instance He chose me to steer the ship through a great crisis." [15]

Steadfastly Lincoln believed in his own destiny. Once after reading Deuteronomy III: 22-27, he remarked that the oftener he read those words "the more, it seems to me, that God has written them for me as well as for Moses. Has He not taken me from my poor log cabin, by the hand, as He did Moses in the reeds of the Nile, and put me at the head of the greatest and most blessed of modern nations just as He put that prophet at the head of the most blessed nation of ancient time?" [16]

During his formative years Lincoln read in his parents' Ostervald Bible the footnotes to Exodus II and Isaiah XLV relating how Moses by direction of Divine Providence had led his people from the tyranny of the Egyptians. In a footnote to Exodus III he found: "Reflection upon this chapter regards the manner of God's calling Moses and revealing His design to make him the deliverer of his people Israel. By the miracle of the burning bush, which Moses saw in flames without its being consumed, God was pleased to engage his attention, and to convince him that He was there in a peculiar manner present."

To Henry C. Whitney, Lincoln confided that when he was a boy he used to wander by himself into the dark, silent Indiana forest. "I knew I was not alone," he said. "I heard voices. Once I heard a voice right at my elbow. Heard it distinctly and plainly. I turned around expecting to see someone. No one was there. But the voice was there." [17] Was the voice the same Moses heard in the burning bush? Did Lincoln ever hear the voice again after leaving Indiana? Following the disastrous Second Battle of Bull Run, Lincoln told a friend: "I have talked with God. It is His cause, and the Union is His. As He willeth, so it will be." [18]

Was Lincoln's feeling of having direct communication with the Almighty derived from what he had heard regarding the Saints of the Lord at Pigeon Creek Church? To the demand that he issue the Emancipation Proclamation at once, he answered the Religious Denominations Committee of Chicago: "If it is probable that God would reveal His will to others on a point so connected with my duty, it might be supposed that He would reveal it directly to me; for, unless I am more deceived in myself than I often am, it is my earnest desire to know the will of Providence in this matter. And if I can learn what it is, I will do it." [19]

Anxious at all times to act wisely in order to re-unite the nation, President Lincoln sought the religious guidance offered him when a boy. Instinctively he looked back to his early experiences for help. Morning after morning, between four and five o'clock, he knelt in the White House and prayed: "Oh God, I cannot see my way clear. Give me light. I am ignorant. Give me wisdom." [20] His appeal to the Almighty closely followed the pattern of words used when, struggling for enlightenment in his youth, he opened "Brush College" by saying to James Grigsby: "There is no darkness but ignorance, Jimmy, and there is darkness in my soul." For him the way had grown dark in 1864 and he was fearful.

But Lincoln did not fear personal harm. Although many about him were panic-stricken in mid-July of that year, when General Jubal E. Early's Confederate infantry and artillery appeared in front of Fort Stevens at the north entrance to Washington, D.C., Lincoln did not flinch. He went to the fort and, while bullets zinged about his head, he calmly watched the battle. "I have all my life been a fatalist," he told Isaac Arnold. "What is to be will be, or rather, I have found all my life as Hamlet says,

> 'There is a divinity that shapes our ends
> 'Rough-hew them how we will'." [21]

Like his mother and like Generals Washington and Marion, whose biographies he had read during his boyhood, President Lincoln had little fear of death. When his friends, thinking assassins might attack him, tried to persuade him to cease his lonely strolls in the dead of night he was heedless. In his heart he continued to cling to the simple Primitive Baptist doctrine of his Pigeon Creek neighbors.[22]

Yet while Lincoln had little fear of death for himself, he refused to sign the death warrants of twenty-four deserters, arguing, "There are already too many weeping widows in the United States." His religious training, received while attending Pigeon Creek Church, and his attitude toward the values of life, gained from books he read in that neighborhood, had asserted themselves. In Dr. Matthew Hole's *Practical Discourses Upon All the Collects, Epistles and Gospels,* which he had borrowed from the Tuley family north of Gentryville, Lincoln read Hole's explanation for the tenth Sunday after Trinity: "From our Saviour's weeping over Jerusalem, we may observe his tender Sense and Concern for the Miseries of other Men. We learn of his . . . Willingness to pardon." In his Scott's *Lessons* he had read the speech of Lucius: "Already our quarrels have fill'd the world with widows and orphans. Sythia mourns." Lincoln's concern for the miseries of other men showed itself in his numerous refusals to add to the increasing number of weeping widows and in his many other acts of mercy.

Despite those acts of mercy, however, and despite his public acknowledgments that he considered himself an instrument of Providence and relied for guidance upon a Higher Power, Lincoln's enemies raised the cry that he had no religion. Without rancor he answered them: "My religion is like that of an old man named Glenn, in Indiana, whom I heard speak at a church meeting. 'When I do good, I feel good; when I do bad I feel bad. And that's my religion.' "[23]

During his growing-up days in Indiana, Lincoln attended about three full terms of the community's subscription schools. To attain his goal of being somebody, as he put it, he supplemented his brief formal schooling with reading books and establishing "Brush College" where he further taught himself by reading aloud to James Grigsby. To learn some elements of the law he borrowed and read Constable David Turnham's *Revised Laws of Indiana* and Sheriff John Pitcher's *Commentaries* by Blackstone. He always strove to improve his education. "I will study and get ready and some day my chance will come," he said at sixteen, while working for Elizabeth and Josiah Crawford.

He attained his highest ambition and entered the Presidency just as the Civil War threatened to destroy the Union. To the quarreling North and South he cautioned: "Suppose you go to war, you cannot fight always; and when, after much loss on both sides, and no gain on either, you cease fighting, the identical old questions of intercourse are again upon you. My countrymen, one and all, think calmly and well upon this whole subject. Nothing valuable can be lost by taking time. We are not enemies but friends."

Those words were similar to the ones he had used so effectively in the gray goose trial back at Gentryville when he made use of his meager knowledge of the law for the first time. To his quarreling Hoosier neighbors he had said, "After you have had your trial today, no matter which way it goes what has either of you gained? I tell you that whichever one wins is going to lose! You'll lose your friendship for one another. I'd get together here and now. Make up and be friends." But, unlike the folk at Gentryville, the North and South would not get together and be friends. Consequently, Secessionist batteries fired upon Fort Sumter, April 12, 1861, and the War Between the States opened.

In his mature life Lincoln sometimes felt the handicap of not having a formal legal training. He had picked up his knowledge of law here and there, just anywhere he could find it. And this hit-and-miss method of education reminded him of the similar hit-and-miss feeding of wild hogs in the Indiana wilderness: rooting here and there for acorns, pignuts, beechnuts, and other mast. He remembered, too, that they made a poor showing when compared with regularly corn-fed farm animals. So when a prominent lawyer, visiting him in the White House, said, "We do not forget that you too, Mr. President, are a distinguished member of the bar," Lincoln humbly ranged himself alongside the wild hogs. "Oh, I'm only a mast-fed lawyer," he replied.[24]

Of all the prominent lawyers who came to the White House asking favors, perhaps the one Lincoln least expected was John A. Breckenridge, defense attorney in the hog-stealing murder case at the Boonville, Indiana, courthouse. Mr. Breckenridge offered his hand to the President. "Yes, sir," said Lincoln, "I'll shake hands with you even if you would not shake hands with me." Recalling Breckenridge's impassioned plea to the jury, Lincoln added: "Mr. Breckenridge, that was the best speech that up to that time I had ever heard. If I could, as I then thought, make as good a speech as that my soul would be satisfied."[25]

In December, 1862, John Pitcher, former sheriff at Rockport, Indiana, the man who had lent young Lincoln law books, came to the White House at Lincoln's invitation. Pitcher, now a judge, talked about his son, Thomas G., a Regular Army captain. The officer had been cited for gallantry in action in both the Mexican and Civil Wars and had been so severely wounded at Cedar Mountain that he was still in a hospital. Lincoln, wanting to do something for the captain, asked the judge for suggestions. In a letter written Christmas Day while on his way home, the Judge explained that it was a "most embarrassing duty" to answer the President's request. "In regards to my son's renomination," he wrote, "I have not been in the habit of asking favors and don't [know] how to do it well." Lincoln overlooked the judge's embarrassment and promoted Thomas to the rank of brevet brigadier general.[26]

In his eloquent and immortal Gettysburg Address the following November Lincoln described the United States as "a new nation conceived in liberty and dedicated to the proposition that all men are created equal." He had first read the words "all men are created equal" in David Turnham's copy of *The Revised Laws of Indiana*. Later he referred to that phrase as the "electric cord in the Declaration." And when in his Gettysburg Address he averred that "this nation, under God, shall have a new birth of freedom," he reached back, perhaps subconsciously, to a phrase he had read in Josiah Crawford's copy of David Ramsay's *Life of Washington*. While the British Army lay at Staten Island, General Washington had told his countrymen: "The time is near at hand which must probably determine whether Americans are to be freemen or slaves—the fate of unborn millions now depends, *under God,* on the courage and conduct of this army."

When Lincoln closed his Gettysburg speech with "that Government of the people, by the people, for the people" he rephrased Daniel Webster's reply of January 18, 1830, to Robert Y. Hayne in the U.S. Senate: "It is, sir, the people's government, made for the people, made by the people, and answerable to the people." Lincoln admired Webster's speech so much he called it "the grandest specimen of American oratory."[27] From it he gleaned many of his arguments for the preservation of the Union. Lincoln's attention had been called to Webster's speech by the editor of the Vincennes *Western Sun*.

Even in his rugged humor, for which he became well known, Lincoln showed much evidence of his Hoosier life and education. One morning, after considerable hominy had been ordered for Federal troops, the President casually remarked to his Cabinet that at last he saw how the word hominy originated. He noticed "it came from the Latin word *homo*, a man," he said. Then pleased that his scholarly Secretary of State, Governor Seward, appeared astonished, Lincoln explained:

"When we decline *homo* it is:

> *homo*, a man
> *hominis*, of man
> *homini*, for men

"So you see hominy being 'for men' comes from the Latin." [28]

Eating hominy along Pigeon Creek had left an indelible mark on Lincoln's memory. Nattie Grigsby wasn't exaggerating when he told friends: "Abe and me many a time et hominy and fat pork together." [29]

Throughout his life Lincoln ate sparingly, adhering to the advice of Socrates he had read in Scott's *Lessons*: "We should eat and drink in order to live, instead of living as many do, in order to eat and drink." In the White House President Lincoln seldom had more than an egg and a cup of coffee for breakfast and a glass of milk, some bread and fruit for luncheon. Whether it was due to his careful eating or his other temperate habits, Lincoln retained far into manhood much of the great physical strength of his youth. With thumb and forefinger the President once grasped the extreme end of the handle of a heavy axe and held it at arm's length—an almost unbelieveable feat of strength. [30] "When I was eighteen years of age I could do this," he told General Egbert W. Veile. "And I have never seen the day since I could not do it." According to numerous stories, Abraham Lincoln was unbelieveably strong from about seventeen years onward.

Besides his great strength and early eating habits, the "blab-school" practice of his youth carried over into Lincoln's mature life. Occasional evidence of this practice was especially noticed by Superintendent Chandler of the War Department telegraph office. To keep in touch with Grant and his other generals, Lincoln often went to Chandler's office to send them messages. "His lips moving, frequently he spoke a sentence aloud or in a half whisper," Chandler recalled. When satisfied he had the proper expressions the President would write out his messages. Inserts and erasures were few, for he had carefully selected his words and arranged them in proper sequence in his mind before putting them on paper.

Lincoln made such good use of this habit in his early political campaigns that by the time he was nominated for the Presidency in 1860 his speeches were widely recognized as having great power of expression. His House-Divided speech, his debates with Stephen A. Douglas, and his Columbus, Ohio, speech had attracted so much attention in the East that he was invited to New York to deliver the Cooper Union Address. After listening to him, Professor John P. Galliver of Andover, Massachusetts, asked him how he had gained such a knowledge of the English language. "Well," replied Lincoln, "if I have any power that way, I will tell you how I suppose I came to get it. You see when I was a boy over in Indiana, all the local politicians used to come to our cabin to discuss politics with my father. After they left, I'd lay awake for hours just a-putting their ideas into words so that the boys around our way could understand." [31]

While putting political ideas into understandable words for the boys around his way, Lincoln noticed that when the Bible was quoted it produced an emotional effect on his adult Pigeon Creek neighbors. He also saw it happen in his own home when, after listening to visiting preachers on those Sundays his stepmother could not attend church, he returned and quoted to her, verbatim, the sermons he had heard. This habit fastened in his memory many verses of the Bible. All of his great speeches and letters reveal the influence of Biblical phrasing.

Probably his first experiment with Bible idiom was his "Adam and Eve's Wedding Song" written for the marriage of his sister Sarah to Aaron Grigsby in 1826. He made the Garden of Eden short-rib operation fit the version in Genesis and when his neighbors liked it so well that they memorized it he sensed a new and effective use for the Scripture.

Several years later he experimented again. This time he wanted to retaliate for not having been invited to the Grigsby double-wedding infare—he had been at outs with the elder Grigsbys since his sister had died in childbirth—so he wrote a satire and called it the "First Chronicles of Reuben" or the "Book of Chronicles." With calculated artistry he copied the rhythmic, smooth-flowing prose style of the Old Testament. He scattered copies of his piece around Gentryville and heard his neighbors laugh at the Grigsby affair, the precise effect he desired. Eventually differences with the Grigsbys were patched up. "No family after this loved Lincoln so well. We all voted for him," Nathaniel Grigsby proudly related. [32]

Thus, at twenty, Abraham Lincoln had discovered how to arouse a whole community to merriment. His Pigeon Creek neighborhood had become for him a literary workshop where he experimented with words and watched people's reactions to them. His study of the art of phrase-making, begun in Indiana, lasted to the day of his death.

Lincoln's statement that when he was a boy in Indiana "all the local politicians" used to come to his cabin covers a period of time when some of the politicians were emerging as prominent state builders. Some of them even appeared in Lincoln's later races for office. Early contacts with them undoubtedly helped him to appraise their actions and motives.

Only a few days before Lincoln was nominated for President on the Republican ticket in 1860 a former neighbor, Joseph Lane, was nominated for Vice President on the Breckenridge Seceder's ticket. Even though the Breckenridge-Lane ticket put a second Democratic slate of candidates into the field, thereby splitting the party, a less able politician than Lincoln might have been defeated. But Lincoln knew a lot about Lane and Lane's methods; this knowledge he found useful when he felt he had to suggest to visiting delegations how they might pour a little more water on his own political wheel.

Joseph Lane, now a U.S. Senator from Oregon, had attained an office Lincoln had wanted a few years before: Governor of the Territory of Oregon. Back in Lincoln's Pigeon Creek days, Lane had helped considerably in sweetening Ratcliff Boon of Warrick County. Long after Boon quit fighting the local political machine and had been elected Lieutenant Governor of Indiana (subsequently becoming Governor) the spirit of his simple, direct political announcements stuck with Lincoln. During Lincoln's first race for the Illinois legislature in 1832 his appeal had Lane's simplicity: "I have no wealthy or popular relations or friends to recommend me. My case is thrown exclusively upon the independent voters of the country." Boon had told Indiana voters: "In presenting myself to you I have nothing to claim through my ancestors, but alone depend on what may be thought I justly merit." [32a]

As a youngster Abe developed an easy familiarity with Governor Boon, state legislator Joseph Lane, and other members of the governing body of Indiana when they rode by the Lincoln home on their way to the state capital at Corydon. Waving at the Governor and legislators, asking them for the latest news, Abe grew up with a high regard for political offices but with little awe of the men who held them.

In the White House Lincoln was neither servile nor pompous. During the summer of 1863, his secretary John Hay, who was born

in Indiana a little way north of the home of Josiah Lincoln, Abraham's
uncle, wrote that the President "is managing this war, the draft,
foreign relations, and planning a reconstruction of the Union, all in one.
The old man sits here and wields like a backwoods Jupiter the bolts of
war and the machinery of the government." [33]   The model of that
"backwoods Jupiter" could easily have been Ratcliff Boon, whom
young Abe and his Hoosier neighbors called King of Warrick.

In an attempt during the Presidential campaign to play down Lincoln's popularity in order to boost that of Lane, the Evansville
(Indiana) *Enquirer*, June 26, 1860, printed in Lincoln's boyhood
country, editorialized: "The great argument in favor of Lincoln con-
sists of his having split a few fence rails in his earlier days. Joe Lane,
the seceders' candidate for Vice President, used to split cordwood in
Vanderburgh County and if he continues as a candidate we predict
a thousand cords of wood can be found as examples of old Joe's handicraft."

Rivermen who remembered Lincoln as one of themselves because of
of his flatboat trips down the Ohio ignored Lane and took up the
fight for Lincoln. According to the Evansville *Journal* (June 23, 1860),
the men had lashed to the bows of their flatboats "a huge rail, about
twenty feet high, near the top of which appears an axe and maul,
crossed, forming an excellent representation of the Lincoln coat of
arms." Other supporters hired an artist to paint a six-by-ten foot
picture of Lincoln splitting rails in Indiana. Hoisting it on a long pole
they carried it, banner fashion, to political rallies throughout the
Hoosier State.[34] This must have reminded Candidate Lincoln of the
Adams-Jackson campaign of 1828, when he and fellow Pigeon Creekers
set up hickory poles and wildly danced and whooped around them.

As the 1860 Presidential campaign grew hotter Lincoln's political
enemies resolutely dug into his Indiana years for material with which
to substantiate rumors being circulated against him. Some of his old
time Spencer County pro-slavery enemies joined in the fight by
whispering a rumor that thirty years before they had heard Storekeeper Jones of Gentryville swear, "Abe Lincoln has slid! That
damned rascal has run off with my goods!" They referred, of course,
to the notions and other items Abe had obtained on credit at Jones'
store to peddle along the highway from Indiana to Illinois. In the
September 20, 1860, *Rockport* (Indiana) *Planter*, William Jones
denied ever having said it and branded the tale slanderous and a lie.
The tale so angered William Grigsby, the man with whom Lincoln had
quarreled over the spotted pup, that he belligerently stalked Buck

Horn Valley, challenging, "I'll whip anyone who dares to speak one word against my old friend, Abe Linkern."

Temporarily in Missouri, Nathaniel Grigsby wrote to Lincoln. In answering Nattie, after telling the news of his family, Lincoln added: "There is now a Republican electoral ticket in Missouri, so that you can vote for me if your neighbors will let you . . . I would advise you not to get into any trouble about it. Give my regards to your brother Charlie." Charles was one of the double-wedding bridegrooms whom Lincoln had lampooned in the "Chronicles of Reuben." [35]

Over at Springfield, Illinois, Lincoln received material evidence that he had other loyal friends on Pigeon Creek as anxious to help him as his enemies were to find Hoosier experiences to defeat him. Josiah Crawford, in whose home Lincoln had vowed, "I will study and get ready," sent a piece of whiteoak rail to be made into a cane. The Presidential-nominee told newspaper men, "It is part of one of the rails I cut for him in 1825, when I was sixteen years old." [36] From G. W. Rathbone of Evansville, Indiana, Lincoln received this message: "At the request of our mutual friend Wm. Jones of Gentryville, I send you herewith, a cane, the first work on which was done by yourself thirty-five years ago." [37] Obviously, it was Abe's walking stick which Jones had put away so long ago for a keepsake. "I always used to carry a cane when I was a boy," Lincoln explained.

Feeling humble, but prepared for the struggle against Seceders who were determined to keep slavery even at the expense of the Union, Lincoln said: "I know there is a God and that He hates injustice and slavery. I see the storm coming and I know that He has a hand in it. If He has a place and work for me—and I think He has—I believe I am ready." [38]

Many of Lincoln's fixed beliefs may be traced back to his experiences in Indiana. He believed a storm could be an overwhelming force. "Of all the forces of nature," he said, "I think the wind contains the largest amount of motive force . . . to level a forest." [39] He had seen the storm of 1827, predicted by the local Miracle Woman, level a wide swath of virgin timber through Buck Horn Valley. In November, 1860, that swath could still be seen as plainly as the storm of war then about to strike the nation. Lincoln had been elected President hardly three months when angry delegates from planting states met in Montgomery, Alabama, organized the Confederate States of America and on February 11, 1861, chose Jefferson Davis as their Provisional President. President Davis, adding excitement to that rising storm, declared: "If war must come, it must be on Northern and not on Southern soil. We will carry war where it is easy to advance, where food for the sword and torch awaits our armies in the densely populated cities." [40]

With sword and torch North and South attacked each other. After more than three years of strife, worries, disappointments, and betrayals had ploughed deep furrows in Lincoln's tired face; he was more wearied in mind than in body. He tried to rest but, as he expressed it to F. B. Carpenter, "The remedy seemed never to reach the tired spot." [41] He knew that each day more homes, North and South alike, sank into mourning. But still the war must go on if the Union was to be restored.

In 1863 someone warned President Lincoln that if he let Colonel James F. Jaquess go as a religious peace emissary to President Davis it might give France and Great Britain the pretext they were waiting for to recognize the Confederacy. President Lincoln observed that he also feared he might be accused by the Copperheads of showing the white feather and thus discourage loyal people. Recalling a tale from his old *Aesop's Fables*, read as a boy, he said, "You see, I don't want to be like the dog that crossed the brook with a piece of meat in its mouth, and dropped it to catch at its enlarged shadow in the water. I want peace. But I can't afford to discourage our friends and so perhaps make it more difficult to save the Union." [42] Surely he knew France, Great Britain and Spain were giving comfort to the Confederacy and that the ruling classes of those three countries did not want to see the new democracy in the New World succeed. Even before his First Inauguration he knew French leadership had begun to encourage Southern secession.

Back in February, 1861, the *Indianapolis State Guard*, an anti-Lincoln newspaper, gleefully published a letter written by a French Senator, M. Hennocque, to the South Carolinian, Professor Dubos, in which it was stated that Emperor Napoleon III did "not see why South Carolina should not secede from the Union" and that the Emperor "will recognize your government as soon as it is regularly organized and constituted." The letter was mailed from Paris on January 14th.

In David Ramsay's *Life of Washington* and William Grimshaw's *History of the United States*, Lincoln had read, while at Gentryville, how President Washington struggled to keep peace with both France and Great Britain while M. Genet, the French agent to the United States, outfitted privateers at Charleston, South Carolina, to prey on British shipping.

In January, 1824, Lincoln had read in the Vincennes *Western Sun* about President Monroe's hands-off policy; after almost forty years he still maintained a sturdy regard for the spirit of that doctrine. As President, Lincoln was faced with as great a dilemma as had faced either President Monroe or President Washington, for, in June, 1864, the French Emperor set up Maximilian of Austria as Emperor of Mexico. It was plain to Lincoln that Napoleon III had put in motion a three-fold plan: aid the Confederacy, weaken the American Union, re-annex the old Louisiana Territory.

By setting up Maximilian, Emperor Napoleon had taken the first step toward openly defying Monroe's warning that "we should consider any attempt on their [European Powers] part to extend their system to any portion of this hemisphere as dangerous to our peace and safety." Great Britain was watching Napoleon's every move. Spain watched, too, ready to undo the work of Simon Bolivar, the great South American patriot about whom Lincoln had heard and read so much back on Pigeon Creek. Lincoln remembered the ardent sympathy his aged American Revolutionary War-veteran neighbors had expressed for the George Washington of the South American revolutionists. He remembered he had been stirred by Bolivar's proclamation carried in the Vincennes *Western Sun* of March 3, 1827: "The loathsome and sanguinary serpent of discord flees from the center of Columbia! Internal enemies are no more. This day is the triumph of peace. Granadians! Your brothers of Venezuela are the same! Columbians! Forget the days of sorrow and may their remembrances be blotted out!"

Lincoln further remembered that in 1825, his political idol, Henry Clay, while Secretary of State, had boldly defended the South American colonies by declaring, "If the leagued despots of Europe should attempt to aid in the subjugation of Spanish America, the whole energy of the United States would be brought into requisition to repel aggression." Clay proposed a sort of Pan American Union, a system which "would constitute the rallying point of human freedom against all the despotism of the old world." [43] Of this Lincoln said, "Mr. Clay's efforts in behalf of the South Americans are among the finest on record, upon the noblest of all themes—a love of liberty and right, unselfishly, and for their own sakes." [44]

As President Lincoln saw he must exert all possible effort to neutralize the meddling of European powers in both Spanish America's and our own Civil War affairs. With able help from Secretary of State Seward, he succeeded to a remarkable degree by getting one power to suspect the other two.[45] But a day came when even Lincoln's patience ended. At a Cabinet meeting he described the time he went up to the warring Indiana farmhouse to peddle some notions and a woman met him at the door. She told him the angry noises were just a family row, which she could manage without any outside help. "And I don't want no sneaking around trying to find out how I do it, either," she warned. "That's the case here," said the President. "We must let other nations know we propose to settle our family row in our own way." Turning to the Secretary of State, he directed, "Now, Seward, you write some diplomatic notes to that effect." [46]

Treason trials at Indianapolis further harrassed Lincoln. Back there sixty persons had been tried for conspiring to resist the draft, and to set up a Northwestern Confederacy friendly to Southern Confederacy. Federal enrolling officers had been shot. There had been secret murders. A plot had been discovered to kidnap and kill Governor Morton, Lincoln's friend, and to seize the State Government of Indiana.[47] Several conspirators, directing the Knights of the Golden Circle and Order of American Knights in trying to break up the Union, had been condemned to death by a military commission. On being told there were many thousands in the State who were not only politically against him, but who were siding with the "dark lantern knights," as the dis-unionists were derisively called, President Lincoln scoffed at the idea, let his Hoosier spirit get the better of his good judgment, and pardoned the condemned men. "Nothing can make me believe that one hundred thousand Indiana Democrats are disloyal," he declared.[48]

Earlier in the year friends of Lincoln had pointed out to him that Secretary Chase, frantic for the next Presidential nomination, was undermining him. They did admit, however, that Chase was zealously trying to make the Treasury Department function efficiently.[49] It was in this connection that Lincoln told his friends about the time in his boyhood days when he and his stepbrother, John D. Johnston, were plowing corn. A chin-fly got on their slow, old horse and began biting it very hard. Away went the horse, pulling the plow rapidly across the field. Lincoln added that if any Cabinet member "has a Presidential chin-fly biting him, I'm not going to knock it off, if it will make his department go." [50]

In spite of Lincoln's enemies in the North, there were enough Republicans and War Democrats who pledged themselves Union men and re-elected him President.[51] On December 6, 1864, he told Congress, "The war will cease on the part of the Government whenever it

shall have ceased on the part of those who began it." It looked as if
he intended to treat the Secessionist slave-holding leaders the same
way he had treated the Negro slave-bandits who attacked him on his
first flatboat trip to New Orleans: fight them only until they quit.

The specter of the North winning the war and Lincoln subjugating
the South frightened thoughtful Rebels. Some of them suggested
repealing the Declaration of Independence, thereby automatically
returning the South to active protection under the British crown.
They argued that then Lincoln would have a brand new war on his
hands.[52] Before trying out that scheme, however, Confederate President Davis sent Duncan Kenner to France and Great Britain, offering
emancipation of the slaves in exchange for public recognition of the
Confederacy.[53]

With the War of the Rebellion drawing to a close, Lincoln held an
informal Cabinet meeting to discuss what to do with Davis and other
Secessionist officials. Almost everyone was for hanging them. Lincoln
kept quiet and listened. Finally, Joshua F. Speed, who also was there,
asked the President for his views. "Well, Josh," said Lincoln, "when
I was a boy in Indiana I went to a neighbor's home one morning and
found a boy about my size holding a coon by a string. The boy,
fearing his father was going to kill the coon as soon as he returned
home, tearfully said, 'If I let him go, Dad would give me hell. But
if he would get away by himself it would be all right.'" The President
added: "Now if Jeff Davis and those other fellows will only get away,
it will be all right. But if we should catch them and I should let
them go, 'Dad would give me hell.'"[54]

Upon General Lee's evacuation of Richmond, April 2, 1865, Jeff
Davis fled from the Confederate capital. And that was all right with
Abe Lincoln.

*   *   *

In addition to his acquaintance with political stump-speakers and
political-fixers during his formative years, Lincoln also had learned
about the sociological experimenters Robert Owen and his son, Robert
Dale Owen, at New Harmony on the Wabash River, just ten miles
west of Thomas Lincoln's Posey County, Indiana, farm. There on
the river, schemes for the self-emancipation of slaves, for freeing mankind from the "contest between individuals," and for guaranteeing
to everyone an equal chance at education and the pursuit of happiness
were being explored in conference or were actually being tried out by
the experimenters.

The President was wrestling with the idea of a proclamation of amnesty when Robert Dale Owen dropped into the White House one Sunday morning. Sixty-three years old now, Owen was more mature in judgment than when he had taught at the New Harmony Utopian experiment. He had become a leading Indiana Democratic politician and had done a good job of buying arms for his state's troops since May, 1861. Back in September, 1862, he had written President Lincoln, urging him immediately to issue an Emancipation Proclamation to free the slaves. Owen argued that "Property in man, always morally unjust, has become nationally dangerous. Property that endangers the safety of the nation should not be suffered to remain in the hands of its citizens. A chief magistrate who permits it to so remain becomes responsible for the consequences." Owen's letter, according to Secretary Chase, "had more effect in deciding the President to make his proclamation than all other communications combined." [55]

"Mr. President," said Mr. Owen when he called at the White House, "I have here a paper that I have prepared with some care. I wish to read it to you." The President settled himself to listen. When Owen referred to the Whiskey Rebellion in Washington's administration, Lincoln sat up and exclaimed: "What! Did Washington issue a proclamation of amnesty?" Owen: "Here it is, sir." Lincoln: "Well, I never knew that."

Robert Dale Owen read through to the end and handed the paper to the President. As Lincoln accepted it he told his visitor: "Mr. Owen, you have conferred a very essential service both upon me and the country." [56]

On December 8, 1863, the President issued his Proclamation of Amnesty and Reconstruction. In it he made "known to all persons who have directly, or by implication, participated in the existing rebellion, except as hereinafter excepted, that a full pardon is hereby granted to them . . . upon condition that they shall take and subscribe to an oath."

Lincoln's sister-in-law, Emilie Todd Helm, widow of Confederate General Ben Hardin Helm, took the oath and was among the first to benefit by Robert Dale Owen's work. Mrs. Helm had come to the White House to grieve with her sister, Mary Todd Lincoln, over the death of their brother David, a Confederate soldier who had died of wounds received at Vicksburg.

* * *

When President Lincoln was accused by Secretary Chase's friends of attempting "to put down this rebellion with the left hand while

supporting Slavery with the right hand," [57] those fault finders obviously did not realize how deep an impression the slavery issue had
made upon the President during his growing-up years in Indiana.

Lincoln had matured in a border country. He had seen slavery
both at its worst and in a form which some borderland people considered not too bad. Beginning in 1820 he had observed how the
slavery question had threatened the Union: "A sullen gloom hung
over the nation. All felt the rejection of Missouri was equivalent to
the dissolution of the Union." [58]

When the first threats of dissolution were heard at Pigeon Creek
Lincoln had read David Turnham's copy of the *Statutes of Indiana*
and had written: "The Constitution should be sacred; the Union
perpetuated and the laws revered, respected, and enforced." [59] More
than thirty years later he set out to enforce the laws in order to per-
petuate the Union. "So long as I am President," he declared, the
war "shall be carried on for the sole purpose of restoring the Union." [60]
But in restoring it he would also recognize the Constitution's guarantee of the individual's lawful rights to personal property. He would
not allow his own prejudice against human servitude to override the
laws of the land that recognized slaves as property.

When Lincoln was seventeen years old he was charged in a Kentucky magistrate's court with violating the legal rights of Ohio River
ferrymen. There Squire Samuel Pate, a slave-holder, demonstrated
that the precepts of the law should prevail over a judge's financial
gain by finding Lincoln not guilty as charged by the Dill brothers who
rented ground of the Squire for use as their ferryboat landing. Squire
Pate's respect for the law and his devotion to the Constitution sharply
outlined themselves in Lincoln's legal thinking.

On the Squire's plantation, from the big house down to the river
bottoms, Lincoln had seen only kindness to slaves. Still it was
slavery. "If slavery is not wrong, nothing is wrong," he said. In
spite of that wrong he was sure that slavery was lawful south of the
Ohio; otherwise, how could a man of Squire Pate's integrity hold
slaves?

When again a sullen gloom hung over the nation and dissolution
threatened the Union in 1860, Lincoln's early border-country experiences gave him a broad understanding of the slavery problem. "I
believe," he said, "the devotion to the Constitution is equally great
on both sides of the river. The only dispute on both sides is 'what
are their rights.' " [61] Speaking before Congress July 4, 1861, he recalled that Secession advocates had carried their idea of their rights so

far as to invent "an ingenious sophism that any state of the Union may consistently with the Constitution withdraw from the Union without the consent of the Union or any other state. With rebellion thus sugar-coated they have been drugging the public mind of their section for more than thirty years."

In his first inaugural address President Lincoln declared: "No State upon its mere motion can lawfully get out of the Union; that resolves and ordinances to that effect are legally void; and that acts of violence, within any State or States, against the authority of the United States, are insurrectionary or revolutionary, according to circumstances. I, therefore, consider that, in view of the Constitution and the laws, the Union is unbroken."

Back in Indiana days Lincoln had read in David Turnham's copy of the *Revised Statutes of Indiana,* Article I, Section 10 of the Constitution of the United States: "No State shall enter into any Treaty, Alliance, or Confederation; grant Letters of Marque and Reprisal; coin money." If a state were not allowed to do any of those things, Lincoln felt no state or states could withdraw from the Union. Nevertheless, by Inauguration Day, March 4, 1861, the Confederate States or America had been set up and were functioning.

From the outbreak of the Civil War, Abolitionists and Northern fanatics demanded that President Lincoln immediately free all slaves. Steadfastly he resisted them. "What I do about slavery and the colored race, I do because I believe it helps save the Union," he wrote to Horace Greeley. "I would save the Union. I would save it the shortest way under the Constitution." To his way of thinking nothing in nature changed suddenly. Even erosion, which in his boyhood he had seen at work along the Ohio River and Pigeon Creek eating away the banks, was gradual. So, while feeling action against slavery should be as relentless as erosion, Lincoln insisted: "Gradual and not sudden emancipation is better for all." [62]

Adhering to his teen-age conviction that the law should be revered and property rights under the Constitution respected, President Lincoln drew up a plan for the Government to pay owners $400,000,000 for their slaves. He read it aloud to his Cabinet. None voiced approval. Slowly he folded the paper and placed it in his pocket. "You are all opposed to me," he commented sadly. [63] By proposing that masters be compensated for loss of their slaves he had multiplied his enemies and shaken the faith of his weaker friends. "Man has no property in man," many taunted him. Those words were not new to Lincoln. He had read them at Gentryville in 1827 in William Wood's

Telescope. Still the law recognized slaves as valuable chattel. As property, the President reasoned the government should pay the masters for them before freeing the slaves. Since his youth he had believed slavery should be abolished. He had known of legal ways to do it.

Frances Wright's self-emancipation system was working quite satisfactorily at the time Abe's father owned the Posey County farm near Robert Owen's New Harmony Utopian experiment. In a letter to General McClernand, Lincoln seems to have had in mind something of Miss Wright's plan when he suggested that the slave-holding states "adopt systems of apprenticeship for the colored people, conforming substantially to the most approved plans of gradual emancipation." [64] Also he remembered Clay's system. "I had hoped and prayed," the President told McClernand," that the gradual emancipation plan of Henry Clay might soon lead to its [slavery] extinction in the United States." [65] During his only term in Congress he introduced a bill to abolish slavery in the District of Columbia "with the consent of the voters of the District and with compensation to the owners," but the measure was defeated. [66]

Hoping to stop the war, save the Union, and solve the slavery question, President Lincoln told the border slave states on July 12, 1862: "I do not speak of emancipation at once but of a decision to emancipate gradually. How much better for you as seller and the nation as buyer, to sell out and buy out that without which the war could never have been than to sink both the thing to be sold and the price of it in cutting one another's throats!" [67] Did Lincoln believe that if the war were ended at once and the Union saved, slave-holders would sell their slaves? Or did he feel that some masters would take their slaves to free soil and emancipate them as Thomas Clay, of Kentucky, had done in 1823, when he crossed the Ohio River and freed his slaves in Lincoln's own Spencer County, Indiana?

Unfortunately for the country neither the slave-holders of the South nor the immediate emancipationists of the North heeded Lincoln's plea. So the war went on. And mourning invaded home after home, even the White House. Another of Mrs. Lincoln's brothers, Samuel Todd, was killed at Shiloh. As a little girl Mary Todd had cuddled Baby Sam. Bravely now she held back her sobs; the wife of the President of the United States must not betray grief for a Rebel soldier. More sorrow entered the White House. In August, 1862, Lincoln received word that during a skirmish near Baton Rouge, Louisiana, still another of his wife's brothers, Lieutenant Alexander H. Todd, a

Confederate officer, had been killed. When that news reached her, Mrs. Lincoln dropped to her knees on the White House floor, sobbing, "Oh, little Alec! Why had you to die?" [68] And while she wept the scar over President Lincoln's right eye grimly reminded him that on his first flatboat trip to New Orleans, 1829, a Louisiana Negro slave-bandit had struck him with a club and almost killed him. It had happened near that same Baton Rouge where Alec was shot.

Steadfastly holding to his objective of saving the Union regardless of the slavery issue, President Lincoln patiently endured the almost daily visits of Senators Ben Wade, Zack Chandler, and Charles Sumner, who came demanding that all slaves be freed at once. They bitterly opposed Lincoln's plan to pay the owners. They disregarded the fact that immediate emancipation of the slaves would economically ruin at least one-third of all Southerners. They resented Lincoln's suggestion that the North share equitably with the South the cost of emancipation. They could not say with him: "I have no prejudice against the Southern people. They are just what we would be in their situation. If slavery did not now exist among them, they would not introduce it. When Southern people tell us they are no more responsible for the origin of slavery than we, I acknowledge the fact." [69]

Quite likely not one of those three Senators had known slavemasters of the quality of Squire Samuel Pate, Sheriff W. D. Ferguson, and former slave-masters such as James Gentry or William, son of Judge Peter Jones. But Lincoln had known them and he further knew that Jones and the Gentrys were now fighting in the ranks of the Northern Army—not to save slavery, but to save the Union.

One day as the President stood watching Chandler, Wade and Sumner walk toward the White House, he remarked to General Henderson that those three Senators reminded him of a dull little fellow reading the Bible in class in the old log schoolhouse back along Pigeon Creek. The boy, who already had found trouble in pronouncing Shadrach, Meshach, and Abed-nego, cried out when he saw them mentioned again on the page, "Here's them same damn three fellers again!" [70]

When, however, it came to dealing with slave-traders, Lincoln was not at all sympathetic. Nathaniel Gordon, sentenced to be hanged for slave-trading, begged the President to change the sentence to life imprisonment. Lincoln merely granted him a respite of fourteen days to "prepare for the awful change which awaits him." He said the man who would "rob Africa of her children to sell into interminable bondage, I will never pardon." [71] Lingering in his memory were the horrors which Kentucky "patter-rollers" and Indiana "nigger-

ketchers" had brought to free and fugitive Negroes of the Pigeon
Creek region by stealing them and dragging them across the Ohio
River into slavery. A decade after leaving that border country, while
on board an Ohio River steamboat, Lincoln again saw the work of
slave-catchers. About a dozen Negroes were on the boat, shackled
together with irons. "I hate to see the poor creatures hunted down
and caught and carried back to their stripes and unrequited toil,"
Lincoln wrote to Joshua F. Speed. "I see something like it every
time I touch the Ohio or any other slave border." [72] To an Indiana
regiment the President said, "Whenever I hear anyone arguing for
slavery, I feel a strong impulse to see it tried on him personally." [73]

Lincoln's determination to save the Union overshadowed all regard
for any immediate group, race, or section of the United States. He
believed that somewhere along this republic's march of progress,
slavery surely would fall by the wayside because it violated the spirit
of the Declaration of Independence. At Pigeon Creek he had grown
up among veterans of the American Revolution and the War of 1812.
From them he had learned first-hand the high cost of bringing "forth
upon this continent a new nation, conceived in liberty, and dedicated
to the proposition that all men are created equal." More than once
Lincoln quoted Henry Clay's speech of the late 1820s in which he
said Clay "told an audience that if they would repress all tendencies
to liberty and ultimate emancipation, they must go back to the era of
our independence and muzzle the cannon which thundered its annual
joyous return on the Fourth of July; they must penetrate the human
soul, and eradicate the love of liberty; until they did these things they
could not repress all tendencies to ultimate emancipation." [74]

To preserve the Union and the spirit of the Revolutionary patriots
had been Lincoln's ideal ever since he read Weems' *Life of Washington*
in his childhood. As President-elect he told the New Jersey Senate:
"I recollect thinking then, boy even though I was, that there must
have been something more than common that these men struggled for
. . . that something that held out a great promise to all people of the
world for all time to come—I am exceedingly anxious that this Union,
the Constitution, and the liberties of the people shall be perpetuated in
accordance with the original idea for which that struggle was made."

At Philadelphia's Independence Hall Lincoln added: "I have never
had a feeling, politically, that did not spring from the sentiments
embodied in the Declaration of Independence. It was not the mere
matter of separation of the colonies from the motherland, but that
sentiment in the Declaration of Independence which gave liberty not

alone to the people of this country, but hope to all the world, for all future time. It was that which gave promise that in due time the weights would be lifted from the shoulders of all men, and that all should have an equal chance."

While Lincoln's policies displeased Senators Chandler, Wade, and Sumner, it was Wade who usually was irritated by the President's story-telling talent—much of which had been nurtured at Gentryville and on Taylor's ferry at the mouth of Anderson River near Troy, Indiana. Once Wade came to the White House to urge the President to dismiss General Grant. "Senator," said Lincoln, "that reminds me of a story." Wade interjected: "It is with you, sir, all story, story! You are the father of every military blunder that has been made during the war. You are on your road to hell, sir, with this government. You are not a mile off this minute." Good-naturedly Lincoln responded: "Senator, that is just about the distance from here to the Capitol, is it not?" [75]

The accusation that he led the country within a mile of hell seemed not to worry President Lincoln nearly so much as the problem of combating the slave-holding oligarchy. This one-third of the Southern voting population had been a big factor in bringing on the rebellion against the United States Government. Lincoln called the action of that minority "an attempt for the first time in the world to construct a new nation on the basis of human slavery." [76] His experiences among slave-holders had led him to believe that generally they looked upon a hired laborer as being in a static social position. He said they assumed that "whoever is once a hired laborer is fatally fixed in that condition for life. This is the mud-sill theory." [77] Mud-sills were those logs which he had helped lay at the bottom of his Indiana cabin homes and which eventually became a fixed part of both cabin and earth.

Orators of the Confederacy pointed out that their new government's cornerstone rested "upon the great truth that slavery is the Negro's natural and normal condition." [78] To grub out that cornerstone and the "great truth" under it as effectively as he had grubbed out the stumps from Buck Horn Valley land, President Lincoln on September 22, 1862, warned the rebellious states that unless they returned to the Union he would free their slaves. It was plain that while he recognized their property rights in their slaves he had determined to follow the suggestion of his old Indiana neighbor, Robert Dale Owen, and remove from the control of Southern rulers the "property that endangers the safety of the nation."

Less than three months later the entire North was stunned by bloody defeat at Fredericksburg. Gloom once more settled above the Mason-Dixon line. Distrust of Lincoln's policies rapidly mounted. Nevertheless, since not a seceded State had heeded his warning, President Lincoln used his war powers to issue the Emancipation Proclamation on January 1, 1863: "All Persons held as slaves henceforward shall be free." He had fulfilled the promise made as he and Allen Gentry stood watching the sale of "fancy girls" on the levee at New Orleans in 1829. "Allen," he then had said, "If I ever get a lick at that thing I'll hit it hard." [79] John Hanks claimed Lincoln made a similar statement to him in New Orleans in 1831, but Lincoln contradicted this in 1860: "Hanks had not gone to New Orleans, but having a family, and being likely to be detained from home longer than at first expected, had turned back from St. Louis." [80]

The Emancipation Proclamation frightened some slave-owners but not W. D. (Wappanocca) Ferguson, the man for whom Lincoln had chopped tupelo gum in Crittenden County, Arkansas, in 1826 and 1827. Ferguson called at the White House to complain to the President that General Grant's soldiers, wintering at Memphis, Tennessee, had been crossing the Mississippi River and raiding his plantation. He said he had appealed to Grant for relief but had received no response. So would the President do something about the situation? Despite the fact that Ferguson still held slaves, Lincoln accommodated his old employer. He wrote Grant a note which said in effect that all of Mr. Ferguson's property must be respected by the Union forces. [81]

As was to be expected the Emancipation Proclamation quickly engendered such bitterness throughout the Confederate states that their armies fought even harder than before. At Chancellorsville, General Lee's troops staggered General Hooker's Army of the Potomac in one of the worst slaughters of the Civil War. On hearing of the defeat President Lincoln, hands clasped behind his back, paced the White House floor. "My God! My God! What will the country say!" he moaned. [82]

Mrs. Lincoln's frequent headaches increased with each announcement that another of her brothers in Confederate uniform had fallen in battle. Finally she said her dead son, Willie, was coming to comfort her. That alarmed the President. "Her nerves have gone to pieces," he remarked to her sister, Mrs. Helm. One day he led his wife to an east window of the White House and pointed to a hospital for the mentally ill: "Mary, if you don't control yourself, we will have to put you over there." [83] He knew what mental illness could lead to for he had seen one of his brilliant Indiana schoolmates completely break down. "I could not forget the impression his case made upon me," he wrote.[84]

But even while struggling to aid Mary Todd throw off her depression, Lincoln himself gave in to spells of melancholia. Back in his boyhood days Pigeon Creekers—especially James Grigsby, the other half of the "Brush College" student body—had noticed how similar spells affected him. "Abe would get fits of blues, then he wouldn't study for two or three days at a time," said Grigsby.[85] For weeks following Willie's death, the President locked himself in a room on Thursdays in order to grieve over his son's passing, sharing his grief with all other fathers, of North and South alike, who had lost sons in the war. And his grief was heightened as the two contending armies clashed at Gettysburg. Again an anguished Lincoln paced the White House corridors. His fear for the Union grew so great he cried out, "Save, Lord, or we perish!"[86] Into his mind came his mother's last words as she lay dying on the old cornshuck tick at Pigeon Creek: "Remember, Abraham, our God is a prayer-hearing God." He would heed her words. "I went to my room," said Lincoln, "and got down on my knees and prayed Almighty God for victory at Gettysburg. I told Him this was His country, the war His war; but that we really couldn't stand another Fredericksburg or Chancellorsville. And then and there I made a solemn vow with my Maker that if He would stand by the boys at Gettysburg I would stand by Him. And He did and I will."[87]

After three days of savage fighting, July 1 to 3, 1863, General Meade halted General Lee's northern invasion. Then while Meade hesitated to strike what might have been a war-ending blow, the remnants of Lee's army escaped across the Potomac River. More encouraging news reached Lincoln: General Grant had captured Vicksburg on July 4th, opening up the Mississippi River to Union traffic. Knowing from his flatboating days the great value of that river, the President wrote to James C. Conkling: "The signs look better. The Father of Waters again flows unvexed to the sea."

Although the signs looked better to him along the Mississippi, Lincoln was disturbed by the situation in the eastern war zone. To arouse more aggressiveness in his military commanders there the President resorted to use of the Rule of Three Direct, the Golden Rule of Proportion he had learned in Pike's *Arithmetic* while attending Azel W. Dorsey's school near Gentryville. To General H. W. Halleck, Lincoln wrote: "General Meade, as shown by the returns, has with

him, and between him and Washington, of the same classes of men,
well over 90,000. For a battle, then, General Meade has three men
to General Lee's two. If the enemy's 60,000 are sufficient to keep our
90,000 away from Richmond, why, by the same rule, may not 40,000
of ours keep their 60,000 away from Washington, leaving us 50,000
to put to some other use? . . . I can perceive no fault in this statement
unless we admit we are not the equal of the enemy, man for man.
I hope you will consider it." [88]

Whether it was due to his Rule of Three argument or to something
else, signs presently began to look so favorable for a Northern victory
that Lincoln started talking of ways to pardon the Rebels and get
them to return peacefully into the Union. And when James R. Gil-
more asked him, "Do you mean, sir, that as soon as Rebels lay down
their arms you will grant them a general amnesty?" Lincoln replied,
"I do. And I will say to you, individually I should be disposed to
make compensation for the slaves. The blacks must be freed.
Slavery is the bone we are fighting over." [89] Not waiting for the
Southern forces to lay down their arms, Lincoln went ahead and issued
the Proclamation of Amnesty.

Some time afterward the President became worried because the proclamation had neither slackened the fury of the war nor improved the
plight of the slaves. Lincoln was reminded of the contents of his boyhood copy of *Aesop's Fables*. The book contained several woodcuts,
one of which showed three white men scrubbing a Negro in a potash
kettle full of cold water. Lincoln said the men thought scrubbing the
Negro might make him white but just about the time they believed
they were succeeding the Negro took cold and died. "Now," he concluded, "I'm afraid that by the time we get through this war the Negro
will catch cold and die." [90]

The spring of 1864 found Lincoln again in anguish. Lines were
growing deeper in his tired face. Grant had set out to capture Lee.
The opposing armies met in the Virginia wilderness and for a while
Grant made some headway in forcing Lee toward Richmond. Then in
the Battle of Cold Harbor on June 3rd Lee's army mowed down
Grant's men. That jarred the morale of Northern soldiers. "It's no
use. We can't whip Bobby Lee," the cry passed along the ranks. [91]

Night after night, spending scarcely an hour in sleep, Lincoln
slowly walked up and down a narrow passageway, hands clasped
behind him, head dropped forward, staring out of eyes ringed in black.
Republican extremists struck at him because of his Amnesty Proclamation; some accused his wife of being a Confederate spy. Peace

Democrats demanded that he stop the war at once. When pro-slaveryites called him "That bloody butcher!" he remembered how he had loathed being hog-butcher for James Taylor and James Gentry, Sr. Even when, editorially, Horace Greely screamed at him, "Stop these rivers of human blood!" Lincoln would not stop the war. He would free the slaves and save the Union. "I did not consider I had a right to touch the State Institution of slavery until all other measures for restoring the Union had failed," he told F. B. Carpenter.[92]

All the while it was becoming more evident that Lincoln's critics and tormentors were incapable of understanding him, incapable of knowing that within him dwelt the solitude of the forest. Pacing those dark corridors of the White House, his long morning wrapper flapping about his legs, Abraham Lincoln again was walking the dark woodland trails of his boyhood and youth. Back in Indiana he had communed with another world. He had heard voices. His sense of mysticism, his superstitions, his faith in dreams had remained with him—elusive, but ever present. He had talked with God, he said; the war must go on. "We are going through on this line if it takes three years more," he announced.[93] "The Constitution should be saved; the Union perpetuated."

While Grant and Lee continued their fighting in the wilderness, General Sherman left Chattanooga, cutting his way toward Atlanta. At Acworth, Georgia, Lincoln's close friend, William Jones of Gentryville, commanding the 53rd Indiana Volunteer Infantry, joined forces with Sherman. Captain Allen Gentry of the 42nd Regiment Indiana Volunteers, and hundreds of others from that area which Lincoln called "the triangular region between the Ohio & Wabash rivers, including my old boyhood home" were already on the march. Destined to be laid away in a Georgia warehouse but certainly now moving along with those troops was the six-by-ten foot banner depicting Abe Lincoln the Rail-Splitter. According to James M. Justice, a 16th Battery Indiana Light Artillery private who had been wounded at the Second Battle of Bull Run, Southerners hooted every time they saw the banner. Twice Rebels captured it and twice the Hoosiers retook it. An ominous bullet-hole defaced the forehead.[94]

Sherman crossed the Chattahoochee River, was attacked three times by J. B. Hood's army, but finally entered Atlanta, leaving dead on a battlefield Lieutenant Colonel William Jones. Although shot through both thighs early in the July 22nd engagement, the sixty-four year old storekeeper continued to fight until a shell hit his head and killed him instantly.[95] A little while before this John W. Lamar, to whom

Lincoln had remarked at Gentryville, "I wouldn't give a cent for a boy who doesn't know more today than he knew yesterday," had been discharged from Colonel Jones' regiment in "the last stages of consumption." Lamar was a first lieutenant.[96]

Word came that the President's boyhood companion, Second Lieutenant Nathaniel Grigsby, had been disabled while guarding an Alabama railroad over which supplies passed to Sherman's Army. From down there Grigsby wrote to the President: "My old friend. I am in the service of my country contending for the government of our fathers. In the battle of Pulaska we had 33 killed and wounded out of our Regt Co G of the 10 Ind Cavalry." The company "was recruited in old Spencer by myself and Wm. Jones Junior the son of Col. Jones of Gentryville our old and lamented friend." After telling Lincoln that David Turnham's son, Thomas, had attained the rank of orderly sergeant, Nathaniel Grigsby added: "I brought out two of my sons with me, one of them since died of smallpox [twenty year old Henry Clay Grigsby] . . . I have two other sons in the army in 42 Regt Ind vol at Atlanta, Ga." [97]

At the outbreak of the war the elder Jones had written President Lincoln that men of Spencer Legion "swear death or victory is their motto." Sacrifices by Lincoln's former neighbors in this chaotic year of 1864 proved to the President that they were holding to their motto and encouraged him to cling tighter to his resolution to save the Union. Consequently, he paid no attention when General McCellan called him "the original gorilla," [98] or when Secretary of War Stanton called him a damned fool.[99] He paid no attention when Secretary of Treasury Chase referred to him as "born a poor white in a slave state . . . anxious for approval" from those whom he "had been accustomed to look up to." [100] Lincoln turned aside these verbal arrows in the same spirit he had turned aside the sarcastic compliments of Stephen A. Douglas. "I was not much accustomed to flattery," he had told Douglas, "and it came the sweeter to me. I was rather like the Hoosier with the gingerbread, when he said he reckoned he loved it better than any other man, and got less of it." [101]

*   *   *

April 15, 1865, was Abraham Lincoln's parting day. He had finished his work; he had saved the Union. Thirty-five years before as he pulled out of Indiana, crossing the Wabash River into Illinois, tar buckets hooked onto the family wagons rhythmically swung back and forth ticking off the end of one eventful period in his life and the beginning of another—even as they had ticked off his crossing the Ohio River from Kentucky into Indiana, from a slave state to a free state.

Beginning in his childhood, when Sarah Bush Johnston had appeared in his father's dream, Abraham Lincoln had firmly believed dreams foretokened life's happenings. By careful study he had found dreams mentioned in twenty chapters of the Bible. He reached the conclusion that in bygone ages mankind often had received divine guidance by way of dreams.[102]

"I had a dream last night," President Lincoln told his Cabinet and General Grant on Good Friday morning, April 14, 1865. "Ever since the war began I have had the same dream just before every event of great importance. I saw a ship sailing rapidly, badly damaged. It portends some important event which will happen very soon." [103]

Lincoln could not have known the important event would be precipitated by John Wilkes Booth, popular Shakespeare tragedian; that Booth had selected this Good Friday for assassination day. Yet Lincoln knew of Shakespeare's interest in the so-called Mystical Number 7, having read about it in an essay in the Vincennes *Western Sun* he had helped print on March 6, 1830. He was fifty-six and he knew that was eight times seven. From Genesis to Revelation he had seen the number mentioned many times. On his first trip down to New Orleans, in 1829, seven Negro slave bandits attacked his flatboat. One slave nearly killed him with a club.

Although not aware the date of his assassination had been set, there is evidence that President Lincoln felt a singular foreboding of danger while walking to the War Department late that April afternoon with his bodyguard, William H. Crook. He was in such a state of uneasiness that the bodyguard couldn't help but notice it. "Crook, do you know," said Lincoln, "I believe there are men who want to take my life?" Then, half talking to himself he added. "And I have no doubt they will do it."

"Why do you think so, Mr. President?"

"Other men have been assassinated," said Lincoln.[104]

Only a few days before the President had told Mrs. Lincoln and Ward Hill Lamon about a recent dream. He said he dreamed he went into the East Room and saw a corpse resting on a catafalque. He asked one of the soldiers on guard, " 'Who is dead in the White House?' The soldier answered 'The President. He was killed by an assassin!' "

President Lincoln added: "I slept no more that night; and although it was only a dream I have been strangely annoyed by it ever since."

To Mrs. Lincoln's cry, "That is horrid! I wish you had not told it," he calmly replied, "It is only a dream, Mary. Try to forget it." But he could not forget it.

Later he talked about it with Lamon and closed with Hamlet's Soliloquy on death: "To sleep: perchance to dream! ay, there's the rub!"[105] He first had read that line back at Pigeon Creek. It had burred into his mind.

Not only "Hamlet" but still another Shakespearean drama, "Richard III," stalked Lincoln's closing hours. Edwin, brother of John Wilkes Booth, visited the President at the White House. Like John, Edwin excelled in playing the character of Richard the Evil Doer; but with gestures, postures and inflections Lincoln demonstrated to Booth the way he felt parts of "Richard III" should be interpreted.[106] Even before Booth's visit the President had written to the actor, James H. Hackett: "I should like to hear you pronounce the opening speech of Richard III."[107] To the portrait painter, F. B. Carpenter, Lincoln explained how Richard, brother of Edward IV, "appears upon the stage, just after the crowning of Edward, burning with repressed hate and jealousy." According to Carpenter the President repeated Richard's soliloquy with force and power.[108]

Call it designs of Providence or merely coincidence, Abraham Lincoln's first awareness of the Booth family came while he and his Hoosier neighbor, flatboat captain Allen Gentry, roamed the streets of New Orleans in February, 1829. Billed there at the American Theatre was Junius Brutus Booth. "That justly distinguished tragedian, Mr. Booth, will make his first appearance in his own peculiar character of Richard III," ran the announcement.[109] The distinguished tragedian was the father of Edwin and John Wilkes.

Enraged over the way the war of American brothers was ending, John Wilkes Booth prepared to do for Lincoln, that Good Friday evening, what Richard planned for his brother:

"Simple, plain Clarence! I do love thee so,
"That I will shortly send thy soul to heaven."

Armed with dagger and loaded pistol Booth sneaked to the Presidential box in Ford's Theater, where President and Mrs. Lincoln sat laughing at Laura Keen in Tom Taylor's comedy, "Our American Cousin." Booth pushed open the door and fired a bullet into the back of Lincoln's head. The bullet lodged close behind the scar made by the Louisiana slave bandit's club.[110]

Long since that parting day the world has acknowledged Abraham Lincoln's greatness without realizing that a large share of that greatness was built upon a foundation laid in Indiana. It was there he grubbed out much of his basic education, developed his self-reliance, acquired his attitudes toward slavery and the Union. There he underwent his first intense sorrows. There he felt his earlier concern for the miseries and calamities of mankind and for all living creatures. There he found his faith in God. And there he made up his mind he was going to be somebody someday.

NOTES
(For full titles of works cited see Sources)

PREFACE

1. Nicolay & Hay, Abraham Lincoln: A History (hereinafter referred to as History), Vol. I, 42.
2. Original in Manuscript Division, Library of Congress.
3. President-elect Lincoln's address to New Jersey Senate, Feb. 21, 1861.

CHAPTER ONE

1. Tarbell, Early Life, 42. Thomas Lincoln of Hardin County, Kentucky, appointed road surveyor in place of George Redmond, May 13, 1816. (The name Redmond sometimes spelled without final "d"). In Indiana the county office was called supervisor. Lincoln Lore No. 657: Factors contributing to the 1816 Lincoln migration.

2. Gladly land was hilly ground crusted with rich topsoil. Eli L. Grigsby affidavit describes the meeting of Reuben Grigsby, Sr. and Thomas Lincoln on a trail in Southern Indiana (near present village of Santa Claus) in the summer of 1816.

3. Discovery of Baby Thomas Lincoln's grave, National Republic, Feb. 1934, an article by author; Lamon, Life, 20.

4. Barrett, 21-22; Gridley, 48.

5. Herndon-Weik MSS, Vol. 14, N. Grigsby, Sept. 4, 1865, and John W. Rowbottom, June 24, 1865, letters; Grigsby affidavit; Barrett, 22; Holand, 26; Thayer, 77; Rockport Journal, Oct. 2, 1902; Huntington Library Herndon-Lamon Collection, LN 2408, Vol. I, 223-224; Warren, 297.

6. Armstrong's Notes: "Pocket Reminiscences," p. 2; Herndon & Weik, I, 13.

7. Grigsby affidavit.

8. Gridley, 48, 52; statement of John J. Hall, nephew of Thomas Lincoln.

9. Grigsby affidavit; Cockrum, 161; Brooks, 12-13; Gridley, 142-143; Esarey's Home, 18-19; Herndon-Weik MSS, Vol. 13, D. F. Hanks, June 8, 1865, statement and Vol. 23, D. F. Hanks undated letter; Ehrmann, 91 (Murr statement)

10. W. D. Doak's letter, Greenville (Ohio) Advocate, Aug. 8, 1929; on wall of Clarence Hall's home, Charleston, Illinois (Mr. Hall is grandson of President Lincoln's stepsister, Matilda Johnston Hall); Lincoln Lore No. 767 (slightly different).

11. Oldroyd, 121; Holland, 436.   12. Nicolay & Hay, History, I, 639.

13. Grigsby affidavit; Peter J. Wahl statement, Richland, in author's collection.

14. Grigsby affidavit.   15. Ibid.

16. The Reverend Mr. Frederick Ostervald, a Swiss divine, born in 1663, died in 1747, pointed out in the Preliminary Discourses that "Many it is true, for want of learning, may not be in a capacity to read the Scriptures; which is a great misfortune, and a shame to Christians." This statement may have prompted Nancy Hanks Lincoln to say she would rather Abraham learn to read the Bible than to own a farm.

17. Brockett, 743.

18. Grigsby second affidavit: F. F. Browne, 63-64. ("Proud to meet you" is still a

common salutation among older people of the Indiana Lincoln country.)

19. Lindley, 188 (Morris Birbeck, July 23, 1817).

20. Tarbell, Early Life, I, 35; Dr. Christopher Columbus Graham's Reminiscences.

21. Grigsby affidavit (The site of the cabin is about three-fourths of a mile south of Nancy Hanks Lincoln's grave).

22. Nicolay & Hay, History, I, 639; Howells, 22.   23. Grigsby affidavit.

24. R. H. Browne, 86; Nicolay & Hay, History, I, 639.

25. Western Sun, Sept. 5, 1818.   26. Grigsby affidavit.

27. Herndon & Weik, I, 13; Herndon-Weik MSS, Vol. 15, D. F. Hanks, Feb. 22, 1866, letter: "I am a Base Born child. My mother was Nancy Hanks the ant of A Lincoln mother."

28. Credit Number F. C. 2566 (under) General Land Office, Vincennes Office, Department of the Interior, Washington, D.C.

29. Davis Inlow to author at Lincoln City, Nov. 1930. Mr. Inlow, then ninety, had as a boy often seen the Lincoln home.

30. Brooks, 29.   31. Herndon & Weik, I, 44.

32. Henry Watterson in Cosmopolitan Magazine, March, 1909, p. 369.

33. Brooks, 29.   34. See Note 28 above.

35. There still are mild outbreaks of "the trembles" in the Lincoln country.

36. "Milk Sickness, the Result of Richweed Poisoning," by Dr. James F. Couch, Journal of the American Medical Association, July 28, 1928, Vol. 91, 234-236; "The Toxic Constituent of Richweed or White Snakeroot (Eupatorium urticaefolium)" by Dr. Couch, Journal of Agricultural Research, Vol. 35, No. 6, Sept. 15, 1927; "Tremetol, The Compound that Produces 'Trembles' (Milksickness)" by Dr. Couch, Journal of the American Chemical Society, 51 (1929), 3617. John Tuley to John W. McCoy.

37. Holland, 30.

38. The Creed reads: "the doctrine of election by grace and that the elect were chosen in Christ Jesus before the world began." This doctrine members called, "the designs of Providence."

39. The will of Thomas Sparrow is on file in the Spencer County courthouse, Rockport. It also is published in Lincoln Lore No. 383.

40. See Note 37 above; Herndon & Weik, I, 26-28.   41. Hobson, 18-19.

42. Redmond Grigsby to Charles F. Brown, Rockport; Herndon-Weik MSS, Vol. 14, William Wood statement, Sept. 15, 1865.

43. Oldroyd, 121; Holland, 436; Arnold's Lincoln, 20; Herndon-Weik MSS, Vol. 13, Dennis Hanks, June 13, 1865, letter.

44. "David Elkins" by Dr. J. Edward Murr in the Christian Advocate, Oct. 17, 1935, p. 938; Cockrum, 331.

45. Judge Ralph E. Roberts, grandson of William Roberts, Rockport, and John Gentry, son of Joseph Gentry, Lincoln City, to author. Ehrmann, 92; Herndon-Weik MSS, Vol. 15, N. Grigsby, March 15, 1866, letter.

46. Hobson, 18.

CHAPTER TWO

1. Rockport Journal, Feb. 11, 1898, statement by Henry C. Whitney, friend of President Lincoln; J. B. McClure, 273-274.

2. Huntington Library Herndon-Lamon Collections, LN 2408, Vol. I, 234.

3. McMurtry, 9.

4.   J. B. McClure, 273-274; Lamon, Life, 29; Samuel Haycraft letter to Herndon, Dec. 7, 1866, in Herndon & Weik, I, 29.

5.   Herndon-Weik MSS, Vol. 15, D. F. Hanks, March 12, 1866 letter.

6.   Ibid., Vol. 14, Matilda Johnston Hall Moore (Lincoln's stepsister), Sept. 8, 1865, statement.

7.   Brooks, 29.   8.   Nicolay & Hay, History, I, 639.

9.   S.W.I.H.S. manuscript Jonesboro by Jeanette Bullock.

10.   Herndon-Weik MSS, Vol. 22, folio 3824, Mrs. Thomas Lincoln statement; Vol. 14, her Sept. 8, 1865, statement; Murr, XIV, 180.

CHAPTER THREE

1.   Lindley, 188 (Morris Birbeck, July 23, 1817).

2.   John Tuley, boyhood friend of Lincoln, to his grandson, John W. McCoy.

3.   Clerk's Records of Cumberland (now Monroe) County, Kentucky; Burkesville, Kentucky: Cumberland County surveyor's Book "A", 309, 396.

4.   Grigsby affidavit.   5.   Arnold's Lincoln, 15-16.   6.   Grigsby affidavit.

7.   S.W.I.H.S. "Life of James Gentry, Jr." by his granddaughter, J. Helen Rhodes (manuscript); Goodspeed, 452; Joseph Gentry to his son, John Gentry.

8.   Herndon-Weik MSS, Vol. 14, N. Grigsby, Sept. 4, 1865, letter.

9.   Ibid., Vol. 15, D. F. Hanks, Jan. 26, 1866, letter; Murr, XIV, 181.

10.   Atkinson, 29.

11.   Nicolay & Hay, History, I, 640; Murr, XIII, 343 and XIV, 154.   (The site of the Noah Gordon mill is about one-half mile south of Old Pigeon Church on the Hevron-Spurlock farm.)

12.   Lamon, Life, 68.   13.   Herndon & Weik, I, 50-51.

14.   Original in Oliver R. Barrett's Lincoln Collection, Chicago; Herndon & Weik, I, 14, and Lamon, Life, 62, quote this poem but both have edited it slightly.

15.   Marriage Record Book No. 1, page 2, Spencer County courthouse, Rockport, Indiana; Rockport Sentinel, June 13, 1883, interview with Mrs. Margaret McFarling (McFarland) Cissna, written by her daughter, Mrs. M. F. Crooks.   Map and sketches of Bureau County, Illinois, by N. Matson, 1867, page 108.

16.   Told to author by old settlers of Lincoln City and published in National Republic Magazine, February, 1931.

17.   John W. McCoy, grandson of John Tuley, to author.

18.   Herndon-Weik MSS, Vol. 15, David Turnham, Feb. 21, 1866, letter.

19.   Gridley, 48, interview with John J. Hall.

20.   Angle, 29-30; Ehrmann, 74   21.   Armstrong, Notes.

22.   Herndon-Weik MSS, Vol. 14, Matilda Johnston Hall Moore (Lincoln's stepsister) Sept. 8, 1865 statement; Vol. 22, folio 3822-3823.

23.   Western Sun, Feb. 15, 1823.

24.   David Inlow statement to author at Lincoln City, Nov. 1930:   Joseph Gentry told story to Mr. Inlow.

25.   Murr, XIV, 33.

26.   John Tuley in Rockport Journal, Feb. 12, 1897; Lamon, Life, 57; Herndon-Weik MSS, Vol. 14, John R. Dougherty, Sept. 17, 1865, statement.

27.   William Jones told Joseph D. Armstrong in 1858, "I have been a regular subscriber to the Vincennes Sun since I came to Spencer county." Of Lincoln, Jones said to Armstrong, "Abe was fond of reading, especially the Whig papers. And any-

thing about Henry Clay was eagerly read and digested by Abe." In the Oakland City Enterprise, Nov. 16, 1899, Joseph D. Armstrong states that "The facts were noted by me during the year 1858, when Mr. Lincoln first came into national prominence, and again in 1860, when he was made the standard bearer of the Republican Party." Mr. Armstrong, a Democrat, made notes of Lincoln during the political campaigns. His penciled notes and published papers are in the possession of his daughter, Mrs. Mina Armstrong Cook, Rockport.

28. Western Sun, Feb. 8, 1817.

29. Peter Jones' Estate, Sept. 1819, Knox County. Clerk's Office, Box 7.

30. *Ibid.*, Minutes of Board of Trustees, Vincennes University, Feb. 18, 1817.

31. *Ibid.* 32. Carpenter, 256.

33. Huntington Library Herndon-Lamon Collection, LN 2408, Vol. I, 235.

34. Hobson, 23.

35. Herndon-Weik MSS, Vol. 15, David Turnham, Feb. 21, 1866 letter.

36. Joseph D. Armstrong in Oakland City Enterprise, Nov. 16, 1899, from William Jones' statement to Armstrong in 1858.

37. Herndon-Weik MSS, Vol. 15. David Turnham, Feb. 21, 1866, letter; Lamon, Life, 24.

38. Hobson, 24-25.

39. Herndon-Weik MSS, Vol. 15, D. F. Hanks, March 22, 1866, letter.

40. Grandview Monitor, Sept. 12, 1935. 41. A. K. McClure, 23.

42. Jacob Reynolds statement to author at Lincoln City, November, 1930 (Mr. Reynolds was the grandson of Joseph Gentry from whom he had the story), National Republic, February, 1931.

43. Roberts, 116.

44. Armstrong's Notes, 1874; Herndon-Weik MSS, Vol. 14, William Wood, Sept. 15, 1865, statement undoubtedly meant this episode.

45. Lowry, 328. 46. Indiana Magazine of History, XXIV, 68.

47. Lowry, 490. 48. Nicolay & Hay, History, I, 14.

49. George Bonnie Enghof, grandson of Betsy Ray Grigsby, to author. Nov. 22, 1935. In calling the colt Bulger it is believed that Sarah Lincoln was using the Indiana backwoodsman's pronounciation of the old Scotch word "buller" which, it is said, meant to rear. Several of Lincoln's neighbors were Scotch immigrants.

50. Tracy, 121. 51. Rice, 458.

52. Scripps, 14-15; New York Herald, Oct. 20, 1860.

53. Murr, XIII, 338; Herndon-Weik MSS, Vol. 16, Elizabeth Crawford, Sept. 7, 1866, letter; Will F. Adams in Grandview Monitor, Aug. 1, 1935; New York Herald, Oct. 20, 1860.

54. Hertz, II, 791 (Lincoln to St. Marie Brass Band and St. Cecelia Society).

55. Herndon-Weik MSS, Vol. 16, Elizabeth Crawford Sept. 7, 1866 letter.

56. Gentry, 269; Nicolay & Hay, History, I, 87-88; Indianapolis Star, March 12, 1939; Lincoln Lore No. 529 (reprint of Lincoln's original manuscript in Library of Congress).

57. Herndon-Weik MSS, Vol. 14, John Romine, Sept. 14, 1865 statement. After talking for several years with Lincoln's old neighbors, Joseph D. Armstrong, in 1874, in his Spencer County and Its Prominent Citizens, 1874, wrote of Lincoln: "By those of his comrades who did not appreciate study he was considered lazy; by others he was pronounced industrious."

58. Mrs. Elizabeth Crawford's public statement at Lincoln City, July 4, 1881,

reprinted in Rockport Journal, June 9, 1916. The well which Lincoln dug for Crawford is still in use.

59. Huntington Library Herndon-Lamon Collection, LN 2408, Vol. I, 136.

60. *Ibid.*, 135.   61. *Ibid.*, 136.   62. Tarbell, 67.

63. Herndon-Weik MSS, Vol. 14: Mrs. Joseph Crawford states that by 1828 Lincoln felt himself destined to be a great man and remarked that he would be President someday. Lamon, Recollections, 110: "From early youth he seemed conscious of a high mission . . . a vision of grandeur and of gloom."

64. Tarbell, Early Life, 62; Lamon, Recollections, 110.

65. Original in Manuscript Division, Library of Congress.

66. Grigsby affidavit. (In the Pigeon Creek neighborhood are three Indian workshops containing stone hoes, drills, pipes, arrowheads, tomahawks, earthenware, jewelry, mortars and pestles.)

67. Norfolk, 129.

68. Barton, 49-50; Butterworth, 39-54: "a true pcture in a framework of fiction."

CHAPTER FOUR

1. Murr, XIII, 323-325; Dr. Murr to author.   2. Angle, 211.

3. Esarey, 425; Herndon-Weik MSS, Vol. 15, N. Grigsby, Jan. 21, 1866, letter.

4. Murr, XIV, 182.

5. Lamon, Life, 49-50; Hobson, 22; Herndon-Weik MSS, Vol. 14, Green B. Taylor Sept. 16, 1865, statement.

6. Townsend, 34-39; Mrs. A. H. Bergenroth's manuscript in author's collection. (Mrs. Bergenroth, deceased, lived in Troy, and was the granddaughter of Reuben Bates who established a store at Bates Landing below Troy in 1812. Mr. Bates was well acquainted with Abraham Lincoln and the Taylor family.)

7. Henry Whittinghill of Boonville to author.

8. Spencer County, Marriage Record Book, No. 1, 1816-1843, p. 20.

9. Grigsby affidavit.

10. Herndon-Weik MSS, Vol. 15, Mrs. Elizabeth Crawford, May 3, 1866, letter.

11. Indiana Magazine of History, XV, 140-141; Lindley, 308-310.

12. Abraham Lincoln's complete "Adam and Eve's Wedding Song" was remembered by Mrs. Elizabeth Crawford and quoted in her May 3, 1866, letter (see Note 10 above).

13. Kidson, 153; Sharp, II, 272, has slightly different version sung by Mr. Jasper Robertson at Burnsville, N.C., Sept. 29, 1918.

14. Grigsby affidavit.

15. Mudge, 57-58; Selby, 59; Murr, XIV, 18-19; Ehrmann, 86; Dr. Murr's 1892 interview with Jefferson Ray, Jr., son of the flatboat captain, and William Forsythe who stated the trip ended at Memphis, Tennessee; statement of William Jefferson Ray, Santa Claus, to author.

16. Cummings, 92.

17. William Jefferson Ray to author. On his return to Indiana, 1827, Jefferson Ray remembered Lincoln's philosophy and on it built a great flatboating business which flourished for many years.

18. Fletcher Chenault in Arkansas (Little Rock) Gazette, July 4, 1927, "Abe Lincoln Lived and Worked in Arkansas." Mr. Chenault interviewed Judge Jesse N.

Cypert, whose father served in the Arkansas Senate with William D. Ferguson, then a State Senator. "Wappanocca" Ferguson told Cypert the story.

19. General Egbert L. Veile in New York Independent, April 4, 1895.

20. Herndon-Weik MSS, Vol. 14, William Wood, Sept. 15, 1865, statement; Murr, XIV, 182.

21. "Spencer County and Its Prominent Citizens," by J. D. Armstrong, 1874; Warrick County Brief, 53—W. H. Scales affidavit; Carpenter, 256; W. H. Scales and Henry C. Whittinghill to author.

22. Herndon-Weik MSS, Vol. 14, David Turnham, Sept. 15, 1865, statement; Lamon, 58-59.

23. Holland, 33; J. B. McClure, 22; Lamon, Life, 58; Arnold, Life, 27. In Hoosier vernacular the word "clever" means kind, neighborly, sociable.

24. Herndon-Weik MSS, Vol. 15, Mrs. Elizabeth Crawford, Feb. 21, 1866, letter.

25. Hobson, 51-52: states that the Reverend Mr. Farmer was a United Brethern preacher who recently had held a big camp meeting in a grove near Gentryville; Herndon-Weik MSS, Vol. 14, William Wood, Sept. 15, 1865, statement; Vol. 16, David Turnham, Sept. 5, 1866, letter.

26. Ordinance Book of Board of Trustees in City Clerk's Office, Vincennes: slave ordinance passed May 15, 1815.

27. Hobson, 29. The Lincoln-Brooner gun is in the Chicago Historical Society Museum.

28. Grigsby affidavit. 29. Warren, 298.

30. Armstrong, Notes, 1874 manuscript; John Tuley to his grandson, John W. Mc-Coy. (Tuley was boyhood companion of Lincoln in Spencer County). The path of the 1827 hurricane was visible as late as 1870. 1827 always afterward was spoken of as "the year of the hurricane."

31. Rockport Journal, Feb. 11, 1898, "Lincoln Heard Phantom Voices and Believed in Destiny" by Henry C. Whitney.

32. Mrs. Mary J. Scott interview in Grandview Monitor, Aug. 26, 1920; Indiana Magazine of History, XXI, 6.

33. Grigsby affidavit.

34. Publication of the Illinois Historical Society, 1907, XII, 165-167.

35. Hobson, 21-24; Charles T. Baker, Grandview, an authority on the Barker-Lamar families genealogy, letter to author. Nettie Barker married John W. Lamar.

36. Grigsby affidavit; Herndon-Weik MSS, Vol. 14, N. Grigsby, Sept. 4, 1866 letter.

37. See Note 35 above. 38. Murr, XIV, 53-55.

39. Gentry affidavit. E. Grant Gentry, Rockport, had the Gentry-Lincoln flatboat story from his grandmother, Katy Roby Gentry, wife of Allen Gentry and schoolmate of Abraham Lincoln. Mr. Gentry's sisters—Misses Anna, Hannah, and Rose, of Rockport—told the same story to author; Herndon-Weik MSS, Vol. 14, N. Grigsby, Sept. 12, 1865 statement.

40. Gentry affidavit.

41. John Gentry, son of Joseph Gentry, to author at Lincoln City.

42. S.W.I.H.S.: "The Honorable Daniel Grass" by Laura Mercey Wright (manuscript).

43. Ehrmann, 21; S.W.I.H.S.: letter by John Grass, M.D.

44. Gentry affidavit.

45. George Burton Cunningham, Chenault, Kentucky, to author. Mr. Cunningham,

in Rockport Journal, July 13, 1928, tells how his father, James H. Cunningham, received the trunk from Lincoln.

46. Gentry affidavit; Gentry, 269.

47. G. B. Cunningham, Rockport Journal, July 13, 1928.

48. *Ibid.*   49. Western Sun, Dec. 13, 1828.

50. Gentry affidavit.

51. Herndon-Weik MSS, Vol. 14, William Wood, Sept. 15, 1865 statement; Murr, XIV, 150.

52. Lamon, Life, 74.

53. Mrs. Josiah Crawford Stapleton statement in Evansville Daily Courier, July 5, 1881; Herndon-Weik MSS, Vol. 14, Jos. C. Richardson, Sept. 14, 1865 statement.

54. Statement of Betsy Ray Grigsby (Mrs. Reuben Grigsby, Jr.), one of the double-wedding brides, Rockport Journal, Feb. 12, 1897.

55. *Ibid.*   56. *Ibid.*

57. Herndon-Weik MSS, Vol. 14, Joe C. Richardson, Sept. 14, 1865, statement.

58. Mrs. Reuben Grigsby, Jr., Rockport Journal, Feb. 12, 1897, statement; Mrs. Elizabeth Crawford's version puts bridegrooms in bed with wrong brides; Herndon-Weik MSS, Vol. 14, C. A. Crawford, Jan. 4, 1866 letter; Vol. 15, N. Grigsby, Feb. 12, 1866, letter.

59. Murr, XIV, 41.   60. See Note 54 above.

61. Herndon-Weik MSS, Vol. 14, N. Grigsby, Sept. 12, 1865, statement. Shortly after the assassination of President Lincoln an old house belonging to the Grigsby family was being torn down. A boy poking around in the loft found the "Book of Chronicles"—a roll of faded, musty papers. Asked what he was doing, he answered, "I am reading a portion of the Scriptures that haven't been revealed yet." About 1892, James Gentry said to Redmond Grigsby, brother of Reuben, Jr. and Charles, "Red, everybody's dead now but you. By gum, I'd let them (the Chronicles) come out." Redmond Grigsby replied, "Jim, there is plenty of time for that yet." (Murr. XIV, 41). In the summer of 1936, Mr. Eli L. Grigsby, Gentryville at the request of the author, made a diligent search for the original copy of "The Chronicles." Mr. Grigsby, who had not seen the Lincoln manuscript for several years, finally reported that he was convinced a cousin of his, in poor mental health, had burned it a year or so before.

62. Murr, XIV, 38-39; Herndon-Weik MSS, Vol. 14, N. Grigsby, Sept. 12, 1865, statement.

63. Herndon-Weik MSS, Vol. 16, N. Grigsby, Sept. 19, 1866, letter.

64. See Note 61 above; Herndon-Weik MSS, Vol. 14, J. C. Richardson Sept. 14, 1865, statement; David Turnham, Sept. 15, 1865, statement.

65. Armstrong Notes, 1875; Herndon-Weik MSS, Vol. 14, Green B. Taylor Sept. 16, 1865, statement; Lamon, Life, 64-65, attributes the Lincoln-Grigsby fight to hard feelings aroused by the "Chronicles of Reuben." Dr. J. Edward Murr interviewed Joseph Gentry, Redmond Grigsby, and Wesley Hall, all of whom saw the fight; all felt Lamon was mistaken. (Murr, XIV, 38-39)

66. Herndon-Weik MSS, Vol. 14, N. Grigsby, Oct. 25, 1865, letter.

67. Grigsby affidavit.

68. Mrs. Reuben Grigsby, Jr. to her grandson, Charles Todd Enghof, Grandview.

69. Herndon-Weik MSS, Vol. 14, N. Grigsby, Sept. 12, 1865, statement.

CHAPTER FIVE

1. Johnson, 156; Murr, XIV, 60-61.
2. Lincoln Lore No. 49 (quoting Lincoln to John Locke Scripps).
3. Johnson, 157.
4. The Lincoln family Bible is preserved in the Lincoln Museum, Ford Theater, Washington, D.C. Six inches wide, nine and a half inches long and three and a half inches thick, it weighs about three and a half pounds. It was printed in 1799; its binding of board and calf-skin is still in good condition. Great sections have been carefully torn out; it is believed this was done to buy other Lincoln relics. Owners of those pages, it is hoped. will return them to the Lincoln Museum to be rebound in this, one of the most precious Bibles in America. Missing parts are Exodus IX to XVIII, inclusive; II Maccabees XII; all of St. Matthew and to St. Mark VIII, 6. Lincoln was especially fond of Isaiah. Consequently, Chapters XLV, XLVI, XLVIII of Isaiah and their footnotes are thumbed and worn. II Esdras and Ecclesiasticus (Prologue of Wisdom of Jesus the Son of Sirach) of the books called the Apocrypha indicate a great amount of usage.
5. Lamon, Recollections, 113-114.
6. The custom of mass funerals in June, prevailed at Old Pigeon Creek meeting-house until the late 1930's. Elder Thomas France invited author to attend such a service.
7. Brooks, 21; Hobson, 20; Arnold, Life, 20; Lincoln Lore No. 606; J. B. McClure, 251; Tarbell, Early Life, 64; Murr, XIV, 178.
8. "Funeral Sermon for Nancy Hanks Lincoln" Dr. J. Edward Murr, Christian Advocate, Oct., 1935; Lincoln Lore No. 69; J. B. McClure, 251-253; Herndon-Weik MSS, Vol. 13, D. F. Hanks, June 13, 1865, letter.
9. Holland, 29-30.
10. Tarbell, Early Life, 64 (Joseph Gentry statement)
11. J. B. McClure, 251-252.   12. Western Sun, Oct. 9, 1819.
13. Warrick County Brief, 43—James W. Phillips affidavit; J. D. Armstrong's "Pocket Reminiscences, Number 2;" Armstrong, Notes; Hobson, 22; Lincoln Lore No. 84.
14. Spencer County and Its Prominent Citizens by J. D. Armstrong, 1874; Armstrong, Notes; Lincoln Lore No. 661.
15. J. D. Armstrong's "Pocket Reminiscences, Number 2." Sometime around 1870 a tramp spent the night in the log church; being too lazy to gather fuel from the woods, he used Thomas Lincoln's wild-cherry pulpit for firewood.
16. Lamon, Recollections, 119-120.
17. Elder Thomas France's sermon at Pigeon Creek meetinghouse, Nov. 3, 1935: the customary statements and inquiries made by preachers there for more than a century.
18. Huntington Library Herndon-Lamon Collection, LN 2408, Vol. I, 82; Herndon-Weik MSS, Vol. 14, David Turnham, Sept. 15, 1865, statement.
19. Herndon-Weik MSS, Vol. 14, Matilda Johnston Hall Moore, Sept. 8, 1865, statement.
20. Murr, XIII, 343.
21. Huntington Library Herndon-Lamon Collection, LN 2408, Vol. I, 227. Detailed account of Lincoln's religious activities, by Thomas B. McGregor, National Republic,

Washington, D.C., Oct. 15, 1921; Herndon-Weik MSS, Vol. 15, N. Grigsby, Jan. 21, 1866 letter.

22. James Grigsby to Professor Andrew M. Sweeney, who knew Grigsby many years.

23. Reverend Caleb A. Obenshain of Dewey, Oklahoma, in Kansas City (Missouri) Journal, Jan. 22, 1909. Reverend Obenshain, a Baptist minister, climbed into the loft of the Old Pigeon Church during 1866, and "discovered in a crevice between two of the upper logs an old, faded memorandum book." Lincoln Lore No. 767.

24. Herndon & Weik, I, 79-80, footnote; Murr, XIII, 344; A. K. McClure, 20-21.

25. After rare book experts, bibliographers, Roman Catholic and Church of England scholars, and the Library of Congress and the British Museum had failed to identify the book—all pages before 259 were missing—for author, 1936-1937, he gave a photostat of page 401 to Dr. Anson Phelps Stokes, Canon of Washington Cathedral, who took it to Europe and turned it over to Dr. Willard Connelly, Director of the American University Union of London and Paris. On December 15, 1937, Dr. Connelly wrote to Dr. Stokes that the book had been identified. Dr. Connelly had taken the photostat to Oxford University and "put it in the hands of my good friend, Dr. Caster, Bodley's Librarian" who "put the problem under the scrutiny of his Senior Assistant, Mr. J. C. Hindle. After a search of three weeks Mr. Hindle solved the puzzle. The photostat is a leaf from Practical Discourses upon all the Collects, Epistles, and Gospels, to be us'd thro-out the year. Volume IV, Part II. By Matthew Hole, D.D., Rector of Exeter College in Oxford. London, 1716, Octaveo." Mr. Hindle wrote Dr. Connelly that "fortunately the Bodleian acquired this particular set of Hole's books only shortly before the question came in. Otherwise he would have looked in vain." The copy which Lincoln read was loaned to author by John W. McCoy, grandson of John Tuley.

26. Warrick County Brief, 31—Sarah Gray affidavit.

27. Lincoln Lore No. 76.

28. Herndon-Weik MSS, Vol. 14, Matilda Johnston Hall Moore, Sept. 8, 1865 statement and her undated statement, Vol. 22, folio 3823-3824; Lamon, Life, 40.

29. Herndon-Weik MSS, Vol. 14, folio 2314, Mrs. Thomas Lincoln, Sept. 8, 1865 statement; Vol. 14, N. Grigsby, Sept. 4, 1865 letter; A. K. McClure, 276.

30. William Fortune's Notes and Collection, Indianapolis.

31. Rockport Journal, Feb. 11, 1898: "Lincoln the Fatalist, Heard Phantom Voices and Believed in Destiny" by Henry C. Whitney "a close personal friend."

32. Drake, 125-126: Drake's wording differs from the traditional version of Tecumseh's reply to Harrison.

33. Western Sun, Sept. 6, 1828.   34. Arnold, 81.

35. Thomas B. McGregor, National Republic, Oct. 15, 1921: quotes Minute Book.

36. Selby, 224; A. K. McClure, 304; will of Jesse Howell, Orange County, Dec. 17, 1822, Indiana State Archives, Indianapolis.

37. Herndon-Weik MSS, Vol. 14, William Wood, Sept. 15, 1865, statement.

38. Western Sun, Sept. 5, 1829.

39. "Minutes of the Salem Baptist Association Held at New Hope Meeting House" the Fourth Lord's Day in Sept. 1829.

40. Lamon, Life, 63.

41. Minute Book of Pigeon Church, owned by Mr. Hilbert Bennett, member of the Spencer County Historical Society, Rockport, Lincoln Lore No. 767.

42. Whitney, 38.

CHAPTER SIX

1. Tarbell, Early Life, 62 (Whipple, 52, quotes Tarbell's Early Life, 62).
2. Huntington Library Herndon-Lamon Collection, LN 2408, Vol. I, 87.
3. Nicolay & Hay, History, I, 596.
4. Grigsby affidavit; Herndon-Weik MSS, Vol. 14, N. Grigsby, Sept. 4, 1865, letter.
5. Still a common salutation among older people of the Indiana Lincoln country.
6. Lamon, Life, 34-35; A. K. McClure, 219; Stoddard, 42-43; Indiana Magazine of History, XIV, 70; statements to author by Anna Caroline Roby Gentry's granddaughters, Misses Anna, Hannah, and Rose Gentry, Rockport.
7. Herndon-Weik MSS, Vol. 14, N. Grigsby, Sept. 12, 1865, statement.
8. Daily Alta Californian, San Francisco, March 8, 1888.
9. Whipple, 45; Williams, 9; Indiana Magazine of History, XIV, 43.
10. Herndon-Weik MSS, Vol. 14, N. Grigsby, Sept. 12, 1865, statement.
11. Bounty Land Claim Wt. 83168-120-'55, Veterans Administration, Washington, D.C.; Lincoln Lore No. 65.
12. Rice, 458.   13. See Note 10 above.
14. Original in Manuscript Division, Library of Congress.
15. Unnamed newspaper clipping, apparently dated 1881, entitled "Recollections of ex-President Lincoln—at Lincoln City, July 4th" in William Fortune Collection, Indianapolis; Herndon-Weik MSS, Vol. 14, Joseph C. Richardson, Sept. 14, 1865, statement.
16. F. F. Browne, 44-45.
17. Oldroyd's Album, 35, quoting from "Sketch of Abraham Lincoln by Hon. Isaac N. Arnold."
18. Journal of Illinois Historical Society, October, 1929, Vol. XXII, No. 3, p. 447; Herndon-Weik MSS, Vol. 14, John R. Dougherty, Sept. 14, 1865 statement.
19. Herndon-Weik MSS, Vol. 14, Jos. C. Richardson, Sept. 14, 1865 statement.
20. *Ibid.* John R. Dougherty, Sept. 17, 1865, statement; James Grigsby to Professor Andrew M. Sweeney.
21. Herndon-Weik MSS, Vol. 23, John Hanks undated statement; Vol. 14, Matilda Johnston Hall Moore, Sept. 8, 1865, statement.
22. F. F. Browne, 52.
23. Lamon, Life, 37, footnote: "He read at Turnham's house Scott's Lessons and Sinbad the Sailor;" Lincoln Lore No. 512. Mr. Ora Brown, Dale, owns Scott's 1806 edition which was known to Lincoln's neighbors.
24. Nicolay & Hay, History, II, 393.   25. Carpenter, 162.
26. Herndon-Weik MSS, Vol. 14, Mrs. Thomas Lincoln, Sept. 8, 1865, statement.
27. *Ibid.*, Vol. 22, folio 3825, Mrs. Thomas Lincoln statement.
28. Indiana Magazine of History, XV, 140-141; Arnold, 21.
29. Sherman T. Briscoe affidavit, Exhibit No. 21 in the Corydon, Lincoln Highway Association Brief. Mr. Briscoe, a great-grandson of Josiah Lincoln, knew Professor J. M. Johnson, son of William B. Johnson, who gave Briscoe the story about Abraham Lincoln borrowing *Pilgrim's Progress.* Briscoe's statement to author at Milltown, Indiana.
30. Murr, XIV, 53: interview with Lincoln's boyhood neighbors; Rockport Journal, Feb. 11, 1898, Henry C. Whitney statement.

31. Cave-stone country of Indiana see booklet "A Brief History of Crawford County" by John H. Weathers, New Albany, 1936.

32. See Note 28 above: Briscoe affidavit.

33. New York Herald, Oct. 20, 1860; Scripps, 14-15. There is a dispute over whether it was Ramsay's *Washington* or Weems' *Washington* which was damaged. Lincoln is said to have approved Scripps' work, making it Ramsay's. Herndon-Weik MSS, Vol. 14, Mrs. Crawford, Sept. 16, 1865, stated it was Weems.

34. Nicolay & Hay, History, I, 171; Oldroyd, 49.

35. See Note 19 above. New York Herald, Oct. 20, 1860.

36. Huntington Library Herndon-Lamon Collection. LN 2408, Vol. I, 137.

37. Abraham Lincoln's autographed copy of the Columbian Class Book is in the Frank G. Logan Collection, Chicago Historical Society.

38. S.W.I.H.S.: letter by John Grass, M.D.; Ehramann, 21.

39. Herndon-Weik MSS, Vol. 14, William Wood, Sept. 15, 1865 statement.

40. Nicolay & Hay, History, II, 366.

41. Rockport Journal, March 20, 1896 and Feb. 12, 1897. The bookcase, which Abraham Lincoln made, is in the Temple of Fine Arts, Evansville. After the Lincolns moved from Indiana in 1830, the bookcase fell into the hands of Abraham's close neighbor, John W. Lamar, Buffaloville. Captain Lamar gave the bookcase, in 1876, to Captain J. W. Wartman of Evansville, who gave it to the Temple of Fine Arts. Shallow holes burned out by Lincoln's candles are quite noticeable in the table top.

42. Hobson, 24.

CHAPTER SEVEN

1. Grigsby affidavit; Professor Andrew M. Sweeney of Indianapolis to author. Sweeney boarded with James Grigsby in 1870.

2. *Ibid.*; Herndon-Weik MSS, Vol. 14, N. Grigsby, Sept. 4, 1865, letter.

3. Andrew M. Sweeney to author.   4. *Ibid.*

5. Fortune, Notes.

6. Herndon-Weik MSS, Vol. 18, John W. Lamar, May 18, 1867, letter.

7. Dunn, Greater Indianapolis, I, 554.

8. Indianapolis Gazette, April 5, 1823.

9. Unpublished manuscript of William L. Barker (deceased), Boonville, in the possession of his son, John Barker of Boonville. After many years of research William L. Barker reconstructed this murder story from material found in three authoritative sources.

10. Huntington Library Herndon-Lamon Collection. LN 2408, Vol. I, 124-125.

11. James Grigsby to Professor Andrew M. Sweeney. Mr. Seth Seacat to author, July 13, 1937: "My mother was Mary Ann Crutchfield, daughter of Barbara Lincoln, daughter of Josiah Lincoln. My mother told me the Breckenridge story lots of times. That man Breckenridge!" This is the one story 80 year old Mr. Seacat, living then at DePauw, Harrison County—just over the ridge from the home of William B. Johnson, who loaned Lincoln Pilgrim's Progress—said remains fresh in the memories of the Indiana branch of the Lincoln family. Herndon-Weik MSS, Vol. 14, S. T. Johnston, Sept. 14, 1865, statement.

12. Rice, 458.

13. Townsend, 34-39; Mrs. A. H. Bergenroth manuscript in author's collection; S.

Grant Johnson statement in Dale Reporter, Feb. 8, 1945; Barton, Women, 141-148. Barton says the girl's name was Caroline Meeker.

14. Hon. and Mrs. R. G. Higdon, Frankfort, Kentucky, to author: Harrison Pate, Negro slave was present at Lincoln-Dill brothers' trial. Mrs. Higdon, granddaughter of Squire Samuel Pate. S. Grant Johnson letter to author, March 18, 1945; Murr, XIV, 150-153.

15. Townsend, 40; Lamon, Life, 37; Herndon-Weik MSS, Vol. 14, N. Grigsby, Oct. 25, 1866, letter. David Turnham's copy of Revised Laws of Indiana, which Lincoln read, is owned by Hon. William H. Townsend, Lexington, Kentucky.

16. Cumberland County Clerk's Records, Burksville, Kentucky; Cumberland County Surveyor's Book "A", pp. 309, 396; letter by G. H. Hoffman, Burkesville, Kentucky, in Grandview Monitor, Oct. 25, 1928.

17. Herndon-Weik MSS, Vol. 15, David Turnham, Feb. 21, 1866, letter.

18. William Fortune's Notes; Ehrmann, 74.

19. Herndon-Weik MSS, Vol. 28, folio 4661-4664, O. C. Terry, July 14, 1888, letter containing Judge John Pitcher's statement.

20. S.W.I.H.S.: Judge John Iglehart's papers; S.W.I.H.S., Bulletin No. 16, p. 55.

21. Vincennes Sun, Dec. 10, 1916, Section 4, describes the volume of Blackstone which Abraham Lincoln borrowed from Sheriff Pitcher and read. In 1916 it belonged to LeRoy M. Wade, member of the law firm of Wade & Padgett, Vincennes. State Senator Jesse E. Wade, Mount Vernon, in referring to the Blackstone newspaper item, wrote on April 18, 1935, "This is a correct statement as given to me by Mr. Engler." (Wade statement in author's collection)

22. Ibid. and Note 20 above. The 1803 edition of Christian's Blackstone's Commentaries which Abraham Lincoln read in Indiana, its pages still badly stained with Spencer County's muddy water, was given by Judge (former Sheriff) John Pitcher to the Reverend Richard Flower, a farmer-preacher, living across the Wabash River from New Harmony and near Albion, Illinois. Reverend Flower gave the book to Colonel Alfred Dale Owen, son of Robert Dale Owen of the New Harmony Utopian experiments and friend of President Lincoln. Colonel Owen gave the book to Captain George W. Engler also of New Harmony. On Dec. 25, 1902, Captain Engler gave the book to Hon. LeRoy M. Wade of the law firm of Wade & Padgett, Vincennes.

23. Herndon-Weik MSS, Vol. 14, William Wood, Sept. 15, 1865, statement; Vol. 16, David Turnham, Sept. 5, 1866, letter; A. K. McClure, 276.

24. Murr, XIV, 73-75.

25. Herndon-Weik MSS, Vol. 22, folio 3825, Mrs. Thomas Lincoln statement.

26. Ibid., Vol. 14, Mrs. Thomas Lincoln, Sept. 8, 1865, statement.

CHAPTER EIGHT

1. See Note 16, Chapter Seven above.
2. Buckley, 96.
3. Fortune, Warrick, 73; Lincoln Lore No. 597: The Lincolns and Audubon.
4. Ibid.   5. Atkinson, 8.
6. Fortune, Warrick, 77; Goodspeed, 251.   7. Western Sun, July 27, 1816.
8. Benton, I, 5-6; Western Sun, July 27, 1816.
9. Western Sun, May 8, 1819.   10. Dunn, 40.
11. Goodspeed, 272-273.   12. Carpenter, 256.
13. Fortune, Warrick, 78: Joseph Lane letter.

14. Armstrong, Notes, 1870; Joseph D. Armstrong in Oakland City Enterprise, Nov. 16, 1899.

15. *Ibid.*   16. *Ibid.*

17. Grigsby affidavit; Herndon-Weik MSS, Vol. 14, N. Grigsby, Sept. 12, 1865, statement.

18. Western Sun, July 24, 1824.   19. *Ibid.*, May 15, 1824.

20. Joseph D. Armstrong in Oakland City Enterprise, Nov. 16, 1899.

21. Stanwood, 136, 140.   22. Prentice, 225.

23. Western Sun, March 19, 1825.

24. Warrick County Courthouse, Complete Record, pp. 128-129, Sept. 1825, Boonville.

25. Hart, 251.   26. Western Sun, May 6, 1826.

27. *Ibid.*, Oct. 14, 1826.   28. *Ibid.*, March 3, 1827.

29. *Ibid.*, Oct. 6, 1827.   30. Dewey, 182.

31. Western Sun, May 31, 1828.

32. Herndon-Weik MSS, Vol. 15, Mrs. Elizabeth Crawford, Feb. 21, 1866, letter.

33. "Lincoln's Early Political Education" by M. L. Houser (Lester O. Schriver, Peoria, Illinois), 1944, 13.

34. Western Sun, Sept. 20, 1828.   35. Stanwood, 149; Channing, 342.

36. Huntington Library Herndon-Lamon Collection, LN 2408, Vol. I, 92.

37. Western Sun, Nov. 22, 1828.

38. Cincinnati (Ohio) Daily Gazette, May 9, 1829, typical of the papers.

39. Western Sun, June 27, 1829.

40. Hobson, 23; Herndon-Weik MSS, Vol. 18, John W. Lamar, May 18, 1867, letter. Lamar says the braggart's name was James Larkins. Samson may have been the nickname given him by Lincoln and others in ridicule. This affair took place near present Santa Claus (Murr, XIV, 37-38).

41. Herndon-Weik MSS, Vol. 22, folio 3825, Mrs. Thomas Lincoln, undated statement.

CHAPTER NINE

1. Lindley, 325; Lockwood, 9-11 and 20-21.

2. Atkinson, 28.   3. *Ibid.*

4. Robert Owen's "Essay on Common Wealth", published in 1822 by the New York Society for Promoting Communities.

5. "A Discourse on a New System of Society; As Delivered in the Hall of Representatives of the United States" by Robert Owen, February 25, and March 7, 1825. First and Second Discourses printed for Robert Owen by Gales & Seaton, Washington, 1825.

6. New Harmony Gazette, Oct. 1, 1825, reprinting Robert Owen's April 27th speech in the Hall of New Harmony.

7. For details of Owen's experiments see The New Harmony Movement by George B. Lockwood, Appleton and Company, New York, 1905; also A Visit to the Colony of Harmony in Indiana by William Herbert, printed for George Mann, London, 1825.

8. New Harmony Gazette, Oct. 1, 1825.   9. Atkinson, 28.

10. Vincennes Credit F. 2566 (under) General Land Office, Department of the Interior, Washington, D.C.

11. Goodspeed, History of Posey, 408.

12. Posey County Marriage Record Book No. 1, p. 48, County Clerk's Office, Mount Vernon; Goodspeed: History of Posey, 288.

13. Posey County Probate Court Order Book "A", p. 213, County Clerk's Office, Mount Vernon.

14. *Ibid.*, 291.

15. Posey County Old Records Box No. 4088: James McCrary's original bond, as guardian, executed Aug. 30, 1826, for $400. Guardians of estates, at that time, generally were bonded for twice the value of the estate, which in this case would be $200. Since Thomas Lincoln bought only one-half of the farm, the "valuable consideration" he paid undoubtedly was not more than $100 cash.

16. The Posey County Lincoln farm is owned by James Garris, Fredonia Strauss Joest, Jane Scherer, *et al.* It is about two and a half miles northeast of Wadesville, Indiana. For description of the 1806 survey of this land see Plat Book, Township and Range Book No. 1, page 2, Posey County Recorder's Office, Mount Vernon.

17. New Harmony Gazette, April 4, 1827.

18. Lockwood, 172.   19. Western Sun, April 5, 1828.

20. Lockwood, 132; Lindley, 415.   21. Lockwood, 251.

22. See Note 10, above.

23. Deed Record Book No. 81, p. 197, Spencer County Recorder's Office, Rockport. At the time the United States Government described the land as being in Perry County, not yet having officially recognized the new Spencer County unit.

24. Lindley, 414-415.

CHAPTER TEN

1. Whipple, 50.

2. A. K. McClure, 219; Lamon, 34-35; Stoddard, 42-45; Indiana Magazine of History, XIV, 70; Misses Anna, Hannah and Rose Gentry, granddaughters of Anna Caroline Roby Gentry, to author.

3. Charles Todd Enghof, grandson of Betsy Ray Grigsby, to author at Grandview. (Mrs. Charles Todd Enghof had known Mrs. Grigsby, and heard her repeat this episode.)

4. *Ibid.*

5. S. Grant Johnson in Dale Reporter, Feb. 8, 1945. Mrs. Samuel Pate lived to see Lincoln become President: S. Grant Johnson, March 3, 1945, letter to author. Barton, Women (148-156), claims the girl's name was Caroline Meeker.

6. Charles Todd Enghof to author.

7. Herndon-Weik MSS, Vol. 29, John M. Lockwood, Jan. 4, 1896, letter.

8. Mrs. Elizabeth Tuley Hesson statement in Rockport Journal, Feb. 12, 1897; John Walker McCoy to author.

9. *Ibid.*

10. *Ibid.;* S.W.I.H.S. T. H. Masterson interview with Mrs. Elizabeth Tuley Hesson (manuscript).

CHAPTER ELEVEN

1. Western Sun, Dec. 14, 1816.   2. Rockport Democrat, Sept. 29, 1860.

3. Western Sun, Oct. 17, 1818.   4. Armstrong, Notes.

5. Tax receipt for "1 black" in Dr. Claude C. Lomax Collection, Indianapolis, signed by A. Newland, deputy for William Taylor, Spencer County clerk.

6. Knox County, Indiana, First Book of Court of Common Pleas, Robert Buntin, Clerk, 1805, Vincennes; Dunn, 434-435.

7. Western Sun, Feb. 9, 1817.

8. Peter Jones' Estate, Sept. 1819, Knox County Clerk's Office, Box 7, Vincennes.

9. Western Sun, Nov. 28, 1818; Oct. 9, 1819.   10. Dunn, 223-224.

11. *Ibid.*, 246-248.   12. *Ibid.*, 224, Lindley, 257-258.

13. Cockrum, 572.   14. *Ibid.*, 571.

15. Western Sun, Oct. 11, 1823.

16. "The Life, Travel, and Opinions of Benjamin Lundy" published by his children, Philadelphia, 1847, 223.

17. "The African Slave Trade," by George C. Mason in American Historical Record, Vol. I, 1872.

18. Spencer County Marriage Book No. 1, shows that Reverend Adam Shoemaker performed marriage ceremonies for Lincoln's neighbors, 1822 to 1827.

19. Deed Record Book "A", page 71, Spencer County Recorder's Office, Rockport.

20. Armstrong, Notes, 1870; Joseph D. Armstrong in Oakland City Enterprise, Nov. 16, 1899.

21. Western Sun, July 19, 1824.

22. Angle, 190; reprint from Carlinville (Illinois) Democrat, Sept. 2, 1858.

23. "Influence of Riley's Narrative upon Abraham Lincoln" by R. Gerald McMurtry, Indiana Magazine of History, XXX, No. 2, pp. 133-138, June, 1934; New York Herald, Oct. 20, 1860; Scripps, 14.

24. Cockrum, 570.   25. *Ibid.*

26. Nicolay & Hay, History, I, 252.   27. Goodspeed, 668-672.

28. Telescope, June 24, 1826.

29. Indiana Magazine of History, XXXV, No. 2, 151; Gilbert, 24.

30. Telescope, July 28, 1827.   31. Dewey, 181.

32. Western Sun, June 22, 1822.   33. Goddell, 30.

34. Cobb, 3.   35. *Ibid.*, 96.

36. Georgia Historical Quarterly, XIV, 39, Savannah, Georgia.

37. See Note No. 14, Chapter VI, above.

38. Georgia Historical Quarterly, XIV, 36-39. Savannah, Georgia.

39. "The Crisis or Essays on the Usurpations of the Federal Government" Oct. 27, 1827, p. 124, by Brutus (Robert James Turnbull), Charleston, S.C., printed for A. E. Miller, 1827.

40. Rockport Journal, Feb. 11, 1898, "Lincoln the Fatalist, Heard Phantom Voices and Believed in Destiny," by Henry C. Whitney.

41. Register of Debates in Congress, 1st Session, 1827-1828, Vol. 41, Jan. 4, 1828, pp. 899-975.

42. Gentry affidavit; Herndon-Weik MSS, Vol. 14, John R. Dougherty, Sept. 17, 1865, statement; Lamon, 71; Nicolay & Hay, History, I, 640; Rice, 462; Selby, 59-60; Stoddard, 63.

43. Gentry affidavit.

44. *Ibid.;* also John Gentry, son of Joseph Gentry (Lincoln's boyhood companion) to author at Lincoln City.

45. Where Lincoln and Gentry roomed in New Orleans, 819 Saint Ann Street (traditional).

46. New Orleans Louisiana Courier, Feb. 16, 1829.

47. Olmsted, 680-681.   48. New Orleans Louisiana Courier, Feb. 19, 1829.

49. Gentry affidavit.   50. Moore, 117.

51. Herndon-Weik MSS, Vol. 14, John Romine, Sept. 14, 1865, statement.

52. Weik, 25-26.

53. Lafayette Johnson affidavit in author's collection. Abraham Lincoln told this tobacco warehouse episode to his close friend and political crony, Colonel Richard W. Thompson of Terre Haute, Indiana. Following the Civil War Thompson and Lafayette Johnson served together in the Indiana Legislature. Thompson told Johnson the story.

54. Tracy, 128.

CHAPTER TWELVE

1. Herndon-Weik MSS, Vol. 15, D. F. Hanks March 7, 1866, letter; Lamon, 74.

2. The Enlow mill was at the present city of Jasper. The wild cherry lift-top desk made by Thomas Lincoln is owned by Louis P. Joseph, President of the Jasper Desk Company.

3. Spencer County Deed Record Book "B", pp. 63-64, Rockport, Indiana.

4. Hobson, 80-81.

5. Lincoln-Douglas, 75, a broadside issued by M. W. Delahay, Leavenworth, Kansas, about 1870, and republished by Daniel E. Newhall, New York, 1939, quotes Lincoln as saying to Delahay near Edwardsville, Illinois, 1858, that while living in Indiana he (Lincoln) "tended a 'short worm' distillery, at eighteen dollars per month." The site of this distillery is on the Henry Steineker farm four miles south of Huntingburg.

6. Ibid.   7. Nicolay & Hay, History I, 59.

8. Warrick County Brief, 24—Captain William Jones, son of Storekeeper William Jones, affidavit; A. K. McClure, 342-343; Hobson, 28-30.

9. Warrick County Brief, 38—Jacob Clark and Bartley Inco affidavits; Murray XIV, 47-48.

10. William Jones in Rockport Planter, Sept. 20, 1860; Lamon, 57.

11. Lamon, Life, 9. Some old people in Southern Indiana and members of the Indiana Lincoln family still pronounce Lincoln as Linkern.

12. Herndon-Weik MSS, Vol. 14, Jos. C. Richardson Sept. 14, 1865, statement.

13. Western Sun, Feb. 20 and 27, 1830.

14. Warrick County Brief, 41—Francis M. Carlisle affidavit.

15. Ibid., 27—Allen Gentry affidavit; Gentry, 269.

16. James Grigsby to Professor Andrew M. Sweeney; Ehrmann, 93-94 (Dr. Murr interview with Wesley Hall and other Lincoln neighbors).

17. Original in Manuscript Division, Library of Congress.

18. Herndon-Weik MSS, Vol. 15, D. F. Hanks, April, 1866, letter; Nicolay & Hay, History, I, 640; Lincoln Lore No. 480.

19. Warrick County Brief, 27—Allen Gentry affidavit; 37—Bartley Inco affidavit; 38—Jacob Clark affidavit; 22-25—William Jones affidavit. Herndon-Weik MSS, Vol. 14, David Turnham, Sept. 15, 1865, statement.

20. Ibid., 25—Captain William Jones, Jr. affidavit; 27—Allen Gentry affidavit; 51 —Cordie Hagan Thompson affidavit; Rockport Planter, Sept. 20, 1860; Armstrong,

Notes; James Gentry, Jr., statement to Judge Ralph E. Roberts, Rockport; Herndon-Weik MSS, Vol. 15, David Turnham, Feb. 21, 1866, letter.

21. Warrick County Brief, 25—Captain William Jones, Jr., affidavit.

22. *Ibid.*, 29—Robert M. Gentry affidavit; 37—Bartley Inco affidavit.

23. *Ibid.*, 27-28—Allen Gentry affidavit; 37—Bartley Inco affidavit.

24. *Ibid.*, 39—L. B. Baker affidavit; 44—James W. Phillips affidavit; 53— W. H. Scales affidavit; 30—Robert M. Gentry affidavit; 51—Cordie Thompson affidavit; W. E. Williams statement, Boonville Standard, May 14, 1915.

25. Grigsby affidavit. After Lincoln was assassinated Redmond Grigsby said to his grandson, Eli L. Grigsby, Gentryville, "I am going to destroy it," meaning the diary. Eli Grigsby stated to author at Gentryville, June 4, 1939: Redmond Grigsby "burnt up a lot of old papers" and the diary probably was among them.

26. Boonville-Vincennes U.S. mail schedule, by stage coach, Western Sun, Sept. 27, 1828.

27. Warrick County Brief, 36—Mary E. Floyd affidavit (Mrs. Floyd, daughter of Joseph Langford); 34—Elizabeth A. Goad affidavit.

28. A. K. McClure, 342.

29. Warrick County Brief, 48—Louella Ashley affidavit (Mrs. Ashley helped tear down the Turpen log house after the Civil War, when the Lincoln pocket-book was found); 34—Elizabeth A. Goad affidavit. The Indiana Lincoln Memorial Highway Commission reported, "The Commission is very frank to admit that it does not have and is thoroughly convinced that there is not now available proof as to the route traveled by the Lincolns during either of the migrations." The author feels that the affidavits of reliable citizens of Spencer and Warrick counties, Indiana, which he cites in Notes 18 to 27 and 29 of Chapter Twelve do prove now beyond a reasonable doubt that the Lincoln 1830 migration followed the then busy, well-supervised Gentry-ville-Boonville-Vincennes highways. For additional comment of the Commission see Lincoln Lore No. 161.

30. *Ibid.*, 34—Elizabeth A. Goad affidavit; 21—statement of Reverend Jefferson W. Richardson. In Lynnville cemetery on slate tombstone: Nancy S. Hanks Died Oct. 1st 1842 Aged 32 years 6 m. & 12 d.

31. Vincennes Commercial, Centennial Edition of the Lincoln Migration, March 6, 1930, under Winslow; John Ashby, grandson of Benjamin Ashby, to author.

32. Petersburg Press, Oct. 7 and 10, 1930.   33. A. K. McClure, 343.

34. Henry W. Slawson, descendant of Jesse Slawson, to author at Bruceville. Henry W. is fourth generation of blacksmiths in Slawson family.

35. See Note 27, Chapter Two, above: Tarbell, Early Life, 87.

36. The Adam Ramage hand printing press in use in the Vincennes Western Sun Office, March, 1830, was sold in 1842 to John R. Jones, who took it to Perryville, Indiana, 125 miles up the Wabash River. Jones published the Perryville Eagle on it. Various people owned it until in 1861 when George Sellers bought it and took it to Tuscola, Illinois. For further details on this press see "History of Iroquois County, Illinois" by C. F. McNeill, p. 35. Albert T. Reid, artist, commemorated Lincoln's visit to Western Sun office with a pen-and-ink sketch, calling it "First Meeting of the Two Great Emancipators," National Republic cover, Feb. 12, 1921. Since then Mr. Reid has done an oil painting, historically correct in detail, of this meeting: National Republic, Dec., 1947, p. 13, article by author. The March 6, 1830, issue of the Vincennes Western Sun is known as the Lincoln Number.

37. Oldroyd, Mystic, 7.   38. Western Sun, Aug. 29, 1829.

39. Lindley, 297-298 (William Faux journal).

40. Nov. 11, 1826 Vincennes Western Sun called Saint Xavier's church a cathedral. Bishop Brute was first Bishop. Late as 1870 ruins of old fort still lay 150 yards from cathedral (Charles Vachet interview, Vincennes Sun Commercial, March 10, 1935).

41. Letter: Peter Smith, Petty's P.O., Lawrence County, Illinois, July 17, 1860, to J. Warren Keifer, Springfield, Ohio, reprinted in Lincoln Lore No. 480; same dog story, slightly altered, in Hertz Hidden Lincoln, 227. In times of high water the Wabash River at Vincennes still floods the Illinois prairies.

42. Nicolay, 364.   43. Nicolay & Hay, History, I, 597.

CHAPTER THIRTEEN

1. Nicolay & Hay, History, I, 646. For a survey of the theory that during a human being's early years much of the basic personality is formed see: Child Behavior and Development, edited by Roger G. Barker, Jacob S. Kounin, and Herbert F. Wright (McGraw-Hill, New York, 1943); Conceptions of Modern Psychiatry by Harry Stack Sullivan (William Alanson White Psychiatric Foundation, Washington, D.C., 1947); A Study of Interpersonal Relations edited by Patrick Mullahy (Hermitage Press, New York, 1949); Physiological Psychology by Clifford T. Morgan (McGraw-Hill, New York, 1943).

2. Nicolay, Personal Traits, 282.

3. Herndon-Weik MSS, Vol. 14, Doct. Houghland, Sept. 17, 1865, statement, quoting William Jones; Murr, XIV, 48.

4. Oldroyd, 82.   5. Nicolay & Hay, History, I, 673.

6. Rockport Journal, July 13, 1928, a statement of George Burton Cunningham, son of James H. Cunningham.

7. Coggeshall, 30.   8. Ibid.

9. A. L. S. Irregular T-82 L.R., S.W. autographed letter received by Secretary of War, Washington, D.C.

10. Original in Mitten Collection, Indiana Historical Library, Indianapolis: reprinted in Indiana Historical Publications Vol. 8, No. 8, pp. 145-146.

11. A.G.O. records pertaining to Lieut. Col. William Jones, 53rd Indiana Infantry Volunteers.

12. Carpenter, 247.   13. Hill, 271.   14. Oldroyd, 94.

15. Atlantic Monthly, April, 1887, 437.   16. Johnson, 138-139.

17. Rockport Journal, Feb. 11, 1898, "Lincoln the Fatalist, Heard Phantom Voices and Believed in Destiny" by Henry C. Whitney.

18. Chapman, 380.   19. Roe, 240.

20. Quoted in sermon by Reverend John Falkner Blake, Rector of Christ Church, Bridgeport, Conn.,April 19, 1865.

21. Arnold, 81.   22. Johnson, 156.

23. A. K. McClure, 304; Selby, 224.   24. Rice, 240.

25. See Notes 9, 10, 11 of Chapter VI above.

26. Nicolay & Hay, History, I, 258, 533.

27. Herndon, 386. His appetite whetted by what he had read in the Vincennes Western Sun, Lincoln later read the whole speech at New Salem, Illinois.

28. A. K. McClure, 340.

29. Ehrmann, 75; William Fortune's interview with Nathaniel Grigsby; Fortune's manuscript in author's collection.

30. General Egbert L. Veile in New York Independent, April 4, 1895.

31. Buckley, 95-96.

32. Herndon-Weik MSS, Vol. 14, N. Grigsby, Sept. 12, 1865, statement.

32a. Nicolay & Hay, History, I, 4; Western Sun, May 8, 1819.

33. W. R. Thayer, I, 199-200.   34. J. B. McClure, 475.

35. Murr, XIV, 39; Tracy, 163.

36. New York Herald, Oct. 20, 1860.

37. Papers of Abraham Lincoln, Library of Congress: G. W. Rathbone to Lincoln, June 1, 1860.

38. Whitney, 280.   39. Hertz, II, 800-801.

40. Rhodes, 5; Davis, 60; Channing, 443.   41. Carpenter, 217.

42. Atlantic Monthly, April, 1887, 437.   43. Mallory, 429; Prentice, 256-259.

44. Nicolay & Hay, History, I, 174.

45. Detailed account of President Lincoln's troubles with foreign powers: *Diplomat in Carpet Slippers* by Jay Monaghan.

46. A. K. McClure, 343.   47. Nicolay & Hay, History, VIII, 3-9.

48. Ibid., VIII, 13.   49. Hendrick, 369-374.

50. A. K. McClure, 25.   51. Channing, 496; Stanwood, 301-306.

52. Coulter, VII, 194-195.   53. Monaghan, 398-399.

54. Lamon, Recollections, 243-244.

55. Appleton's Cyclopaedia of American Biography (1888), Vol. IV, 616.

56. Carpenter, 99-101.

57. Salmon P. Chase Papers, Library of Congress, Cyrus Pitt Grosvenor letter to Chase, July 28, 1862.

58. Nicolay & Hay, History, I, 172-173.

59. Herndon-Weik, MSS, Vol. 14, William Wood statement, Sept. 15, 1865; A. K. McClure, 370.

60. Oldroyd, 133 (1864).   61. Nicolay & Hay, History, I, 581.

62. *Ibid.*, 129; 274.   63. Nicolay, 349.

64. Nicolay & Hay, History, II, 296; letter to General J. A. McClerand.

65. Tracy, 128.   66. Nicolay & Hay, History, I, 147.

67. Oldroyd, 80.   68. Helm, 213.

69. Lincoln's Peoria speech, Oct. 16, 1854.

70. Daily Alta Californian, San Francisco, March 8, 1888.

71. Nicolay & Hay, History II, 121; Rice, 583.

72. Nicolay & Hay, History, I, 216.

73. Roe, 226 (March 17, 1865 address to an Indian regiment).

74. Nicolay & Hay, History, I, 557.   75. Lamon, Recollections, 182-183.

76. Pillsbury, 14; Channing, 444.   77. Nicolay & Hay, History, I, 581.

78. Rhodes, 5.   79. E. Grant Gentry affidavit.

80. Nicolay & Hay, History, I, 641; Herndon & Weik, I, 76.

81. See Note 18, Chapter Three above.

82. Brooks, Washington in Lincoln's Time, 57-58.

83. Nicolay, Personal Traits, 225; Evans, 338-339; Lincoln Lore No. 220.

84. Nicolay & Hay, History, I, 87-88; Gentry, 269.

85. James Grigsby to Professor Andrew W. Sweeney.

86. Hill, 286.   87. Oldroyd, 123.

88. Nicolay & Hay, History, II, 409.
89. Atlantic Monthly, April, 1887.   90. A. K. McClure, 283.
91. Rhodes, 312.   92. Carpenter, 30; 76.
93. Nicolay & Hay, Complete Works, X, 129.
94. McClure, Abraham Lincoln's Stories and Speeches, 475.
95. A.G.O. records pertaining to Lieut. Col. William Jones, 53rd Indiana Infantry Volunteers; War of the Rebellion Official Records, Series 1, Vol. 38, part 3, p. 588.
96. A.G.O.records pertaining to 1st Lieut. John W. Lamar, Company "C", 53rd Indiana Infantry Volunteers.
97. A.G.O. records pertaining to 2nd Lieut. Nathaniel Grigsby and Private Henry Clay Grigsby, both of Company "G", 10th Regiment Indiana Cavalry.
98. Hendrick, 289.   99. Stephenson, 355.
100. Hendrick, 372-373.   101. Lincoln-Douglas, 78.
102. Lamon, Recollections, 113-114.
103. *Ibid.*; Carpenter, 292. These two accounts differ slightly.
104. Crook, 65-66.   105. Lamon, Recollections, 113-116.
106. Dr. E. V. Wilcox. President of Shakespeare Society of Washington, D.C. letter to author, Nov. 5, 1950, in which Dr. Wilcox tells of his conversation with Charles Hanford, a veteran actor in Edwin Booth's Shakespeare Company which played in Washington during 1864. Booth said President Lincoln recited from memory the great soliloquies from *Macbeth, Othello, Hamlet, Henry V* and *Richard III*. Booth told Hanford he had "never heard them recited so well on any stage."
107. Nicolay & Hay, History, II, 393.   108. Carpenter, 51-52.
109. New Orleans Louisiana Courier, Feb. 19, 1829.
110. Pitman, 81-82: Testimony of Dr. Robert King Stone, May 16, 1865. Dr. Stone examined President Lincoln shortly after Booth shot him.

SOURCES

A.G.O. Records pertaining to Civil War soldiers, Adjutant General's Office, Old Records' Section, Department of the Army, Washington, D.C.

ANGLE: New Letters and Papers of Lincoln. Compiled by Paul M. Angle. Boston: Houghton Mifflin. 1930.

ARMSTRONG: Notes pertaining to Abraham Lincoln in Indiana which Joseph D. Armstrong began collecting in and around Gentryville, Indiana, 1858, and continued until about 1879. Papers, notes, and manuscripts are in the possession of his daughter, Mrs. Mina Armstrong Cook, Rockport, Indiana. (Now deceased).

ARNOLD: Sketch of the Life of Abraham Lincoln. By Isaac N. Arnold. New York: John B. Bachelder, 1869.

ARNOLD: Life of Abraham Lincoln. By Isaac N. Arnold. Chicago: McClurg, 1891.

ARTHUR & CARPENTER: History of Kentucky. By T. S. Arthur and W. H. Carpenter. Philadelphia: Lippincott. 1856.

ATKINSON: The Boyhood of Lincoln. By Eleanor Atkinson. New York: McClure. 1908.

AVENT: Lincoln Addresses and Letters. Edited by John M. Avent. New York: Allyn and Bacon. 1928.

BARRETT: Life of Abraham Lincoln. By Joseph H. Barrett. Cincinnati: Moore, Wilstach & Baldwin. 1865.

BARTLETT: The Life and Public Services of Abraham Lincoln. By D. W. Bartlett. New York: H. Dayton. 1860.

BARTON: The Soul of Abraham Lincoln. By William E. Barton. New York: George H. Doran. 1920.

BARTON: The Women Lincoln Loved. By William E. Barton. Indianapolis: Bobbs-Merrill. 1927.

BENTON: Thirty Years View In the U.S. Senate 1820 to 1850. By Senator Thomas H. Benton. Two Volumes. New York: Appleton. 1854.

BROCKETT: The Life and Times of Abraham Lincoln. By L. P. Brockett. Philadelphia: Bradley & Co. 1865.

BROOKS: Abraham Lincoln and the Downfall of Slavery. By Noah Brooks. New York: Putnam's. 1894.

BROOKS: Washington in Lincoln's Time. By Noah Brooks.. New York: Century Co. 1895.

BROWNE, F. F.: Every Day Life of Abraham Lincoln. By Francis F. Browne. New York: Thompson Publishing Co. 1886.

BROWNE, R. H.: Lincoln and the Men of His Time. By Robert H. Browne. Cincinnati: Jennings & Pye. 1901.

BUCKLEY: Extemporaneous Oratory. By James M. Buckley, New York: Eaton & Mains. 1898.

BUTTERWORTH: In the Boyhood of Lincoln. By Hezekiah Butterworth. New York: Appleton. 1892.

CARPENTER: The Inner Life of Abraham Lincoln. By B. F. Carpenter. New York: Hurd and Houghton. 1868.

CHANNING: A Student's History of the United States. By Edward Channing. New York: Macmillan. 1931.

CHAPMAN: Latest Light on Abraham Lincoln. By Ervin Chapman. New York: Fleming H. Revel. 1917.

COBB: Scriptural Examination of the Institution of Slavery in the United States. By Howell Cobb. Georgia: Printed for the Author. 1856.

COCKRUM: Pioneer History of Indiana. By Colonel William M. Cockrum. Oakland City, Indiana; Press of Oakland City Journal. 1907.

COGGESHALL: The Journeys of Abraham Lincoln, 1861-1865. By William T. Coggeshall. Columbus, Ohio: Ohio State Journal. 1865.

COULTER: The Confederate States of America, 1861-1865. By E. Merton Coulter. Louisiana State University Press. 1950.

CREELMAN: Why We Love Lincoln. By James Creelman. New York: Outing Publishing Co. 1909.

CROOK: Through Five Administrations. By Colonel William H. Crook, bodyguard to President Lincoln. Compiled and edited by Margarita Spalding Gerry. New York: Harper. 1910.

CUMMINGS: The Western Pilot, Containing Charts of the Ohio River and of the Mississippi. By Samuel Cummings. Cincinnati: N. & G. Guilford. 1829.

DEWEY: Financial History of the United States. By David Rich Dewey. New York: Longmans, Green, and Co. 1903.

DRAKE: Life of Tecumseh and His Brother the Prophet. By Benjamin Drake. Cincinnati: Applegate & Co. 1852.

DUNN: Indiana: A Redemption From Slavery. By J. P. Dunn, Jr. Boston: Houghton Mifflin. 1888.

DUNN: Greater Indianapolis. By Jacob Piatt Dunn. Two Volumes. Chicago: Lewis Publishing Co. 1910.

EHRMANN: The Missing Chapter in the Life of Abraham Lincoln. By Bess V. Ehrmann. Chicago: Walter M. Hill. 1938.

ESAREY: History of Indiana. By Logan Esarey, Ph.D. Indianapolis: W. K. Stewart Co. 1915.

ESAREY: The Indiana Home. By Logan Esarey. Crawfordsville, Indiana: R. E. Banta. 1943.

EVANS: Mrs. Abraham Lincoln: A Study of Her Personality and Her Influence on Lincoln. By W. A. Evans. New York: Knopf. 1932.

FORTUNE: Warrick and Its Prominent People. Edited by Will Fortune. Evansville, Indiana: Courier Co. 1881.

FORTUNE: William Fortune's Notes and Collection. Indianapolis, Indiana.

GENTRY: The Gentry Family in America 1676 to 1909. By Richard Gentry. New York: Grafton Press. 1909.

GENTRY AFFIDAVIT: E. Grant Gentry affidavit in author's collection.

GILBERT: Memoir of Frances Wright The Pioneer Woman in the Cause of Human Rights. By Amos Gilbert. Cincinnati: Longley Brothers. 1855.

GODDELL: The American Slave Code. By William Goddell. New York: American and Foreign Anti-slavery Society. 1853.

GOODSPEED: History of Warrick, Spencer & Perry Counties, Indiana. Chicago: Goodspeed Bros. 1885.

GOODSPEED: History of Posey County, Indiana. Chicago: Goodspeed Publishing Co. 1886.

GRANT: Personal Memoirs of U.S. Grant. Two Volumes in One. New York: Webster & Co. 1894.

GRIDLEY: The Story Life of Abraham Lincoln. By Eleanor Gridley. Chicago: Kuhlman Co. 1900.

GRIGSBY AFFIDAVIT: Eli Lewis Grigsby affidavit in author's collection.

HART: Formation of the Union, 1750-1829. By Albert Bushnell Hart. New York: Longmans, Green, and Co. 1909.

HAWLEY: The Assassination and History of the Conspiracy. Cincinnati: J. R. Hawley & Co. 1865.

HELM: The True Story of Mary, Wife of Lincoln. By Her Niece, Katherine Helm. New York: Harper. 1928.

HENDRICK: Lincoln's War Cabinet. By Burton F. Hendrick. Boston: Little, Brown & Co. 1946.

HERNDON: Life of Lincoln. By William H. Herndon and Jesse N. Weik. Notes by Paul M. Angle. One Volume. New York: Albert and Charles Boni. 1930.

HERNDON & WEIK: Herndon's Lincoln The True Story of a Great Life. By William H. Herndon and Jesse William Weik. Three Volumes. Springfield, Illinois: Herndon's Lincoln Publishing Co. 1888.

HERNDON-WEIK MSS: The Herndon-Weik Lincoln Collection of Manuscripts in the Library of Congress, Washington, D.C. This is the original source material collected by William H. Herndon, Lincoln's law partner and close associate. The Library of Congress bought the collection from George Baker & Company.

HERTZ: Abraham Lincoln A New Portrait. By Emanuel Hertz. Two volumes. New York: Horace Liveright. 1931.

HILL: Abraham Lincoln Man of God. By John Wesley Hill. New York: Putnam's. 1922.

HOBSON: Footprints of Abraham Lincoln. By J. T. Hobson. Dayton, Ohio: Otterbein Press. 1909.

HOLLAND: The Life of Abraham Lincoln. By J. G. Holland. Springfield, Massachusetts: Gurdon Bill. 1866.

HOWELLS: Life of Abraham Lincoln. By William Dean Howells. Springfield, Illinois: Abraham Lincoln Association. 1938 (reprint of the 1860 edition)

HUNTINGTON LIBRARY HERNDON-LAMON COLLECTION: The Herndon-Lamon Lincoln Collection LN 2408, Vol. I of manuscripts in the Henry E. Huntington Library and Art Gallery, San Marino, California. All references in Notes are of manuscripts in Vol. I, LN 2408. This material was collected by William H. Herndon and sold to Ward H. Lamon prior to 1872. All items herein are reproduced by special permission of the Director of Research, Henry E. Huntington Library.

JACKSON: Lincoln's Use of the Bible. By S. Trevena Jackson. New York: Eaton & Mains. 1909.

JAMES: The Life of George Rogers Clark. By James Alton James. Chicago: Chicago University Press. 1928.

JOHNSON: Abraham Lincoln the Christian. By William J. Johnson. New York: Eaton & Mains. 1913. Cincinnati: Jennings & Graham. 1913. (Revised edition: Abraham Lincoln the Christian. By William J. Johnstone. New York: Abingdon Press. 1928).

JOHNSON AFFIDAVIT: Lafayette Johnson affidavit in author's collection.

KIDSON: Traditional Tunes, A Collection of Ballad Airs, Chiefly obtained in Yorkshire and the south of Scotland. By Frank Kidson. Oxford: Charles Taphouse & Son. 1891.

LAMON: Life of Abraham Lincoln. By Ward H. Lamon. Boston: Osgood and Co. 1872.

LAMON: Recollections of Abraham Lincoln 1847-1865. By Ward Hill Lamon. Edited by Dorothy Lamon. Chicago: McClurg. 1895.

LINCOLN-DOUGLAS: Political Debates Between Hon. Abraham Lincoln and Hon. Stephen A. Douglas. (These speeches were edited by Lincoln) Columbus, Ohio: Follett, Foster, and Co. 1860.

LINCOLN LORE: Edited by Dr. Louis A. Warren and published each week by the Lincoln National Life Foundation, Fort Wayne, Indiana, 1929 to date.

LINDLEY: Indiana as Seen by Early Travelers Prior to 1830. Edited by Harlow Lindley. Indianapolis: Indiana Historical Commission. 1916.

LOCKWOOD: The New Harmony Movement. By George B. Lockwood. New York: Appleton. 1905.

LOSSING: Eminent Americans. By Benson J. Lossing. New York. Hurst & Co. 1886.

LOWRY: A Complete History of the Marquis de Lafayette. By Robert Lowry. New York: Printed for and published by Robert Lowry. 1826.

McCLURE, A. K.: Lincoln's Yarns and Stories. Collected by Col. Alexander K. McClure. Chicago and Philadelphia: John C. Winston Company. (No date of publication indicated. According to Ward Hill Lamon, Col. McClure was "a friend, confidant, and adviser" of President Lincoln.)

McCLURE, J. B.: Abraham Lincoln's Stories and Speeches. Edited by J. B. McClure. Chicago: Rhodes & McClure. 1897.

McDONALD: History of Freemasonry in Indiana from 1806 to 1898. By Daniel McDonald. Indianapolis: Published by the Authority of the Grand Lodge. 1898.

McMURTRY: The Lincolns in Elizabethtown, Kentucky. By Gerald McMurtry. Fort Wayne, Indiana: Lincolniana Publishers. 1932.

MALLORY: The Life and Speeches of the Hon. Henry Clay. Compiled and Edited by Daniel Mallory. Two Volumes. New York: Van Amringe and Bixby. 1844.

MARTIN: A Defense of the Mother Conversion and Creed of Abraham Lincoln. By James M. Martin. Minneapolis. 1921.

MONAGHAN: Diplomat in Carpet Slippers. By Jay Monaghan. Indianapolis: Bobbs-Merrill. 1945.

MOORE: The Civil War in Song and Story. Collected and Arranged by Frank Moore. New York: Collier. 1889.

MUDGE: The Forest Boy: The Sketch of the Life of Abraham Lincoln. By Z. A. Mudge. New York: Carlton & Porter. 1867.

MURR: Lincoln in Indiana. By Dr. J. Edward Murr. Bloomington, Indiana: Indiana Magazine of History, XIII, No. 4; XIV, No. 1 and No. 2; (December, 1917; March, 1918; June, 1918.)

NEWCOMB: In the Lincoln Country. By Rexford Newcomb. Philadelphia: Lippincott. 1928.

NICOLAY: Personal Traits of Abraham Lincoln. By Helen Nicolay. New York: Century Co. 1919.

NICOLAY & HAY: Abraham Lincoln, Complete Works. Edited by John G. Nicolay and John Hay. Two Volumes. New York: Century Co. 1894.

NICOLAY & HAY: Complete Works of Abraham Lincoln. Edited by John G. Nicolay and John Hay. Ten Volumes. New York: Tandy Co. 1894.

NICOLAY & HAY: Abraham Lincoln: A History. By John G. Nicolay and John Hay. Ten Volumes. New York: Century Co. 1890.

NORFOLK: Gleanings in Graveyards—A Collection of Curious Epitaphs. Collated, compiled, and edited by Horatio Edward Norfolk. (Third Edition) London: John Russell Smith. Soho Square. 1866.

OLDROYD: Words of Lincoln. Compiled by Osborn H. Oldroyd. Washington, D.C.: O. H. Oldroyd. 1895.

OLDROYD: Lincoln Memorial: Album—Immorteles. By Osborn H. Oldroyd. New York: G. W. Carleton & Co. 1882.

OLDROYD MYSTIC 7: The Mystic Number 7 In the Life of Abraham Lincoln: By Osborn H. Oldroyd. Washington, D.C., 1930.

OLMSTED: Our Slave States. By Frederick Law Olmsted. New York: Dix & Edwards. 1856.

PIKE: A New and Complete System of Arithmetic. By Nicolas Pike. Worcester, Massachusetts: The Press of Isaiah Thomas. 1797.

PITMAN: The Assassination of President Lincoln and the Trial of the Conspirators. Compiled by Benn Pitman. New York: Moore, Wilstach & Baldwin. 1865.

PRENTICE: Biography of Henry Clay. By George D. Prentice. New York: John Jay Phelps. 1831.

RHODES: History of the Civil War 1861-1865. By James Ford Rhodes. New York: Macmillan. 1917.

RICE: Reminiscences of Abraham Lincoln. Collected and Edited by Allen Thorndike Rice. New York: North American Publishing Company. 1886.

ROBERTS: Lincoln in Illinois. By Octavia Roberts. Boston: Houghton Mifflin. 1918.

ROE: Speeches and Letters of Abraham Lincoln, 1832-1865. Edited by Merwin Roe. New York: E. P. Dutton. 1912.

SCRIPPS: Life of Abraham Lincoln. By John Locke Scripps. Chicago: Tribune Tracts—No. 6; also The Chicago Press and Co. 1860. (This 32-page pamphlet was authorized and revised by Abraham Lincoln. For convenience, references made to Scripps will be found in the reprinted copy by Edward J. Jacob and M. L. Houser, Peoria, Illinois, 1931.)

SELBY: Anecdotal Lincoln. By Paul Selby. Chicago: Thompson & Thomas. 1900.

SHARP: English Songs from the Southern Appalachians. Collected by Cecil J. Sharp. Two Volumes. London: Oxford University Press. 1932.

STANWOOD: A History of the Presidency From 1788 to 1897. By Edward Stanwood. Boston: Houghton Mifflin Company. 1928.

STEPHENSON: An Autobiography of Abraham Lincoln. By Nathaniel Wright Stephenson. Indianapolis: Bobbs-Merrill. 1926.

STODDARD: Abraham Lincoln: The Man and the War President. By William O. Stoddard. New York: Fords, Howard & Hulbert. 1888.

S.W.I.H.S.: Southwestern Indiana Historical Society file of papers and manuscripts. Rockport and Evansville, Indiana.

TARBELL: The Life of Abraham Lincoln. By Ida M. Tarbell. Two Volumes. New York: Doubleday, 1909.

TARBELL: The Early Life of Abraham Lincoln. By Ida M. Tarbell. New York: McClure. 1896.

TELESCOPE: The Telescope, published each week by W. Beach, Editor and Proprietor. New York. 1824-1829.

THAYER: From Pioneer Home to the White House. By William M. Thayer. New York: Hurst. 1882.

THAYER, W. R.: The Life and Letters of John Hay. By William Roscoe Thayer. Two Volumes. Boston: Houghton Mifflin. 1915.

TOWNSEND: Lincoln the Litigant. By William H. Townsend. Boston: Houghton Mifflin. 1925.

TRACY: Uncollected Letters of Abraham Lincoln. Now First Brought Together by Gilbert A. Tracy. Boston: Houghton Mifflin. 1917.

WARREN: Lincoln's Parentage & Childhood. By Louis Austin Warren. New York: Century, 1926.

WARRICK COUNTY BRIEF: Brief Prepared by the Warrick County Lincoln Route Association of Indiana. Affidavits and papers collected by William L. Barker, Philip Lutz, Jr., and Union W. Youngblood. Boonville, Indiana: Press of the Boonville Standard. 1931.

WEEMS: Life of General Francis Marion. By M. L. Weems. Philadelphia: Carey. 1818.

WEIK: The Real Lincoln: A Portrait. By Jesse W. Weik. Boston: Houghton Mifflin. 1922.

WESTERN SUN: Western Sun & General Advertiser, a newspaper published each Saturday at Vincennes, Indiana. Founded in 1804 by Elihu Stout and edited by him from 1804 to 1843.

WHIPPLE: The Story-Life of Lincoln. By Wayne Whipple. Memorial edition. 1908.

WHITNEY: Life On The Circuit With Lincoln. By Henry C. Whitney. Boston: Estes and Lauriat. 1892.

INDEX